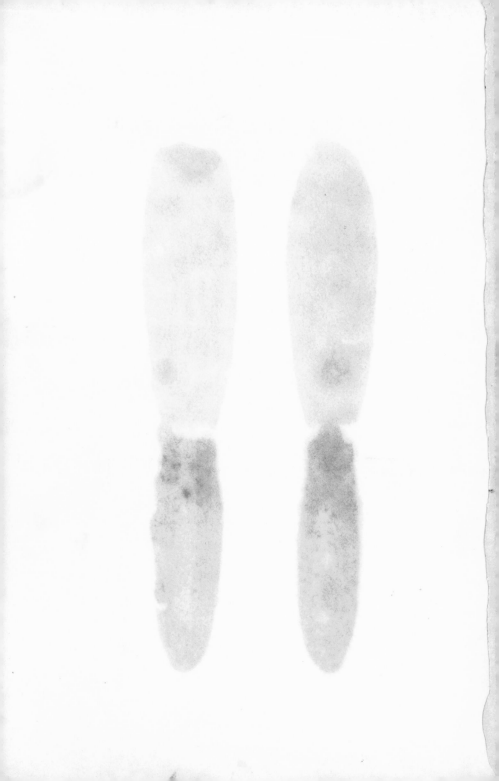

MARTHA'S VINEYARD

An Elegy

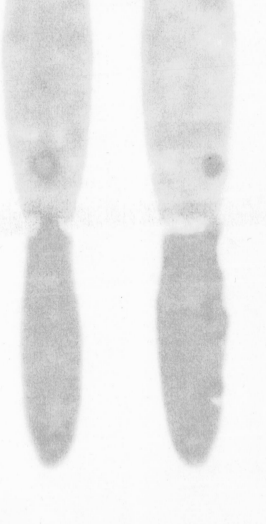

Books by Everett S. Allen

Arctic Odyssey: The Biography of Rear Admiral
Donald M. MacMillan

Famous American Humorous Poets
(For young people)

This Quiet Place: A Cape Cod Chronicle

Children of the Light: The Rise and Fall of New
Bedford Whaling and the Death of the Arctic Fleet

A Wind to Shake the World: The Story of the
1938 Hurricane

The Black Ships: Rumrunners of Prohibition

Martha's Vineyard: An Elegy

MARTHA'S VINEYARD

An Elegy

EVERETT S. ALLEN

LITTLE, BROWN AND COMPANY — BOSTON – TORONTO

FIRST EDITION

The author is especially grateful to Henry Beetle Hough of
the *Vineyard Gazette* for his continuing interest in this effort
and his cooperation in making material previously published
in the *Vineyard Gazette* available.

Permissions for material quoted in the text can be found on
page 308.

LIBRARY OF CONGRESS CATALOGING IN PUBLICATION DATA

Allen, Everett S.
  Martha's Vineyard.

  1. Martha's Vineyard (Mass.)—Social life and
customs.   2. Martha's Vineyard (Mass.)—Description
and travel.   3. Allen, Everett S.   I. Title.
F72.M5A58 1982   974.4'94   82-14004
ISBN 0-316-03257-3

MV

Designed by Susan Windheim

*Published simultaneously in Canada
by Little, Brown & Company (Canada) Limited*

PRINTED IN THE UNITED STATES OF AMERICA

For
Joseph Chase Allen
and
Henry Beetle Hough
whose combined knowledge of and love for Martha's
Vineyard created a friendship of uncommon dimensions

Preface

HEREIN are some nonscientific reflections concerning the island of Martha's Vineyard. The Vineyard, as has been noted by its historian, the scholarly Charles Edward Banks, is situated five miles from the Massachusetts mainland, south of the "heel of the Cape" (Cod, that is). Its longest measurement east and west is about nineteen and one-fourth miles, and its greatest width from north to south is nine and three-eighths miles, within which is contained approximately one hundred square miles, or about sixty-four thousand acres, of land.

This book touches upon matters occurring during the period 1925–1980. It makes no pretense of commenting on everything that happened or even upon everything of importance that happened. It is conceded that, in numerous instances, minor matters are given more attention than major ones and my priorities are, if not capricious, at least indefensible.

The first section of each chapter is concerned with events and atmosphere, based upon personal recollection and perusal of *Vineyard Gazette* files. Each chapter ends with a comment obtained in 1980. In deciding whom to interview, I selected those who knew what the Vineyard used to be like, who have been sufficiently involved to know what it is like now, and who undoubtedly were moved to ponder the changes long before I asked what they thought of them. Most of these people I have known for a long time, some of them since elementary and high school days in Vineyard Haven.

Martha's Vineyard is inhabited, increasingly so. On this

island, Mike Wallace interviewed Thomas Hart Benton for CBS, at the latter's island home. Columnist Art Buchwald, who sojourns in summer in Vineyard Haven, acclaims the place as "what my childhood vacations were like." John T. Hughes, the hatchery director in Oak Bluffs, bothered by the cost of cannibalism among lobsters, is trying to breed "a gentle lobster, meek and mild." Albert "Ozzie" Fischer, Jr., puts out grain for the Canada geese in Chilmark when the ponds are frozen. There are a number of other people on the island, too, and some of them make things like bread, wine, and music. And when the island Baptists got together at Gay Head town hall, the ladies provided a buffet supper that included more than forty homemade casseroles.

I had an idea that thinking about the Vineyard, past and present, might offer an opportunity to hold mankind and the universe at arm's length to see whether they are going in the same or opposite directions. If you doubt that traveling the Vineyard is akin to traveling the world, that is because you never talked with Hattie Tilton, whose people and whose husband's people have been islanders for a couple of hundred years or more.

One Sunday noon, while she was waiting for the potatoes to be done, Hattie said, "I imagine everything that ever happened on earth has happened on the Vineyard at least once. And some things twice."

I imagine that is so.

Contents

MARTHA'S VINEYARD

An Elegy

1. The Move

IF you are going to write about an island, you must begin by coming to grips with the sea that makes it so, not only by definition but because it is as well a catalyst, and beyond that, a perspective. The sea is what makes islands; it is also what makes islanders.

So I have come to this Vineyard beach, admittedly much altered from the years when I first knew it, yet still dear to me, to think alone. There is a certain private advantage in returning to a piece of the world such as this — with which you have been on intimate terms for a long time — because there are so many things that you can associate with every part of it, things that are no longer visible or perhaps not even there anymore.

Beneath this very sand — I cannot remember how many feet down, but not many — there lies the hull of a little schooner that was driven ashore before anyone now living was born. Once, I dug out part of her forward cabin, exposing the graceful curve of planking, now gone silver with age and weather. I built a driftwood fire and roasted a couple of potatoes; it started to rain so I crawled into the cabin and ate them. Such sand as remained in there was damp, yet there was a sense of security in that forecastle — or what remained of it — such as ancient things tend to provide. I wondered who before me had eaten potatoes there and whom they cursed and whom they loved.

{3}

The next high water refilled the cabin with sand and you would never have known that I had dug there. Still, *I* knew that I had and, in so doing, never presumed to defeat the sea's purpose but simply desired to create a moment to remember. Which I did.

Today was another such moment. It was shortly after daylight when I came to the sea here and I thought immediately that it must have been much like this in the beginning of things. The fog of the night remained in the windless morning; most landmarks of field, marsh, and wood it obliterated, and those vaguely seen, dark against light, were so formless as to tempt the imagination, so delicately undefined that they seemed to lack weight and substance.

Except for the short strip of empty beach, there was nothing in the visible world to offer a yardstick for determining relationship or proportion. It occurred to me to wonder whether, if that, too, disappeared in the mist, I could be completely certain that I was not upside down. We do, after all, depend to a great extent upon a relatively few objects — horizon, tree, and others of the human kind — to reassure us that we are right side up. Not one of these was available. In short, it was a time that called for assumption and faith; I assumed my boat was at the mooring just offshore because it had been there the night before.

An hour ago, the sea was still retreating from this beach, which it floods and redesigns at each high water. When the cycle commands, water pours off the land and back into itself, cutting caramel gashes across the sand as it retreats. Now, there are only two sounds in all of this place, some small chuckle of water and a gull's cry, somehow timelessly mournful upon the new day.

The harbor is still in all its parts. Nothing moves and I am coming to reflect upon how many thoughts of various kinds the sea has inspired in mankind and what it has meant to the human creature. With a few outstanding exceptions, I think the professional mariner has not been inclined to philosophize or write poetry about the sea. I submit that is understandable.

If you have business upon the waters and intend to execute it effectively, you must keep the ocean in sharp focus, being mindful of precisely what it is in your terms. First of all, travel upon it requires the regular solution of a mathematical problem concerned with time and distance. If your solution is incorrect, you may be in trouble.

Equally important, as an oceanographer will tell you, the sea is a hostile atmosphere for the human, whether he is on it or in it. I once received a letter from a Coast Guard officer who was in command of a ship that had been for some weeks on offshore patrol. "I must close this," he wrote, "because the wind is beginning to freshen out of the northwest and I have to go topside to make sure that everything is properly secured. I find that I have difficulty convincing my better educated young officers that they must respect the ocean; on the other hand, I have discovered there is nothing like a fifty-foot sea to make an instant Christian out of almost anybody."

These attitudes of the professional, comprehensible and essential though they are, are seldom likely to produce the reflections of an Arnold or a Melville, both of whom were inclined to find within the seascape metaphors relatable to life and to mankind. It is more often the largely shorebound, at arm's length from matters of reefing and sounding, who can see the ocean in its larger perspective; it is they in all ages and most nations who have recorded the sea's vastnesses and truths.

Yet I am moved to remember that there is a third way in which we may come to the sea — not to make a living or a poem but in a manner, largely wordless and formless, that comes close to marriage. That brings me to the old man, who was, I believe, the father of Brad Clough of Vineyard Haven.

He was lean and slow-moving in the manner of great age, yet curiously, he was not old all over. He was as bright-eyed as a catbird and he made a point of doing things and moving about with such care as to make no noise, which is a very civilized habit.

If there was some wind and the morning was fair, he would come down to the beach at Owen Park about ten o'clock, carrying his oars and rowlocks. Usually, he took off his shirt, being naked to the waist because the sun felt good upon his bones but not on his head, which he protected with a floppy-brimmed white hat.

Near the dock, he had a small round-bottomed boat and there was always somebody around to shove her overboard for him. As going to sea is itself an act of faith, the old man assumed there would be someone to help him launch and so there was, especially because in those times, mariners whose sailing years were over came each day to the shore for recollection and refreshment of the aging spirit.

Once afloat, the old man stowed his oars very carefully along the thwarts and set a leg-of-mutton sail about the size of a bandanna handkerchief. The boat, stiff and high-sided, sailed easily, and as the water began to gurgle under her forefoot, you could see peace settle upon his posture; although he did not seem to have moved, there was something newly composed in the curve of back and slant of shoulder.

I have watched him thus many times and came to conclude that what I was observing was an extraordinary equation as expressed in man, boat, and sea, and I suspect that, in the end, even the element of the boat was eliminated. I think this because she was the simplest kind of boat with the simplest rig; she sailed a little, but not a lot — she did not demand, did not get in the way of the experience; one did not have to spend time with her, forever adjusting this or that. She was no more than a fundamental means to an even more fundamental end.

What the boat did was to place the old man in suspension in a plane of such broad proportions, such timeless predictability, such comforting, unchanging familiarity, as to obliterate past, present, and future by making their differences indistinguishable through immersing them in their similarities. Everything contributed to this end — the relative silence of the hour, the soporific of the sun, the soothing sound of water as the hull moved through it; and sometimes, the old man dragged the tips of his fingers in the sea's summer warmth.

If you can achieve this kind of thing, and it may be that age is helpful in so doing, the moment becomes forever in its infinite qualities; truth, as it concerns both man and his relationship to his world, envelops the being — not as a word but as an experience.

One day, when the old man came ashore after his sail, somebody — knowing that he never ventured beyond the breakwater — asked jokingly, "Where have you voyaged to this morning, cap'n?"

If I had been the old man, I would have replied, "Everywhere there is," for islanders know that their sea is all, that their relationship to it is everything — and the old man was an islander.

Not everybody is.

When we got ready to move to the Vineyard nearly sixty years ago, my mother regarded it as consignment to perdition. This had nothing to do with the island people, most of whom she did not even know, but she was a farmer's daughter and to her, salt water was something on which you were seasick and in which you drowned. Vineyard Sound was no protective moat to her, it was a cruel barrier, occasionally made worse by fog, wind, or ice that halted boat service. Whenever my father and I went to sea for a day, it was predictable that she would have a migraine when we returned for she had spent the hours envisioning our disaster.

In such moments of physical and mental distress, my mother's face assumed an expression of reserved magnificence. A sensitive woman, a violinist, organist, and schoolteacher, she had fine English features and pale skin. Her coloring, straight nose, and high forehead were emphasized dramatically if she was wearing dark clothing. More than once, coming home with scup scales on my pants after some hours of hand-lining off Lambert's Cove, I looked at her, thin-lipped in pain, and thought of Lady Macbeth; but under the circumstances, I did not mention it.

Her family regarded the sea in the same way. I once took her brother Charles out in a good substantial twelve-foot skiff. He was a kind and gentle countryman who had "peddled milk" back in the days when they did it with horses, and he was much at home with radishes and rabbits. The island steamer came in to the dock while we were paddling about and I rowed in her general direction to give him a better view, although we remained many yards distant. Charles did not have hands enough to clutch both gunwales for safety and hold his straw hat on at the same time but he tried. When the steamer's wake rolled under us, an easy slop, he went pale and cried hoarsely, "Don't get any closer!" Sweat born of fear trickled down from under his hatband. "Take me to land," he said, his voice sounding like that of someone who is weak from illness. As I started pulling for the beach, wondering how he could be so afraid, he said, "I know of no reason on earth why this boat of yours should stay right side up!"

My father, Joseph Chase Allen, looked upon moving to the Vineyard as going home. His ancestor James Allen was the only one of the original purchasing proprietors of Tisbury who remained on the island as a settler except James Skiffe. Allen probably settled there in 1669 and for forty-five years thereafter was a leading spirit in the towns of Tisbury and Chilmark. He owned at one time or another seven of the original home lots on the west side of Old Mill Brook and his final holdings, which he distributed among his heirs, amounted to about 250 acres.

In 1675, he was an assistant under the Mayhew regime, this being equivalent to a justice on the bench. He was one of the first three justices of the peace after the inclusion of the Vineyard in Massachusetts. He was recommended for this appointment by Simon Athearn, who stated that Allen was "reputed wealthy and having such influence with the people there." Historian Banks says this was the most exalted office to which men in those days could aspire, a justice on the king's bench. James Allen was the first to hold any considerable office of honor or profit on the Vineyard following its settlement who was not connected by either blood or marriage with the Mayhew family — and that in itself was a major distinction. In 1701, James gave Tisbury its first God's acre for burial of the dead and as a location for a projected new meetinghouse.

Ever since James, there has been a family Allen paying taxes in the town of Tisbury. Squire Benjamin Allen, born in 1767, was my father's great-great-great-grandfather. Of him, my father said, "He was the last of the family to use an English title. His land holdings spread clear across the island at the widest point [Note: not quite; they extended from Quansoo to the North Shore, in the Seven Gates Farm area] and were divided into many farms, which he rented to tenants after the English fashion. The American Revolution ended this practice."

Benjamin was drowned in the fall of 1791, when his sloop grounded in foul weather while he was ferrying a load of sheep from Nantucket to the Vineyard. Searchers found his conch shell foghorn and one of his legs in a boot. The leg was buried with proper ceremony in West Tisbury cemetery and the place where his vessel was lost is named Mutton Shoal to this day.

The first Joseph Allen, for whom my father was named, was a selectman of Tisbury during the Revolution.

The oldest Allen house of which I am aware was located near the Chilmark–West Tisbury town line, on the eastern end of the farm once owned by my grandfather, William C. Allen, off the North Road. It had two cellars, which was unusual, but it was understood that rum was kept in one, from which the hired help were barred. My grandfather tore down this house because it was burglarized repeatedly, probably by relatives. A date of 1652 was found on a fireplace tile, which may indicate when it was built.

My grandfather William was typical of those islanders of his day who stayed home. He was born on the Allen farm; as a stock raiser and farmer, he kept his home always there; he was educated at the North Road School and Dukes County Academy in West Tisbury; he was married in the Chilmark Methodist Church, which stood near Tea Lane on Middle Road; he held various town offices, including those of school committeeman and selectman; and he died at eighty-one within a few rods of the site where he was born.

The only thing my grandfather ever gave me was a nickel-plated .32-caliber revolver, which, he said, pointing out the kitchen window, "will shoot to kill, clear to that tree." The only advice he ever gave me was to "stay out of boats," which was several years too late to be effective. He gave me the gun because he was afraid of it.

At a reasonably advanced age, my grandfather Allen had the shingles — which for the benefit of the blessedly uninitiated is an acute inflammatory skin disease of nervous origin marked by, among other things, neuralgic pains — and he was miserable enough so that he thought he was about to die. Having endured more discomfort than he believed he deserved, he decided, at three o'clock in the morning and after several days of not eating, to consume his last meal. I might note here that my grandfather bought all the groceries in his household, principally because he did not propose to have anything in the house that he did not like. Also, he ate with the gusto of Samuel Johnson ("he who does not mind his belly will hardly mind anything else"), although there the resemblance ended.

Accordingly, my grandfather lighted the kerosene lamp on the shelf over the sink, located three pounds of freshly speared eels in the "buttery," stoked up the kitchen range with an armful of wood, whacked up the eels in four-inch chunks, and fried them in a big black iron spider. He ate those eels, every one, together with a quart of home-pickled onions, half a loaf of my grandmother's crusty bread lathered with a quarter-inch of Cronig Brothers' best butter, and all sluiced down with a pot of heavily creamed coffee. He then had what he described as his best night's sleep in weeks, rose in time for a hearty lunch, and lived for many years thereafter.

At fourteen, my father left the family farm in Chilmark where he was born. "It got to be too crowded," he said. "My father and I never got along worth a damn. So I got out and went fishing." He went to Menemsha and sailed as mate with Captain Everett Poole, the elder, aboard the catboat *Goldenrod*, and he said of himself that, as he carried his gear aboard, he was "the saltiest human clothespin wearing boots." I am named for Captain Everett Poole, which suggests something of the depth of the relationship that came to exist between them.

My father's mother, the former Sarah Hammett, was "tastefully dressed in white henrietta en train and wore a veil and orange blossoms" when she married William on New Year's Day in 1891. She was descended from Edward Hammett (probably spelled with one *t* then), who first settled in North Tisbury about 1706. He was a worsted comber, had four sons and seven daughters, and was variously town constable, tithingman, and surveyor of highways. Historian Banks had some difficulty tracing his ancestry:

Nothing has been developed regarding his antecedents. . . . There is a fantastic legend about him to the effect that his mother, a beautiful English girl, was captured from a ship by some Algerian pirates and she became the consort of the chief. A son was born, who bore the name of Hamid and when he grew up, his mother told him the secret of his birth and bade him escape to her own people, which advice he followed. Those who wish to believe the story will probably do so.

I am inclined to believe the story principally because Dr. Banks, a tireless researcher and fastidious scholar, was able to track down the roots of every old Vineyard family but this one. I am also mindful that one of my grandmother's male relatives taught my father, then nine years old, to duel with a cutlass and that my grandmother's father, Humphrey Hammett, had his left ear pierced for a small gold ring, as had all his male forebears.

I remember Sarah Hammett, with her olive skin, graygreen eyes, and dark hair — a lean and quick woman, even though a grandmother several times — hiking the Chilmark hills after blueberries like a poem in motion.

All of this is relevant because how you come to a place determines what you find there and this is especially true of an island. My father returned to the Vineyard with roots as deep as time, eight generations of it.

As for me, I moved to the Vineyard with a different kind of mood.

Bank robbers and wife deserters know, of course, but I think the average law-abiding citizen is unaware of the tremendous advantage that may be gained by a change of location. When I was in the third grade of public school on the mainland, most of the girls liked me (because I was the only boy in the class who would participate in folk dancing without being dragged) and most of the boys didn't, because I liked school. It wasn't so much that I was a good student but that in those days, most of my teachers were female, and I fell in love with them more often than not.

The result of this situation was that I was miserable. An ill-tempered gang of my peers chased me to school every morning, home to lunch every noon, back to school after lunch, and home again when school was over. Long before it was nationally fashionable, I started earnest running at the age of seven. Inevitably, my pursuers finally caught me and tied me to a fire hydrant, where I remained, unhinged and weeping, until a passerby rescued me, just before dark. This situation had gone on for some time and, to such degree as a third-grader can be depressed, I was.

At about that time, my father displayed a borrowed hundred-dollar bill while we were eating supper. He announced that with it we were going to move to Martha's Vineyard, that he had a better job there, and that there was going to be a "slump" on the mainland. I was not surprised. Our city tenement was small, and nights after I had been put to bed, I could hear my father and mother, forever worrying about money. I was old enough to wonder why my mother bothered to write "Food," "Rent," "Coal," and so on, very carefully on those envelopes when there was never anything to put in them anyway. I visualized the coming "slump," whatever it was, as being something peculiar to the mainland that could not cross water. So, in the first instance, I was greatly relieved by the news.

The interesting thing about that childhood reaction is that it was essentially correct economically and socially; the Vineyard of those years was splendidly independent of much that bothered the United States and the world.

I knew little about the Vineyard but I realized that if I were going to join a new peer group they would know about me only what I chose to reveal. All I had to decide was how I wanted to be regarded. From my experience, I concluded that the most pugnacious boys were the most respected because they were the most feared. I decided that I must create for myself an aura of pugnaciousness.

Projecting a new self-image at the age of eight is difficult because the trappings of adulthood — diplomas, credit cards, club memberships, letters of reference, and framed citations — with which reputations can be built and secured are not available. Most evaluations at that level are monosyllabic and subject to daily challenge. I did not wish to start another chapter of being tied to fire hydrants but I had no ideas for creating a tougher I on the day we moved.

The fourth member of our family was my sister Jo, who was six months old. I do not know how she felt about going to live on Martha's Vineyard because she did not say.

We moved to the island on the paddle-wheel steamer *Uncatena*, undoubtedly the most romantic vessel on the line at the time but we took her for economic reasons. My father and mother had money enough to hire just one truck to carry all of our possessions; the *Uncatena*, with an open forward

deck, was the only ship of the fleet that could accommodate a
load that high. Being aware that the hundred-dollar bill —
now spent — was all the money that the family had and that
the truck on deck contained everything we owned, including
my toys, I suffered more than I mused en route. I maintained
a nervous vigil on the boat deck all the way from New Bedford; a dozen times, I fancied that the truck's wheel chocks
moved as the steamer rolled and I expected the whole vanload
to slam through the bulwarks in a cloud of splinters and disappear in the sea.

It didn't.

It was April, 1925, and what I perceived first about Martha's
Vineyard, on the initial ride from Oak Bluffs to Vineyard
Haven and thereafter in and about the property in Cromwell's
Lane that my father had rented, was more aura than physical
detail. I sensed immediately an exciting lack of regimentation,
this because I had spent the first eight years of my life in the
minuscule backyards of a city, each defined by picket fences
that kept somebody in and somebody out. There were none
visible here; more important, I felt that there were no fences
at all, for reasons that I did not understand. What is more,
there were few signs, no billboards, no "keep out" notices, no
trolley tracks, and, in many places, no sidewalks. Some roads
were unpaved, and trees and shrubs, obviously not planted by
a park department, sprawled as freely as cats in the sun.

There was a clean, unfettered vastness that surprised me,
for I had been told that the island had fewer people than the
city so I assumed it was smaller. There was no smell or sound
of industry, nor any man-made staleness; there were no smokestacks upon the horizons and boats, even working boats, moved
with such majesty as could not be achieved by trucks or clanging streetcars. Everywhere, clean water stretched away beyond

seeing. I felt an opening of things that urged me to run to all the parts of this place, to touch, to feel, to smell.

We passed children playing in a field and I wondered how they knew whom to ask whether they could play there. It occurred to me, because there were no signs, that perhaps they had not had to ask anyone and that was enough to set the heart beating faster.

Finally, I stood in the yard of the house where we were to live in Vineyard Haven. My father said it was more than a hundred years old and I tried to relate that to the oldest person I had ever known. He was a retired whaleman, father of the practical nurse who had assisted my mother at my birth. His name was Benjamin — being small, I called him "Mundemund," which was close enough — and he had long curved fingernails as yellow as an old tusk. He was almost a hundred and I tried to think of him as a young man with pale pink fingernails when our house was built.

My father, sweating, irritated, and apprehensive about the future, began moving furniture. Among other things, inadvertently, he tore up the cardboard cab of a new balloon dirigible that I had been given to ease the transition of moving, and he used it to shim the leg of a china closet because not one floor was level. I wept a small amount and he sent me to explore the house.

I had to go to school either the next day or the day after that. I expected that I would be challenged and tested on the playground on my very first day. That brought up again the matter of what I was to do to create a new image. It fretted me as I walked alone in the empty upstairs bedroom that faced the harbor, a place of ancient smells and dust. Suddenly, I came upon something, a most unlikely item that seemed to offer hope.

In this upper room, on a closet shelf, I found a little tin box; curiously, it was full of human teeth, some quite large. Pray do not ask me why people saved their extracted teeth, for people save everything, including bills that they never intend to pay. I put the tin box containing the teeth in the pocket of my corduroy pants.

At recess on my first school day on the Vineyard, the biggest boy in the grade came over to me and grabbed my necktie. At that age level, necktie-grabbing was a favorite way of starting something. "I can lick anybody around here," he said. "I can lick you. You want to try it?"

My heart was bumping inside my shirt and my movements were somewhat restricted because he continued to hold my tie but I reached into my pocket and pulled out the little box. I opened the cover.

"What are them?" asked the fellow who was holding my necktie.

"Teeth," I said.

"Where'd you get 'em?"

"Where I just moved from, I knocked them out of people who held my necktie."

His face underwent a peculiar change for a small boy. He continued to look at the teeth as one might look at a box of corpses.

"Well, watch it," he said, and let go of me.

Nobody ever bothered me after that and I have never been tied to a fire hydrant since.

Having made my place, I returned home in victory after school and, feeling newly positive about the world, I stopped in the backyard to pick a few flowers, reveling in the chance to do so. My mother came to the kitchen door and said, "You don't have to pick them. Just look at them where they are.

We're here to stay." And gradually, the grass started growing over the shortcut in our yard that people had made walking from the lane to Water Street before we moved there.

Generations of islanders have been born since that day of taking my place. The house still stands, the flowers still grow, and when I began this book, Stephen Carey Luce, Jr., who took *his* place in the island community long before I did, was one of the first Vineyarders with whom I discussed it. I did so because Mr. Luce, who died in March of this year, could look back on a long and influential career as a major mover and shaper on the island. Through his stewardship of the Martha's Vineyard National Bank, membership in the Steamship Authority and County Commission, leadership of the Martha's Vineyard Hospital, and a score of other capacities relating to everything from estate settlements to government programs, he made things happen.

Many of these things make the difference between what the island was and what it is, including increasing the size of the Authority's property at Vineyard Haven so that it could handle more traffic, and acquisition and development of the island's airport. I asked a number of Vineyarders who it was who had wielded significant power on the Vineyard during much of the period with which this account is concerned. Several replied, "S. C. Luce and friends." When *Vineyard Gazette* editor Henry Beetle Hough wrote Mr. Luce's page-one obituary, he described him as having "exercised a greater influence on Martha's Vineyard and among Vineyarders than any other individual."

Something of what the island now is, Mr. Luce could take credit for, and he did.

For the sake of the record, I was some kind of cousin to "Carey," because my great-great-grandfather married the daughter of Shadrach Robinson, who was for thirteen days in

1776 a member of Captain John Grannis's militia company on Naushon. Mr. Luce became a member of the Sons of the American Revolution at least in part on the strength of his relationship to Shadrach.

Mr. Luce was a man of many facets. I remember him standing on the bank steps in summer, one of the first in the morning to be downtown for business. In immaculate panama, white flannels, and blue jacket, and always with fresh carnation, he was totally composed and reassuring, a veritable symbol of a symbol, a breathing landmark. Once, I asked his advice about business opportunities on the island; we were in his office at the bank, and he turned slowly in his chair and faced me. "Everett," he said, clipping his words off neatly, like so many blades of grass, "I have sat right here in this office, on this street, in this little town, and made a million dollars." And he smiled, quite far back. That was probably thirty-five years ago.

This was the same man who, in the summer of 1941, drove James Cagney's bay gelding Gold Leaf in the feature race of the Metropolitan Driving Club at the Charles River Speedway. Ten thousand roaring spectators watched Carey nose out Carl Hinckley's pacer to win. In a subsequent Class C event, Mr. Luce, driving his own trotter Calumet Doble, was pocketed by other drivers until he was within a few feet of the wire, when he was able to break out of the field and claim another victory that day, an extraordinary achievement.

The late Francis X. Hurley of Oak Bluffs, attorney, former state auditor and treasurer, and, at that time, chairman of the Steamship Authority, once observed with characteristic humor, "Carey delights in the art of manipulation. If he wants something done, he could probably pick up the phone and ask somebody to do it and that would be that. Instead, he prefers to create a Rube Goldberg sequence in which he contacts

Party A, who gets in touch with Party B, who writes a letter to Party C, who finally gets Party D to do whatever it is that Carey wants done."

In 1980, how did Mr. Luce feel about island change in the last half-century?

"I think Vineyarders are happier and better off than they were in 1925 because they're making more money," he said. "Change had to come because the island was easier to get to, more people had more money, and because more of them kind of got the idea of coming here. These changes have got to continue. There's still a lot of land that's good for something besides raising huckleberry brush.

"There was a time when many of our policies were determined by a small group of people. Now, I think it's a pretty cosmopolitan setup. I think these changes are good because these young people have got to carry on the way they think it should be done and not the way I think it should be done from the cemetery."

I pointed out that in 1975, Mr. Hough, publisher and editor of the *Gazette* since 1920, concluded in his book *Mostly on Martha's Vineyard* that, "considering everything, I should be sorry to have these memoirs end with the slightest note of optimism. Selfishly, I am sorrier about Martha's Vineyard than about the world."

"Obviously," I said to Carey, "Mr. Hough is depressed by the changes that have taken place here during the last half-century."

"I'm sorry that Henry is depressed," Carey said.

Some are delighted, some are dismayed by what has happened; that's about the way it is.

2. The Lane

THE way things used to be does not go out of mind readily, especially because even the smaller sights and sounds were so inextricably and comfortably linked to the larger whole — there was a oneness of spirit about the place that was in no sense intrusive but, rather, subtly beguiling, like the aroma of cinnamon in warm apple pie. And it is as easily recalled.

The unpaved dogleg of a lane in which we lived offered, in all its parts and people, a splendid introduction to what the island was. True, the house had no central heating system, no electric lights, no indoor plumbing, no storm windows, and no heat in the second-floor bedrooms, but a lot of island residences then had none of these things. Besides, it was spring and the cold and shorter days that would make all these factors more burdensome were far away and, more important, eclipsed by the immediate interlude of exploration and discovery.

On May 1, 1925, the *Vineyard Gazette* noted in a page-one item, "Of interest to Gazette readers up-Island, Joseph C. Allen, whose poems and stories of the Vineyard have won him a wide following, will devote his entire time to the Gazette. Mr. Allen is taking up his residence in Vineyard Haven. He is a Vineyarder by birth, tradition, and inclination. His interest in the island, added to his acquaintance

Martha's Vineyard

with its people and his ability as a writer, promise much for the future of the Gazette."

As the year expanded, clumps of tiger lilies exploded against ancient sagging fences. At the rough stone steps leading to the lower front yard, the blue flag bloomed. There were three old trees, gnarled and wind-shaped, for we were only one street removed from the harbor, and they bore apples, pears, and quinces. Heavy with fruit, Mary Abby Norton's cherry tree overhung our yard, and she said we could pick all we wanted. I was impressed by that because it was one of the first clues I had to what island life was going to be like.

Mary Abby, gentle, white-haired, and soft-spoken, lived in what once had been the Revolutionary Claghorn Tavern and the village post office, a rudely finished old place with hand-hewn timbers and handmade cleated doors. She was becomingly reticent, as were most Vineyard ladies of her era — even when Henry Ritter, the high school principal whose garage was across the lane, backed out of his driveway and struck her woodshed something like twice a week. She did not make a speech when she offered the cherries or suggest that we should run in and out of each other's houses. She just said, "Do help yourself," and then she smoothed her white apron and went back into her kitchen with quick, small steps. Her one dramatic statement to society was in a row of pink hollyhocks that erupted each year from earth on which she had dumped her winter's stove ashes. They stretched to such glorious, spiky, bell-waving heights — thirteen or fourteen feet, as I remember — that they were sometimes mentioned in the newspaper, which I think pleased her, although she never said so.

Lucy Cooper used to come through the lane carrying a market basket worn smooth with the years. She was on her way to Smith, Bodfish, and Swift's grocery on Main Street and she walked slowly; I never was sure whether this was because she was elderly or simply so that her cat, which always accompanied her, could keep up. The cat was plump, yellow, and aloof; it carried its tail like a plume, the end always waving slowly, and it chose not to hurry.

At the Beach Street end of the lane, Curtis Athearn, being unmarried, lived with his father and mother. He worked at the grain store, took pride in carrying a hundred-pound sack of feed on each shoulder, and his mother said that he had once swum "a very great distance" underwater when they used to live at Menemsha. Every Sunday, Curtis put on his blue serge suit with a bulging bag of horehound drops in the right-hand jacket pocket and walked purposefully (he leaned forward) up the hill to the Baptist church, where he sang in the choir. Standing against a vestry wall with his feet together and his head to one side, he explained to me that he could sing every part except soprano. Once, H. P. Ayer of Newton read some of my father's verses on a Boston radio broadcast and we went to the Athearns' house to listen to it on their crystal set but the static was heavy and we could make out no more than an occasional word. My father had no use for radio thereafter.

I "ran errands" for Betsy Gifford, being paid a nickel each time. She was in her nineties and lived in a dustless, bare-floored little house on Water Street that smelled musty except for a whiff of kerosene, with which she fueled the portable stove that heated her daily soup. She did not have many errands to run; usually, she would ask me to go to Cronig's for ten cents' worth of stew meat, for her appetite was no more active than her life. She said she had read the Bible completely four times, although usually she could not remember the parts of it that she wanted to.

Periodically, she would ask me, "Now who on earth was the

father of David?" or some such question, and usually, I would not know. I suppose it was not to my credit that I would make up an answer to keep her from getting upset. I would say quickly, as if there were no doubt in my mind, "Elisha," or something similar, and that would satisfy her, principally because she had already forgotten the question and was thinking about something else.

When I crept into her house in late afternoon to see whether she wanted anything done, she would be sitting, straight-backed in a black dress, her hands and Bible in her lap, utterly without motion. Almost every day, I thought she was probably dead, and every time I opened her back door and stepped into that silence so heavy that I was afraid to break it, I whispered to myself, "God, don't let her be dead. Don't let me be the one to find her." And one day, a woman whom I did not even know beckoned me to the fence where Mary Abby's cherries hung over and said quietly, "Mrs. Gifford won't need you anymore. She's gone."

The Cromwells, for whose family the lane was named, lived next door to us — Benjamin Coffin Cromwell II, called "Big Ben" to distinguish him from his son, Benjamin Coffin Cromwell III, "Little Ben," and Emma, the widow of the first Benjamin, who brought up her grandson because his mother had long since died. They lived in a handsomely appointed house with mansard roof, grand proportions, and a sweeping front porch; it was rich yellow and always freshly painted. Emma's husband had been a master mariner of distinction and had created the wealth that continued to give her a certain social position. She wore a pince-nez, drove her own brand-new Model A sedan, albeit erratically, and served tomato bisque with croutons and molded salad at her Lobsterville summer cottage.

Big Ben spent most of his time boating, fishing, and hunting for the fun of it; he was a ruggedly built, handsome fellow, most at home in open-throated woolen shirts, flannel trousers, and hand-sewn leather moccasins. His dogs were thoroughbreds, his cars, always new, were loaded in winter with automatic shotguns, boxes of ammunition, the best oilskins, and burlap sacks of wooden decoys — expertly crafted and painted — which he had made himself. He was capable of building a boat or a boat model with the skill of a professional. He owned a hardware store that specialized in the best tools and sporting goods; habitually, he took new hammers, chisels, shovels, or whatever, from the stock, used them once with consummate skill, and then left them in his ever-open garage or on the lawn to rust. When next he needed a hammer, he took another from the store.

Within the house, many things were reminders of what the family had and stood for, beginning with the oil painting of the grandfather's ship, a handsome, gold-hued clipper that made her salty mark in half the world's seas and oceans. The picture dominated the dining room. "Yes," Big Ben would say, carving a roast black duck at the mahogany table that shone like warm glass, "that was the captain's ship. He'd see a vessel ahead of him on the horizon at daybreak and by sundown, she'd be on the horizon astern." Then he and Emma would chuckle, even though they had heard this a thousand times, principally because, in a competitive world (in which, however, it was assumed that the rich would remain rich and the poor would remain poor), their family had been accustomed to winning. The old captain's vessel was not fast by accident.

Their home was something of a museum of what they were and of what the name Cromwell meant. In the kitchen corner, there were stacked oiled hunting guns, dark and glistening; in the living room, a splendid grand piano that nobody played but that was precisely right for the rug from Aubusson and floor-to-ceiling windows looking upon the harbor. The fireplace fittings were of brass, gleaming, and the Mah-Jongg tiles were of ivory, all 144 of them.

When Little Ben had a birthday, a half-dozen of us who were his playmates were invited to the Cromwell house to eat round golden waffles (which Emma made in great numbers), drowned in maple syrup and quiescent under chunks of melting S. S. Pierce butter. To some extent, it was depressing for the guests to return to their largely unpainted, rented homes and to ordinary pots-and-pans households without a single candlestick, but less so than you might think, because in those days, the notion of economic egalitarianism had not been thought of and would not have been tolerated if it had been.

In summer, Emma was hostess for the annual church bazaar, and her spacious front lawn that extended to Water Street was gay with bright umbrellas; chatting women in pastel silks and georgettes, every one hatted and gloved; a mustached fellow with a monkey and a hand organ, imported from the mainland; and perspiring, smiling men who scooped ice cream filled with chunks of strawberries out of frosted cans. After it was over and the ladies were returning to their cars in the lane, they always lingered to look at Emma's roses in the garden across from the house; the bushes, drooping with fragrant blooms and full of great bumbling bees, dominated the whole corner of the single-track road and were a reasonable expression of what it stood for.

The Cromwell world, to such degree as I was exposed to it, was exciting. One windy Sunday in the fall of 1925, a small seaplane dropped into Vineyard Haven harbor. This was an event of consequence then and a couple dozen of us had gathered to peer at it by the time it had plowed through spray and roared up to the beach. Inside were two men from Boston who had come to visit Big Ben; that in itself was extraordinary but more so was the fact that he flew back to Boston with them. He told me afterward that the "running time" between Vineyard Haven and Boston in the seaplane was about one hour and fifteen minutes, which I assumed was very rapid although I did not really know how far away Boston was.

The Cromwell house was both full and empty; even as a child, I knew that. It was well appointed but it had few books and nobody read them. On rainy days, I enjoyed going to their attic with Little Ben, listening to the water falling on the roof and riding the genuine leather rocking horse with beautiful glass eyes that had belonged to his father. Yet I did think that Little Ben wanted something that numerous expensive presents did not give him.

Henry and Evangeline Ritter were not wealthy but, by contrast, their home — built in the late eighteenth century and now a landmark on Beach Street — combined both taste and antiquity. They deserved the house; the house deserved them, for, as it was outstanding, so were they.

Henry was a basic Teuton, an excellent and determined teacher who acquainted those possessing willingness and fortitude with the value of disciplined thought, especially as this applied to physics, chemistry, and biology. At that time, I had never heard of Millay's "Euclid alone has looked on Beauty bare," but when I did, it was Henry — chalk in hand and attacking the classroom blackboard with symbols of truth — who came to mind at once. He possessed a restless impatience, forever jerking his head and hitching up a shoulder, as if he could not wait for something to be done. He ran his school as a general runs an army, resorting at times to anger and ridicule, abruptly ending both school dances and school classes if he saw fit, and totally dominating teachers, students, and even the atmosphere in which learning took place. On occasion, he was unfair and unreasonable, yet he was basically a man of compassion because when young he had known the need of it, and he taught well, knowing what an education was worth. And when he *did* laugh, it was deep and real.

Evangeline, known by a few intimates as "the Duchess," a name that my father gave to her and that she confessed she liked, was a complementing partner to her husband, not because they were alike in temperament but because they were both intelligent and shared great intensity of feeling. Mrs. Ritter contributed to the town — which was, after all, like most small towns of the period, pretty much a meat-and-potatoes affair — a touch of elegance and sparkle that came naturally to her.

It is significant that the members of the Want to Know Club met at her home, this being one of several such societies on the island at that time that not only constituted social outlets but served to satisfy a certain cultural appetite. There were groups of both men and women who met regularly to be informed by speakers, including their own members, who lectured on their travels or who had prepared papers on subjects of broad interest. In the present instance, the reporter who covered the meeting (concerned with "discoveries and excavations in the valley of the tombs of the king of Egypt in 1923") also saw fit to say something about the Ritter house. It was, said the account, "a very fashionable resort for teas and guest occasions for those not opening their own homes for club and society meetings. The rooms where the meetings and tea were held were done in old blue and yellow colonial paper, braided rugs and old furniture; yellow flowers and candles lighted the tables, which were spread with delicacies and glass and china dishes."

For her personal guests, Evangeline laced her consommé with sherry, served an elegant fish soup in Italian pottery, and offered hot yeast rolls and blackberry wine at ten in the morning in the garden. I find it difficult to remember precisely what she wore and that is because what she wore was precisely hers and of her; one was conscious only of the total taste, flair, and womanliness, without being specifically aware of the items that created the effect. She radiated warmth and life; she dominated the moment without seeming to do so, especially since she was tall and carried herself well; her dark eyes snapped and her smile was always on the verge of roguishness. Opening her front door, she exuded both grace and hospitality in extraordinary fashion; "it was like being dunked naked in hot buttered rum," commented one who experienced the sensation, and that strikes me as being a fair appraisal.

I once heard an admiring male, caught in a flight of fancy, compare her to George Sand, which is interesting but not accurate. Evangeline was prettier, and she was less the leader of a movement than the movement itself. She provided a social oasis in which the arts, crafts, books, paintings, music, good words, imaginative dining — all those things that separate man from beast — were embraced with enthusiasm and without inhibition.

When I was quite young, she had a bookshop in a front room of her house. On the particular day, she had just received a new shipment and, as usual, was unpacking at a snail's pace because she stopped to read excerpts from every volume. She read to me from Elinor Hoyt Wylie: "My lord, adjudge my strength and set me where / I bear a little more than I can bear."

"Do you know what that means?" she asked.

I said that I did.

"Do you agree with it?"

I said that I didn't, that I didn't see anything very good about being asked to bear more than I could.

"You will come to agree with it," she said. "One day, you will." And she smiled at me.

Our lane, through which few vehicles passed in the course of the day, was like the island itself, "somewhat off to one side," as my grandmother Allen would have said, and both its nature and neighbors were comfortably predictable.

If you sat on our back doorstep, which was next to the lane, and heard the sound of an iron wheel on cinders above the scolding of the crows, that would be Clem Cleaveland, lean and quiet, pushing his barrow of celery to Main Street, to sell it to Bert Smith at the S.B.S. grocery. You could float a skiff in Clem's backyard after a heavy rain and that is why he raised such good celery there. Mostly, there was no noise louder than that wheel. Luther Athearn, sitting in a kitchen chair in his workshop, was whittling, and that makes no great sound. Mr. Palm, who had a display of imported pottery in Evangeline's house, might be in Mr. Ritter's driveway, fishing out red and blue bowls from excelsior in a packing case stamped with a foreign name, and that makes no sound, either. And Lucy Cooper's cat stepped quietly.

I soon came to understand that things and people moved slowly and quietly, that all dogs had first and last names that everyone knew, and to believe that nothing changed, although this, of course, was in error. Yet because I was then measuring from day to day, rather than dealing with longer periods, it seemed to me that the wisp of blue breakfast smoke rose precisely at the same time each morning from the kitchen chimney of Prentiss Bodfish, the blacksmith. I assumed it always would and that Prentiss, great-boned man of work, would lumber unchanged forever through our lane, as much an irresistible force as a deep-legged vessel butting through a tide rip. The simple routine of the neighborhood, the lack of great difference from one day to the next, encouraged the belief that only the very young had birthdays and that older people did not, in fact, get any older but instead had come to assume the well-deserved permanence of landmarks. It was comforting to me to know that they were there and always would be.

The seasons, of course, *did* change and people's lives adjusted accordingly, for Vineyarders lived, as Luther said, "close to the weather." I was soon aware that on summer nights, once a week, the brass and reeds of the band concert at Owen Park came to our lane, now louder, now softer on the wind, and that on winter nights, there was no sound at all, except perhaps the hiss of snow sifting in from the northeast. In spring, our lane was mud-rutted and puddles splashed the wooden spokes of my father's brass-snouted Model T touring car. And in the fall, the sky produced a blue not only beyond poets but beyond belief — it was of such clarity that one expected it to ring like a perfect bell.

One of the first ways in which I learned that islanders' lives relate to the seasons came on a fall day when someone at school told me that the hake — these being a cod's cousins — had come in to the steamboat dock. That night, after I had done my homework, I rigged a hank of cod line with a hook and sinker, took a couple of quahaugs for bait and a rock to smash their shells, and walked down past Tom Tilton's house, past the old cellar hole with the abandoned dray in it, past the grain store, to the dock.

I was still young enough so that night was new to me — being out in it and aware of how it changed things. The water was as black as the shadows under the freight shed; yesterday's buildings, lumberyard, coal piles, and the Seamen's Bethel lay foreign in the moonlight, and those who fished on the wharf beside me, no more than hollow voices in the dark, had become strangers since the light of noon.

I caught four fish; my mother baked them for lunch next day. It is good to learn early in life, as islanders do, what to look for in wind and weather, to learn the natural calendar if you are going to do your own food gathering. I did not think of all that at the time but I was impressed by the fact that I had provided a meal and that it had not cost any money.

Moreover, I was early aware that the Vineyarder found ignorance of nature ridiculous as well as deplorable. Attorney John M. Thayer of Worcester appeared in the district court in Edgartown in behalf of the Gay Head selectmen over the question of a herring fishery lease. One of the points involved was the number of herring that might have swum up the Gay Head herring creek during a two-week period in April. It was Mr. Thayer's job to pooh-pooh the claim that herring enough to fill two hundred barrels in all probability went upstream during the fourteen days.

"Why, it's perfect nonsense," argued Mr. Thayer. "It is ridiculous for anyone to attempt to say that a certain number of herring probably went up the creek last April," he said scornfully. "Why, anyone knows that fish won't always bite. It may be too hot or too cold, the wind blows from the north, south, east, or west, or somewhere else, or the sun doesn't shine or the fish are not hungry."

Since herring are caught otherwise than with hook or line, Mr. Thayer's argument was interrupted by general laughter in the courtroom. When it had subsided, Judge Nelson P. Brown, on the bench, said to Mr. Thayer, "You might hang around and learn something more about fishing."

The incident was related with amusement by Vineyarders of all ages, including those at the elementary-school level, for herring on the island were, and are, something special.

At that time, on a day when the year was warming, the word would spread at school that Frankie Vincent had reported the herring were running at Tashmoo. That night, men and boys from the town would line the banks of the creek and this is what it was like, from start to finish:

In the woodshed off the kitchen, where our tiger cat had all her babies, my father blew pale pipe smoke and hunched over the workbench, fashioning a dip net for taking herring. Some families had had their nets for generations because a good bow and shaft are works of art. Shape the curved handle with care and flatten the sides so that it will not turn in the hands when soaked with water and slime. Form the bow of two sections, preferably of natural bends — sometimes roots, carefully barked, smoothed, and seasoned — and see that it describes a shape resembling a snowshoe but curving upward like a Turkish slipper.

Secure bow to shaft with the greatest care and then bore holes in the bow to take the twine, at intervals the length of a bar in the net. The first row of meshes knitted go through these holes, which are bored at an angle to prevent any part of the twine striking sand or gravel as the net is swung to pick up fish. How the smooth, homemade shuttle flashes in the sunlight from the window, and the net grows quickly, until there it is, like an overgrown soup spoon, artfully contrived and light enough to swing all night.

"Now you," said my father, "take care of the rest of the gear." So I found a wooden apple box back of the grocery and painted it white inside. Then I got down the black tin lantern from its nail in the shed, trimmed the wick, washed the glass chimney, and filled the base from the kerosene can. Finally, I found a clean burlap sack, and that was everything.

When it was dark, my father piloted the Ford through the twisting sandy ruts fringed by pines. I fretted that there might be no room left — and as it turned out, more than fifty showed up that night, lining both banks of the creek — but we were fairly early and got a good place. We stood the box on one end, close to the water's edge, lighted the lantern, and put it inside. Its yellow rays carved an oval of light on the fast-running creek water and you could see that the bottom was sparkling gravel. In the offshore dark, somewhere out in the Sound, there was faint splashing and my father said, "If that's a hungry seal, hollow clear down to his ankles, he's going to get more herring than we are."

Yet almost as he spoke, we saw the first fish come into the pool of light, heard the crack of swinging nets upon the gravel, and the spatter of water as they lifted, some with a flopping fish, some empty, all moving shadows against the rows of lanterns in the dark, still night. Some came up empty because the herring passed irregularly, sometimes in twos and threes, darting, and sometimes by the dozens, and the fisherman must keep a sharp eye to catch the sheen in his small light for it will not be there long. The herring is fast; he is lively, and when you make a pass with the net, it must be on the mark, for the fish is good at dodging dippers.

They were like dark-backed torpedoes; some pushed steadily against the out-running current, others spurted to the creekside to rest in the unlighted spots, finning just enough to hold their own. When they turned a little in the mellow light, silver in the clear riffles, framed by the warm blackness, there was created an instant of uncommon beauty, a harmony of creature, time, and place, and a bonus of graceful motion.

"Now, we'll baptize her," said my father, swinging the new net, and I thought it a splendid omen for up it came, the first time around, dripping sparkles, and with two fat fish. "Hah!" said my father with satisfaction, and he slatted them out on the sand behind him, where I grabbed them. And after that, there were more, including some for Luther to salt (proper brine must float an egg) and smoke over a tiny fire of sweet fern and hardwood chips, and three or four with fat roes for Mary Abby, who preferred the roe — sautéed in butter and served with bacon — to the fish.

It was about that time that I discovered weather also had its official aspects. Somebody representing the national government asked my father if he would be willing to have a rain gauge installed in our backyard. "Installed" is probably too high-flown a word because the instrument was no more than a galvanized iron cylinder a couple of feet high that stood on four legs. It had a funnel-type top and a dipstick. The idea was that whenever it rained, my father would insert the dipstick into the cylinder, determine how much precipitation had fallen, and notify the U.S. Weather Bureau.

In retrospect, I assume that the government was assisted in its rain measurements by thousands of such gauges and citizens scattered all over the country. But at the time, the matter loomed large to me, because I was not very old and I had not been much of anywhere, even if you included the Brockton Fair. So that overgrown tin can next to the quince tree was a direct link to far-off Washington, the American eagle, and the might of the nation. Occasionally, I would sit on the grass next to the green wickiups of poled Kentucky Wonder beans in our garden and stare at that can. I really did not expect the voice of President John Calvin Coolidge to come hollowly out of the funnel, saying, "Hello, Everett," but, on the other hand, I thought of the thing as being official. I had, after all, never been so close to the White House in my life.

There came a Saturday afternoon when my father decided that I would split some kindling instead of going to the movies to see Douglas Fairbanks, Sr., in *The Thief of Bagdad,* for which I had saved money that I made by digging quahaugs. I felt the need of expressing my displeasure — in some manner so subtle as to escape punishment, this latter because my father never got over being a sergeant in the regular army and he brooked about as much insubordination as you could stick in your eye.

After I had finished splitting the wood in sullen fashion, I sat staring at the government's rain gauge and, even as I did, the first sprinkles of a gathering storm dropped upon my head. I knew then what I would do. While it was still pouring, I filled a quart milk bottle with water and emptied it into the rain guage. Vaguely, but with satisfaction, I visualized the impending confusion in the country's capital, the incredible distortion of the national statistic.

Of course, it was my father who was confounded first. After the storm had passed, he stuck the dipstick into the can, hauled it up, observed the reading, and exclaimed, "Jehoshaphat!" He dipped the stick again, verified the measurement, muttered, "Damned if I thought it was a cloudburst!" and stomped into the house.

I did not sleep well that night. About 1:00 A.M., it occurred to me with terrible force that my father might be sent to jail for falsifying federal figures. I had no idea what the government did with its rain-gauge information but by daybreak, I had convinced myself that the farmers of the Midwest or even large elements of the U.S. Army and Navy might be affected adversely by what I had done. So I confessed to my father at breakfast.

"Fortunately," he said, "I thought something was wrong with the figure and I did not send it in." Then he said, "I want you to know that the only thing worse than being simply dishonest is being dishonest in such a way that other people have to pay for what you have done." He finished his fried egg and added, "You were willing to put me in a position where I might very well have given inaccurate information to the government of the United States, which trusts me."

I felt awful and yet relieved that Washington had not been misled. I felt that a great burden had been lifted, however, and whistled all the way to Sunday school, even though my father made me bail out the rain gauge and split kindling on the next Saturday, too.

Although I did not know it in the early years, everybody who moves to the island is not accepted by the natives and many of those who eventually are do not achieve this status for a long time. The business of "moving in" has to be low-keyed and leisurely and principally initiated by the Vineyarder or it will never happen at all. It was not a problem for me because my father's family had been there so long; natives ignored the fact that my father ever had been away (probably viewing it as a young man's pardonable mistake) and down-island, I was "Joe Allen's boy" and up-island, I was "Will Allen's grandson." Among older residents, that identification persists today, and I have wondered whether, had I not left the Vineyard, I would ever have achieved an identity of my own.

I remember exactly when I first became aware of acceptance.

C. M. "Duffy" Vincent and his pretty wife, Rose, operated a store on Main Street in Vineyard Haven that sold newspapers, stationery, tobacco, and candy. They offered a pair of brand-new roller skates free to the boy or girl who saved the most Oh Henry candy bar wrappers, which were, as I remember, principally orange. I wanted the roller skates but there wasn't any extra money in our house at the time and certainly not enough for as much candy as I knew it would take to win the contest. For what seemed to me quite a while,

I had only three Oh Henry wrappers in my top bureau drawer. I did not know how many anybody else had but three were certainly not enough.

Then something happened and, to this day, I do not know how it came about. Candy-eating members of the town community, of several age groups, somehow found out that I was trying to get the roller skates and they rallied to my cause. I first became aware of it on the playground at school when a couple of girls gave me their Oh Henry wrappers. I have been interested in girls ever since.

A couple of days later, a deacon of the church gave me one and then there was an elderly lady who stopped me on the street and took one, neatly folded, out of her handbag, saying that she had been carrying it for nearly a week in hopes of seeing me. I even received three in the mail with an unsigned piece of paper saying, "Good luck! Get those roller skates, boy!"

Strangers stopped by the house and left Oh Henry wrappers and once, a fellow who drove one of the town trucks hauled a couple out of his pocket that he had retrieved from the dump. He apologized because they were dirty but he said, "I guess it don't matter. You can still tell what they are."

I won the roller skates because the people in my town, some of whom I did not even know, wanted me to. The city had never been anything like that. I had a feeling, then beyond my power to crystallize or express, that I belonged to them and they to me.

Those were the days when the island was sparsely settled; the county average was about forty people to the square mile. A twelve-room house on four acres of land, with waterfront, on the east side of Vineyard Haven harbor, with a three-car garage, landing dock, boathouse, beach house, four bathrooms, and fully furnished, was for rent for the summer for

$2,700. James W. Lee was offering for sale for $4,000 a West Tisbury farm "on the new state road to Edgartown," consisting of seven acres, an unfurnished house of six rooms and bathroom, modern improvements, a barn, small farm building, small greenhouse, and some farm machinery.

Commercial fishing on the island was big news, especially when Captain Robert Jackson of the schooner *Hazel M. Jackson* of Edgartown brought into Boston a high-line trip — 110 swordfish after three weeks out — and the crew received $359 each. There was still considerable island farming — fresh native pork shoulders were selling for 25 cents a pound — but the central part of the Vineyard was already being described as a "veritable graveyard of farms which are actually dead and buried." There was a good ice business but William G. Manter Company was selling Frigidaires for $190 and up, pointing out that "you can make one trip to market or have one delivery from your grocer in which you can cover your needs for days in advance and save the possible muss and annoyance of using ice."

Mrs. Edward Roth, Jr., arrived at Vineyard Haven from Washington, D.C., on a May Monday, having driven over the roads from that city to Woods Hole. She left the capital at 6:30 A.M. Sunday and "spent only one night on the road, at New Haven. Mrs. Roth is a very accomplished driver, having toured extensively. She said, however, that if conditions had not been so favorable, she would have been unable to make such fast time. She reported the roads in good shape, being compelled to make only a few detours." At that time, you could buy a Hudson seven-passenger sedan with balloon tires, front bumper, automatic windshield wiper, looking glass, and stoplight, delivered to any part of the island, for $2,475.

One of the reasons people dropped into Duffy Vincent's store regularly was to pick up news and the same was true of other places on the island. There were, after all, only sixty radio sets in all of Edgartown and, as late as 1927, I stood with a good-sized crowd before Roger Amidon's radio shop in Vineyard Haven and listened to the Tunney-Dempsey fight through a morning-glory speaker hung on the front of the building, which was a fair indication of how many did not own radios.

Society was still much phonograph-oriented. Approximately two thousand people from all over the island turned out for a Victor Artists Concert at the Tabernacle for the benefit of the Martha's Vineyard Hospital. The concert, very likely offering the greatest aggregation of celebrated artists ever brought together on the island up to that time, was arranged by Calvin G. Child, a Vineyard Haven summer resident, and director of the Victor Talking Machine Company. The artists who contributed their services were Lucy Isabelle Marsh, soprano; Lambert Murphy, tenor; Billy Murray, comedian; and the International Salon Orchestra, under the direction of Alexander Shilkret.

In Oak Bluffs, Selectman Michael J. Keegan took the floor at a special town meeting to argue in favor of lifting a years-long ban against amateur Sunday sports. "Our aristocratic neighbors, Edgartown and Vineyard Haven, are having Sunday baseball and I think Oak Bluffs might as well do so," said Mr. Keegan. William Amaral of the American Legion and senior member of the plumbing firm of Amaral Brothers, said such a move would benefit "men who have to labor six days of the week." The vote was yes, 60, no, 36, and there was "vociferous applause."

Commercial fishing vessels, although still able to carry sail, increasingly were leaving their canvas ashore or stowing it in the hold as "confidence in the gasoline engine" increased. The *Vineyard Gazette* noted in May of 1925 that "for long, it has been the prophecy that Martha's Vineyard would some day take its rightful position among the famous resorts and, for long, it has been the hope and prayer of all good Vineyarders that it might come to pass and that voices might be lifted from the four corners of the earth extolling the beauties and charms of Martha's Vineyard."

At about the same time, my grandfather's heifer gave birth to twin calves and it was so reported in the Roaring Brook items.

I seldom think about my grandfather without thinking about the Poole family, for obvious reasons — if my father had felt able to grow up at home, I would never have known as much about the Pooles as I do, nor would our families have been as close as they have been for all of these years.

Donald LeMar Poole, the elder Everett's son, is a successful commercial fisherman, a short and stocky, pipe-smoking, sea-going Vineyarder, whose house at Nashaquitsa Pond, Chilmark, stands on land that belonged to his great-great-great-great-grandfather. Captain Poole is a traditionalist; he wears gold earrings presented to him by his wife on their golden wedding anniversary in 1976 because his grandfather Anderson Poole, his great-grandfather Captain Otis Smith, and his great-great-grandfather Mayhew Smith all wore earrings.

His wife, Dorothy Cottle Poole, is descended from eight generations of Vineyarders in her mother's family and nine in her father's. Her father, mother, and grandfather were educators and her father and grandfather also were judges; the latter, Beriah Tilton Hillman, also was a member of the state legislature, served on school boards in both Chilmark and Edgartown, and was town treasurer in Chilmark. Mrs. Poole retired in 1965 as principal of Menemsha School, where she taught twenty years. She was a charter member of the Chilmark Community Club, taught Sunday school, organized the first Girl Scout troop in Chilmark, was a charter member of Martha's Vineyard Community Services, and is historian of the Dukes County Historical Society.

She relates to the natural world as do most islanders, naturally; unlike many of them, she is inclined and able to articulate this relationship. "In summer," she once wrote,

we go to the cove to dig a bucket of clams, little ones to steam and larger ones for a chowder. If we don't find clams, there are always plenty of quahaugs. We don't hurry but take time to savor the freshness of the early morning hour. Going up the grass slope toward home, our gaze is arrested by myriad white blossoms and, on close view, dark red berries. We doff our old straw hats, line their crowns with leaves, and gather strawberries, not large, but juicy and sweet. We'll have a shortcake to follow the chowder.

Captain and Mrs. Poole sit in their Chilmark living room, which is dominated by shelves of books, with the accent on maritime subjects and history.

They both conclude that newcomers to the island, essentially elderly retired or young people seeking a particular kind of life-style, have "outnumbered and overwhelmed" the natives. "Some of the young," Captain Poole says, "do not work as we know it; mostly, if they work at all, they go into the building trades and many are heavily dependent on government assistance.

"Many of the retired people come here to live because they think this is a lovely place. They buy and build and then they begin to agitate so that everything will be the same as where they came from, including police force and garbage collection. They demand the extra services; they don't want the tax rate required to provide them."

Captain Poole deplores the fact that fishing and hunting

have been affected adversely by island changes. "Newcomers have become numerous enough to dictate the shellfisheries," he says. "The emphasis is to give visitors the opportunity to take scallops. Open the beds on the first of November when the weather is warm and the bank clerks from New York can get scallops without getting chilly. They try to stop shell-fishermen from working in front of property they own.

"A lot of property that goes to the water has been bought up. Our very best gunning is locked up solid. Walk along the beach between high- and low-water marks and it's all no-trespassing signs. We are still overrun with people renting or trying to buy. An island realtor had a call from a man in New York who wanted to rent a house for four weeks in August and was willing to pay eight thousand to ten thousand dollars. Can you imagine what that does to a Vineyard economy built on potatoes and salt codfish?

"These things change the whole way of life for Vineyard people and I see no possibility of reversing the trend," he says. "I look upon this as one of the last outposts of the insolent, independent Yankee. Yankees have been held up to derision in many ways and perhaps they deserved it, but we'll go down fighting until the last clod of earth is on top of us."

Mrs. Poole believes that the retirees who have made the Vineyard their home "often have much to contribute" but she is concerned because "an island, more than any other locale, can easily become so overpopulated that it loses its identity. That is happening to Martha's Vineyard. The pace of island living has accelerated uncomfortably."

After the interview, on my way down-island, I stopped near Chilmark's Cross Road to watch a pair of Canada geese that were sufficiently accustomed to mankind and motor vehicles to be flying across the highway at just above the treetop level. Black-stockinged and magnificent in their easy grace, they *ka-ronked* and *ha-lunked*, and I reveled in their voices, wondering what it is that geese have to say to each other at high noon on a warm and bright-blue day. Even if I could have understood their language, I was not about to discover the subject of their conversation because it was drowned out abruptly by the braying of the fire station whistle, also announcing noontime in its own way.

The symbolism of the moment — the one sound obliterated by the other — was too poignant to be ignored within the context of the total continuing Vineyard drama: man and nature, yesterday and today, or, in the view of some, not "and," but "versus."

3. The Cycle

IN the late 1920s, my world on the Vineyard — as with many of my age — was in three parts: school, church, and work. One may begin at any point on this fundamental cycle, priorities varying according to day and hour; the whole span will be covered eventually. If it occurs to you to wonder where recreation was, it was there certainly but more spontaneous and casual, more individualistic and less regimented than today. It was less something separate than a part of all else that life was; it related to the way in which an islander lived, whether it was getting a boat ready for spring, making barrel-stave bunks in the shack that we used for a clubhouse, or roaming the Lagoon shore in search of an occasional arrowhead in the broken layered shell of the sandbanks.

It so happens that outside the window as I write, the green of the lilac bushes flutters in the light morning air and I am made suddenly aware of how far along they are toward flowering. I never can think of lilacs, pink and white, heady in their sweet-scented promise of summer's overspilling, without remembering the Memorial Days of childhood, for one was the symbol of the other.

Because the school lunch program had not been invented, we went home to eat at noon, even though for some it meant walking a fair distance. On the class day when we were to honor the nation's war dead — the nearest date to Memorial

Day when school was in session — we cut a handful of flowers in the backyard during the lunch period to carry in the parade. Ordinarily, not much but the lilac was blooming that early and if you did not have a lilac bush in your yard, there was always somebody next door or in your class to give you three or four sprigs.

The simple presence of the flowers transformed the day from that moment. The children returning to school were always like rivers flowing to the sea anyway — one street leading to another, all streets leading to one street, and all the children spilling together, until finally, nearing the school, they were a chattering throng, the little with the little, the larger with the larger, all buzzing and bustling. But on this day as they converged, most carrying flowers — even boys whose voices were beginning to change seemed to have no reticence about bearing flowers on this occasion — the nature of the customary parade to the classroom assumed a new excitement.

In part, of course, it was because one knew we were not to have afternoon classes, but, in the larger sense, it was because of other things. Most days resembled each other in their relative uneventfulness but everyone dressed up for the parade and I remember even now how well-scrubbed, shined, and starched we all looked. One year, I observed with quiet astonishment as we lined up to march downtown that a girl whom I had regarded always as plain was actually pleasantly upsetting in pink. And, too, Memorial Day reminded that the school year was winding down; another grade almost gone by, farewell to another teacher, and to a few who would "stay back," and all of that was both exciting and a little sad.

Those of us who played in the school band wore white shirts, blue ties, and white duck trousers. In the beginning, I played a baritone saxophone lent to me by Mr. Tuckerman, steam fitter, toy merchant, and leader of the town band, because I could not afford to buy my own instrument.

Now here is Mr. Grace, our bandleader; he is lean and serious and he teaches music and does job printing on the side in his cellar. He is quietly calling for attention and for those various other responses of stance, posture, and uniformity that are expected to transform a gaggle of youths into a rhythmic unit. The drum beats and we step off down the Church Street hill toward the center of town, all of the schoolchildren, their waving flowers, and a couple of enthusiastic dogs that recognize somebody in the line, following behind us. Abruptly, there are clusters of fathers and mothers and just people, along the line of march.

As we approach Main Street and prepare to turn the corner at the post office, it is obvious that everyone is there and that everything else in town has stopped. Sam Cronig, in his white apron, has come out of the market because his son David plays the clarinet with us. Over Cromwell's Winchester store, the window of the Barnacle Club is open and a couple of the members have interrupted a cribbage game to lean out and look. Chief of Police Flaherty stands at the intersection, his big hand stopping all the traffic (one car, one pickup truck), and Frank Swift, lean and dapper, is on the front steps of his clothing store, characteristically, with arms folded, rhythmically rising on his toes and falling back on his heels.

It is time for the band to strike up. Mr. Grace holds his right hand aloft and brings it down smartly, the drummer breaks into a ragged roll that nevertheless sends up my hackles as always. And so we launch into "Maryland, My Maryland" and after that, I think something called "Repaz Band." Our music is thin in the more difficult passages, there are occasional reed squeaks, and some parts that ought not to overpower the melody do, in fact, but our audience applauds and cheers because we are theirs. What is more, most of them like a sprightly tune but can't play anything more than waxed paper on a comb themselves, and they look upon it as a pleasant minor miracle that their young ones can. I think it also pleases the ladies that there is a girl in our band, Dottie Brickman, who plays the trumpet.

At the steamboat dock, we march across the great splintered planks, hoof-worn and wheel-worn, and halt near the caplog. Members of the clergy, with their forefingers or little pieces of white paper tucked into their Bibles where they are going to read, stand off to one side, pale in their dark suits.

Next to his low-slung dray loaded with cartons of soap, corned beef hash, and baking powder for the grocers uptown, there is Al Luce, big-boned and bent in his baggy-kneed overalls, a chew of tobacco in his cheek. He stands beside his brown-eyed horse and pulls off his hat, limp and shapeless, in respect for the occasion. The fellows who work in the bottling plant on the dock have come to watch, standing in the open doorway. On the spile next to me, a hook-nosed gull stands on one leg and cocks a beady eye; I suppose he wonders whether the flowers we carry are edible.

A good many have walked down from Main Street to watch us. The principal and some teachers are scurrying about: "Now get the sixth grade right in here; no, no, not there, over here"; when it comes time to throw the flowers, it is done by grades, starting with the youngest, because they get tired of holding their flowers first. Finally, everybody is standing in the right places and a fat man in khaki pants turns off the engine of his truck and it is as quiet as Sunday. The principal motions to the clergymen and one of them clears his throat and comes to stand in front of us.

"If it had not been the Lord who was for us, / When men rose up against us," he reads, "Then they had swallowed us up alive. / When their wrath was kindled against us; / Then the waters had overwhelmed us, / The stream had gone over our soul. . . ."

(I accepted that kind of thinking as reasonable because I assumed from what I had heard and read that we had always been on the right side of any war in which we ever had been engaged. Everybody I knew felt the same and I would have been startled to hear anybody express a different view. And if you were on the right side, obviously, the Lord had to be with you, and if He was, it was equally obvious that you would win, which we always had. The moral certainty of the whole business was sufficiently reassuring so that you could spend your time thinking about other things, such as understanding Latin verbs. And girls. It was, in fact, an age of moral certainty, even though some were more certain than others.)

Finally, we throw our flowers overboard. It always makes me feel sad to see masses of them floating in the harbor, rising and falling in undulating blobs, because I think that is the way a drowned man floats, although I have not yet seen one.

The principal dismisses us and we go up to Main Street to get a cone of ice cream and listen to the people tell us how nice we looked.

It really doesn't matter at what point you start talking about school, church, and work — or play, for that matter — because the same people were everywhere and you knew them all. Things as well as people were interrelated similarly since the whole was a microcosm of simplicity. So it is that lilacs also remind me of a classroom (and one classroom of another and another), and bear in mind that about this time, the Vineyard had an average of approximately twenty-one pupils per teacher, a ratio that allows a lot of personal relationship between educator and educated.

The first school building was a drafty old box, lower grades downstairs and upper grades upstairs. In the fall, when the traditional "line storm" struck and the wind blew from the northeast for two or three days, dumping enough rain so that the town had to put the portable wooden footbridge across the bottom of Centre Street, that building tested the teachers newly arrived from the mainland. It was too early in the year to start the coal furnace, so they taught, red-nosed, homesick, and bundled in sweaters, to the plink-plunk accompaniment of water leaking through the roof and falling into pans on the floor. I still associate *plink* and *plunk* with *amo* and *amat*.

I have to begin with Lillian Jacobs, not because I loved her more than any other teacher, although love her I did and do, but because of the time in our respective lives when we shared her classroom. I was in the sixth grade and ready, without knowing it, to pass from the task of acquiring by rote the fundamental tools of learning to something more flexible and exciting. She was in her early twenties and it was her first year of teaching. Thus, in a sense, we started together at a threshold of new challenge.

Some ties that bound us had nothing to do with education and I doubt that they would have existed to the same degree in a larger community. Early in that year, there was a death in Miss Jacobs's immediate family; greatly shaken, close to tears, she asked for our help. We had not known death so near, and we would have wept at our desks all day for her. This slender, blue-eyed young woman, red-haired and freckled, seemed so alone in the world that we rallied to her as if we had been her children, or even her brothers and sisters, for her grief and courage narrowed the gap of years between us. We were determined to do well in her classroom because we were all she had left; affection begets affection, and she responded in kind.

I suppose it would not be well thought of professionally today, but occasionally, she took those of us who got an A in spelling to Luce's ice cream store for a caramel sundae sprinkled with salted almonds. As I think of it, I do not know how she could have afforded to do so; perhaps she couldn't really, but love affairs are never wholly logical. Luce's is long gone and I do not eat caramel sundaes anymore because I do not need the calories, but I remember what it was like sitting there next to her — we took turns sitting next to her — just as I remember "*i* before *e*, except after *c*," which has always had romantic overtones (however strange you may find that) because she taught it to me.

On one of my last days in her classroom, shortly after we had hung her a May basket, I took to Miss Jacobs purple and white lilacs picked in our backyard and almost wished that I had not passed to the seventh grade.

But the seventh grade was something else and I would not have missed that either.

First, I remember the room, because it was not until later, when her spirit came to dominate, that the woman teaching there emerged as more important than the place. Essentially, this first impression was of her own doing; she did not project self and this, I suppose, was because she visualized her task as more important than the individual who undertook it. Yet like a gentle, true-toned bell that is rung persistently, what she was eventually became everything there was in that place.

The floor of the room was oiled hard pine; the ceiling, which must have been twelve feet high, supported largely useless gilded chandeliers with frosted shades. The windows were enormous. Chairs and desks were screwed to the floor.

There was about the place something more than mere orderliness. It possessed a tested formality that discouraged the notion of physical change. Each green shade was pulled down to cover one-third of a window. Blackboard erasers, all right side up, were roughly at six-foot intervals in the wooden trough. The only decoration, if that is not too frivolous a word, was a framed print of George Washington. For the first week or two, I had a feeling that if anyone moved anything in that room, George would say crisply: "Don't!"

The teacher was Vesta Maury. She was a tall woman of generous feature and strong jaw. Women teachers then were not encouraged to use makeup. Since her characteristically composed face was virtually without lines and very pale, it gave the impression of having been chiseled in stone. As her room was orderly, her person was disciplined. She did not raise her voice, betray emotion, cross her legs when seated, or wear anything likely to attract attention. She controlled what went on in her class but without light remarks, laughter or histrionics.

That room was her universe. The purpose of that universe was to educate. In her view, the pupils would not have been there had they known more about her subjects than she did. Each working day, she attempted, almost relentlessly and with great reliance on frequent examination, to balance the equation. I believe she would have felt it professionally unethical, perhaps even dangerous from the standpoint of jeopardizing evenhandedness, to permit a less formal relationship with her pupils. She did not ask to be "liked" or to be considered "likable" but to be respected and regarded as competent.

Even now, I can hear her saying: "The vegetation of Egypt is confined largely to the Nile delta, the Nile valley, and the oases. The most widespread of the indigenous trees is the date palm. Others include the sycamore, tamarisk, acacia, and carob. . . ."

As the days went by, one paid less attention to the room and more to the woman, because, never insisting but persisting, she was exposing us to the building blocks of basic knowledge.

One day, almost by accident, I learned something about her that she had never revealed in the classroom. Basically, I was well-behaved; neither my father nor my mother would have stood for less. But in this instance, I was in trouble because a school official suspected me of some misdemeanor. Mrs. Maury was surprised and hurt; she took me out into the corridor and asked: "How could you have done it?" I told her honestly that I had not done it but that the only way to clear myself would be to tell who did — and I did not wish to because the guilty party was a troubled boy from a troubled home and I was sorry for him.

She put her arm about my shoulders and looked at me with tenderness such as I had never seen in her. "Perhaps I can help you," she said, and I assume she must have because I went back into the classroom and nothing ever came of the affair. I thought about Mrs. Maury in a new light after that, not being able to put it into words very well but realizing how much of herself she concealed in the name of professionalism.

More than fifty years later, I wrote to this woman, who was born ten years before the U.S. battleship *Maine* was sunk in Havana harbor, to tell her what her teaching had meant to me. I was not sure that she was still able to see or write but I received her reply within forty-eight hours. The handwriting was firm, still reminiscent of the precise Palmer method that she taught; the letter was couched in those restrained and civilized phrases that her background commanded: "I consider the years of my teaching a rare privilege. . . . It is pleasant to be remembered. It is very pleasant to be well remembered, as you have been kind enough to suggest that I am."

There was nobility in the woman, uncommon then, more uncommon now.

And I must think of Alice Hackett, lean and bright, who

coached girls' basketball and taught Latin and English, all with enthusiastic effectiveness, and who, somewhere in the struggle through *Ivanhoe*, or perhaps shortly after "The stag at eve had drunk his fill, / Where danced the moon on Monan's rill," concluded that, as a class, we did not know a verb from an adverb. Therefore, we abandoned the luxury of literature and concentrated for weeks on learning grammar.

I found the business of taking sentences apart and memorizing rules of proper construction both boring and exasperating but somewhere along the line, as a result of these exercises, I came to love the English language and to revel in its effective usage. It was Miss Hackett who inspired that love, very likely on some run-of-the-mill teaching day when she least expected it.

At the end of that year, I discovered that she was leaving us to get married. I composed what I thought then was a compelling speech, and memorized it, urging her to postpone her wedding for another year so that I would continue to have her as an English teacher. Throughout a half-day in late May, during which I assisted her in putting textbooks in the closet, I tried to find the courage to deliver this speech but the straightforwardness of her gaze undid me and I concluded it was too much to ask of her.

Which I suppose it was, all things considered.

Church and school were intimately related because Henry Ritter, the high school principal, was our Sunday school teacher. On warm-weather days, we often sat out on the parish-house lawn in kitchen chairs, leaned up against the cobblestone wall of the church property, and listened to Mr. Ritter tell us about "In the sweat of thy face shalt thou eat bread, till thou return unto the ground; for out of it wast thou taken: for dust thou art, and unto dust shalt thou return." Then very likely, he would get off onto his story about the frankfurters, which was so awful that I never forgot it.

"I went to the county fair when I was a boy," he said, "and I didn't have any money; all I could do was look. I was hungry and I went to the frankfurter stand and stood there, smelling them cooking, and my mouth watered.

"A man came along and saw me. He took some money out of his pocket and said, 'Get a frankfurter in a bun for me and one for yourself.' I ran to do it, hurried back, and handed his to him. Then I raised my bun quickly to take a bite of frankfurter and he knocked the whole thing out of my hand and stepped on it, grinding it into the dirt.

" 'You didn't say thank you,' the man said, and walked away, eating his frankfurter.

"I have remembered to say thank you ever since," said Mr. Ritter.

Then maybe if the weather was very good and there weren't too many of us, Mr. Ritter would take us to Tashmoo in his touring car and we would get out near the pumping station and watch the goggle-eyed carp or the yammering crossbred black ducks paddling about, until it was time to go home.

I am not suggesting that the church experience was either superficial or casual. In those years, I went to church in the morning, assisted in taking the collection as a junior deacon, sometimes pumped the organ for a quarter a Sunday, played in the orchestra between church and Sunday school (we did a great deal of four-four time stuff, which was lively and liberal for a Yankee church so long ago that Spain had not even become a republic), and then went to Sunday school. In the evening, I went to the Christian Endeavor youth group meeting (to this day, whenever I sing the hymn "Now the day is over, / Night is drawing nigh," I think of Augustus

Crowell, pale, thin, and mustached, who walked the State Road at least two miles round trip to play for us, reverentially and mathematically, while a stuffed gray squirrel on top of the piano stared unblinking into space) and then to evening church services. It was a full day but there was no sense in *not* being there because everybody I studied and played with was; moreover, it was largely pleasurable, even though taxing. I mean no irreverence whatever when I suggest that I ate my most substantial breakfast of the week on Sunday, preparing myself for the day's demands.

Sometime during this period, a fellow named McCarthy wrote a letter to the editor of the *Christian Register* that was entitled "To Be Happy in New England." In part, Mr. Mc-Carthy wrote, "You must eat beans on Saturday night and fish balls on Sunday morning. . . . You must make sure in advance that your obituary appears in the *Boston Transcript*. There is nothing else."

Well, there is not even that much now, because the *Transcript*'s own obituary was written when the proletariat stormed the Bastille, as it were, ushering in a heady new pace and style of journalism in which there is more gin and less ginseng. Better the *Transcript* is dead; if it were living, it would be miserable, having to put up with author interviews of less than a page in length, sandwiched between advice on marital infidelity and advertisements on behalf of bagged tea.

However, beans and fish balls remain with us (which would not have surprised the ladies and gentlemen of the *Transcript*), and in those days, I ate fish balls on Sunday morning. Fish balls have constituted a significant part of my background. I suppose, in evaluating what they have done for my staying power and attitude toward life, I would have to rate them about even with the last half of the third grade, in which I learned the multiplication tables. It is my belief that people who eat fish balls regularly have a great deal of equanimity, which is very helpful when playing a saxophone.

So much for school and church; as for work, I got a job at an early age because I knew that my father and mother were worried about money.

It was early summer. I was on my way to the steamboat dock to see if I could catch a bucket of tinkers, and cutting through the field with the ancient cellar hole full of oxeye daisies, I came upon Maurice Delano, who was in my class. "I have a pain in my stomach," Maurice said. "I think maybe I have an appendix or maybe I strained myself. So I have quit my job with Captain Packer." And he walked on toward his house.

I ran home, leaned my fish pole against the woodshed, and went in to see my father, who was in his office whacking away at his old Oliver upright with two or three fingers and a thumb. He did not like to be bothered when he was writing but I risked it and said very quickly, "Would you let me get a job if I could?"

He leaned back and chewed his pipe stem a little. "I believe I would," he said. "If you wanted to. And if you could." I said thanks, rushed out, and ran all the way to Captain Ralph M. Packer's plant, which was called the Tashmoo Springs Bottling Company.

It was on the dock, with the gulls always mewing just outside, and the company made soft drinks and bottled beautiful water in green glass carboys that was shipped away to people whose water was not so beautiful. I walked in and the bottle washer, with its brass, rubber-shod spindles on which the up-ended bottles sloshed through the hot water on an endless belt, was chugging away, and a fellow whose name was Roxy was rocking a metal tank of something on a wooden cradle — to ensure even carbonation, I suspect now, but I didn't know then. When he rocked the cradle with an upright wooden handle, back and forth, back and forth, evenly, he sang part of something over and over; I think perhaps it was "Sweet Jennie Lee," which was popular then.

I thought this must be a fine place in which to work. The singing, the hot water, gurgling and steaming, and the shiny bottles coming up all dripping; the gulls crying just beyond the open door; steamers full of brightly dressed people arriving all day; and, against the wall, stacked cases of soft drinks, pink, orange, green, and chocolate, sparkling in the sun and waiting to be guzzled in pleasant places where children laughed.

I was afraid Captain Packer might not hire me because I had never worked anywhere before. I was nervous about asking somebody where I could find him, so for the moment, I was staring through a square trapdoor in the floor at the green water of the harbor below, trying to think what I dared to do next. I saw a pair of well-shined shoes standing next to my sneakers; I looked up and there he was. He looked pleasant.

I asked him if he thought I could do Maurice's job. He made some small show of feeling my right biceps and he said, "I'll bet you can." I couldn't believe I was hired so quickly so I asked him if I was and he said, "Yes, sir. If you want to work with me, you're hired." I thought it was something that he said "work with me" and not "for me," so when he asked if I would like to start the next day, I said I would rather start right then. And I did, beginning with something like a broom, and for three dollars a week, which was a lot of money. I think my father was surprised that I had been hired but he didn't say anything.

So the cycle of life, simply constituted, simply constructed, emerged; my peers and I were kittens in a basket, and destined to remain so for several years, without even knowing it. I did not journey much to other island towns in those days — and I think many did not; I did not even find a need to go beyond my particular part of town because it had everything I required, including companionship. Many did not go into all the stores on Main Street regularly, and there were not that many stores, because one did not need what they sold and had no money to buy what was not needed.

The way in which we lived, simply and routinely, was the way in which many islanders lived, especially because the average income was low. My father's was above average and on a twelve-month basis, but many whom I knew charged their groceries in winter and paid for them the following summer. And had it not been for rabbit hunting, a number of families would have had a lot less meat.

Because life was simple, I recall as major certain incidents that broke the pattern. In those days, if anyone in the family contracted scarlet fever, town officials tacked an ugly red sign with black letters on the side of the house nearest the street and everyone within was quarantined for four weeks. My sister Jo, very small at the time, was one of only two people in town to have it, and so severely that there was concern for her hearing and eyesight. My mother burned sulfur in her darkened room and stayed by the bedside night and day. My father had gone to live with Tom Tilton's family, so that he could continue to work; after dark, he would come to see my mother and me, standing out in the shadows of the lane and talking to us through the screen of the kitchen window.

I did what cooking was done, my mother coming halfway down the front-hall stairs to explain to me the intricacies of flour, eggs, and shortening. It seemed to me a sad time. My father's visits each night reminded me that we were prisoners and I envied my cat, who came and went each day as usual. Perhaps she wasn't supposed to, I do not know to this day, but no one told me to confine her and she would have hated it anyway.

I assumed that a great deal was going on in town of which I was unaware — which was absurd — and that I would not be promoted to the next grade because of the school I had been forced to miss. I did not wish to be as ill as my sister was but I thought occasionally that since I had to be shut away anyway I might just as well have had something. Eventually, Tad Athearn, who lived next door, came by on his bicycle, whistling as usual, and tossed my report card over the fence. I had passed for the year and felt much better; that afternoon, I made my first apple pie.

There were one or two other experiences that were extraordinary in a life bounded by Church Street, Cromwell's Lane, and the waterfront — a brisk walker could cover this area easily in thirty minutes, with time out for a couple of sidewalk conversations.

Across the lane from our house, there was a shed that belonged to the Cromwells. Three or four of us, including Little Ben, were allowed to build bunks in it and to sleep there occasionally, especially on the night before the Fourth of July. How does one communicate to today's world the degree to which those were times of innocence? Principally, news was not world news or national news but island news, and very often the item worth relating was not something that never had happened before but, rather, something reassuring that happened every year at about the same time and guaranteed that the clockworks of the universe were still in order. It was news each spring when Captain Hartson H. Bodfish reported the first mayflowers and if he found them on a Saturday, he wore a few blossoms in his buttonhole when he went to church next day, and that was news, too.

When we "slept out," we did not dare to leave the shed

before our families had gone to bed for fear that somebody would come to check on us — if we were gone, that would mean back into the house for the night once we returned. And probably, no more sleeping out. Our homes were all close by and it was exciting to watch their lights wink out, one by one. By eleven o'clock, newspapers had been read, cats had been dumped on the back steps, the last shade had been drawn, and we were alone with the night.

Then we left the shed to prowl. It says something about the nature of the times that there never were any other groups of young men abroad at that hour. Even the one policeman on duty was nowhere in sight when we walked down the middle of the empty main street. And because of the times, we walked as quietly as possible and talked in whispers; adults of those years, if vexed by what they considered unreasonable behavior on the part of the young, were inclined to be forthright — something that was about to be proved on this particular occasion, although we were not aware of that.

The night was benign but there were rags of fog patches along the beach when we went down to locate a skiff that we had permission to use. Oars, rowlocks, and bailer were in it, as usual, as they were in most of the hauled-up boats; we shoved off and paddled down toward the town beach. We intended to go ashore near the vegetable garden of Captain Bodfish, an Arctic whaleman for more than three decades, take a couple of handfuls of scallions, two or three cucumbers, and a few tomatoes, row out into the anchorage basin, and eat them. We counted on the night and the fog to conceal our presence.

Crawling in on our bellies, we were both noisy and clumsy. Also, I rather think the captain had several windows open and had barely turned out his lights, for he was not even undressed. We learned that he was not when he turned on his porch light, appeared at the top of the steps, yelled something very loudly, and fired a shotgun twice. I assume that he did not fire at us because I never knew him to miss anything that he wanted to hit. Still, lying there facedown among the squash vines, I found the bark of the gun distressing; obviously, "Hartie" Bodfish found our behavior unreasonable. We accepted his judgment and ran, after the second shot, assuming that he had a double-barreled gun and would then have to reload. It is no more than fair to add that Captain Bodfish was one of the most generous and agreeable residents of the town and that, had we asked him, he would very likely have given us the vegetables. But that would not have been much of a way to celebrate the night before the Fourth; as it was, we had done something so daring, in a relatively undaring age, that it could be discussed privately (with as much titillation as if the mission had succeeded) for at least a year.

Finally, in those gentle times when I wore knickers, parted my hair in the middle, and had begun to wonder about the ladies' underwear pages in the Sears, Roebuck catalogue, I had an unforgettable experience with gambling.

I discovered to my astonishment one evening when I went into Tilton's drugstore to buy ten cents' worth of chocolate peppermints for my mother that somebody had installed a slot machine in the place. "Hutch," who got the peppermints for me, told me that it paid off in brass slugs worth a nickel apiece in merchandise at the store.

The idea of getting something for nothing was incredible. It was contrary to everything that Henry Ritter, the school principal, or Henry Ritter, the Sunday school teacher (or my father, for that matter), had ever told me. I studied the slot machine very closely because I had never seen one before and I do not think many in town had. I concluded that it must work like an alarm clock; when it was the right time, it spewed slugs. I do not know to this day whether that is a reasonable parallel.

The first person I ever saw play the machine was a short, fat woman who lived in an apartment over one of the Main Street stores. She had whitish-yellow hair that looked as if it had been struck by lightning. She was about Napoleon's height and when she stood before the machine, she struck a militant stance, one foot forward, toe out, and right arm raised as if she intended to strike the thing. Every time she pulled down the handle, she shot her lower jaw forward and pursed her lips. I confess I got to staring at her, even though I had intended to watch the slot machine.

"You want to look, young man," she said, "get to my left side. You get to my right side, you get in my arm's way. Behind me, you make me nervous."

So I did, and she shoved in slugs at a great rate. Once in a while, she would get a few back; she didn't even stop to pick them out of the tray but just kept feeding the machine, lost in the spell of the business. And there was a spell to it. The rhythm and the ritual were mesmerizing: slug in, arm down, slug in, arm down; she had a red-stoned ring on her right hand and it sparkled as she grabbed the handle and swung it. And then the clicking and spinning, the colored fruits whirling prettily behind the glass, and, at last, the almost unbearable instant of waiting as, one after another, the revolving cylinders came to a halt.

Finally, the woman had used up all the change in her handbag and had put back into the slot machine all but one of the slugs that she had won. When she put in the last slug, she winked at me and said, "This has got to be it." And when the whirling was done, there, in terrible finality, were one cherry, one apple, and one orange, and she said a word that I was aware of and stormed out of the store, looking more like Napoleon than ever.

So I knew that it was possible to lose all of your money in the thing and I ignored it for days, not daring to risk what little I had. Until one day . . .

One afternoon in October, I was walking home from school with an armload of books, kicking golden leaves and fallen mahogany horse chestnuts. At one point when I kicked, something shiny turned up. Of all unbelievable things, it was a quarter.

By the time I got down the hill to Main Street, I had decided I would stop at the drugstore for a double cone of maple walnut, which I did. After I got it, I had fifteen cents left and I thought, "I could play the slot machine three times and even if I lost it all, I would still be ahead because I started with no money of my own and I already have the ice cream." I bought three slugs.

I stepped up to the machine. There was no one in the drugstore except Hutch and I was glad of that because I still felt guilty about risking the fifteen cents. I put in a slug. The machine spun, clicked, and stopped. Nothing. At that point, totally uncharacteristic madness seized me; I had a fierce impulse to shove in the other two slugs and I did. I pushed in the first and hardly waited for the cylinders to stop before I popped in the last.

Something like remorse rose within me, with the inevitability of the flood tide. The fifteen cents was gone and I had nothing to show for it. I picked up my books and walked toward the door before the machine stopped spinning.

I was at the door when the shower of slugs came, filling the tray and spilling onto the floor. My heartbeat accelerated, my hands began to shake, and I was so elated that I never did find out what I got three of to make the thing pay off.

Hutch was not so easily moved. "All day, it's been getting ready to pay," he said laconically. "Last guy was in here I said that to. If he'd played three more times, he'd a had it. Here's a bag to put the slugs in."

When I got home and dumped them on the kitchen table, my father said agreeably, "Well, I'll be damned!" and for quite a while after that, when I went to the store for my father's Half and Half or my mother's peppermints, I took slugs instead of money, although never without feeling rather odd about doing so. Something for nothing was a heady experience but I never played the slot machine again because I never found any more money.

In the larger and less personal sense, there were other indicators of where the Vineyard and Vineyarders were as the 1920s ended. William Shaw Thomson, speaking at the Bankers Industrial Exposition in New York, observed, "Incredible as it may sound, there is not an advertising sign or a hot dog stand on the island." One island contractor said his business had increased since the crash of the stock market and another businessman quoted a West Tisbury resident as saying, "Mainland panics never affect the Vineyard . . . a gallon jug will hold only a gallon and there's always a panic here."

The bluefish and striped bass were coming back after an absence of years. Captain Arthur West of Edgartown caught 610 bluefish between July 7 and October 20, 1929; the largest weighed slightly more than 13 pounds and the biggest day's catch was 51 fish, on October 7. He caught 67 striped bass during the same period, the largest weighing 22 pounds.

Scholarly H. Franklin Norton concluded that the effect of isolation on the language of the Vineyard people was to preserve it. As examples of island speech differing from that of the rest of New England, he cited: *fleet,* used in the sense of to move from one place to another; *lockram,* an improbable story; and *wequashing,* of Indian derivation, referring to the method of spearing eels at night from a boat, the eel being attracted by the light of a torch.

There was some published controversy as to whether or how much summer people were missed during the off-season. Chester M. Poole of Chilmark observed, "Some of the very best friends I have are summer people. Nevertheless, when they are all gone, the Vineyard still lives and lives pleasantly. From some time in the fall to the first of June, the Vineyard again becomes a Vineyard place. Then come those days that are so precious to a real Vineyarder and no misunderstanding crank need ruffle his feathers if we choose to speak of them occasionally. They are ours."

Some islanders look upon population growth with equanimity, accept some change as inevitable, and suggest that such change may be more limited than many believe — and perhaps not necessarily related to growth anyway.

Erford W. Burt of Vineyard Haven is a native islander; his wife, Alice, is the daughter of the late Captain Henry Stevenson of that town, and has lived on the island virtually all of her life. Mr. and Mrs. Burt are parents and grandparents of islanders. Mr. Burt, now retired, is a master craftsman; he has designed boats, built boats, and created and operated his own boatyard, with the assistance of Mrs. Burt. He has served the town of Tisbury as assessor and school board member, and the island generally as a member of that committee which recommended and worked for establishment of the Vineyard's regional high school.

Both Mr. and Mrs. Burt were subjected to bitter criticism at the time when the proposed high school, now generally accepted as a major asset but once opposed by those fearing loss of local autonomy, was a matter of controversy, especially in their town.

Mrs. Burt finds the results of island growth mixed, "but mostly positive.

"Wars have created mobile populations," she says, "and this, together with the terrific amount of free cash given out by our government, has enabled people to come here, decide it was a good living, and anchor. Scratching for a living on this island never afforded much more than the basic necessities but in more recent years, with all the government aid, younger people have come here and entered into the life-style. With regard to those of retirement age, women in this category seem to feel the need of being involved in something, so they turn to town affairs, some good and some not so good."

She thinks many things that some people regard as changes on the island were the same seventy years ago.

"You hear it said that working people cannot find places within reason to live in," she says, "and that teachers cannot find homes because of summer rentals. When my folks came to the island looking for a house to rent in 1909, they were not able to find a house for rent with central heat or plumbing facilities. In the late twenties and early thirties, teachers could not find homes unless they would get out in early June.

"However, times never stand still; changes come and go."

Mr. Burt "likes people," so he is not "fussing" about the steady growth in numbers. "Perhaps I should be alarmed about the number of people coming here," he says, "but I'm old-fashioned. If they want to come here and have the money, it bothers me to think that people can't come here if they want to."

But the increase in "paper-pushing" does bother him.

"I find something very upsetting when we have so much

organization and pressure groups," he says. "Some people seem to have nothing else to do but pick up pet projects so that bylaws and regulations can be carried out.

"I made this place where we live. It wasn't accessible. I dug out a harbor and had to obtain only a simple state permit to do so. It was my property; I could do as I saw fit. It's very discouraging today if it deals with property. You have to get into paperwork before you lift a spoonful of earth. Imagine what it would be like to establish a business today such as I did. And I did it without harm; this was just a swamp hole; I created upland, with a business and a badly needed harbor. It is better off because of what I did. How would you go about it today? I wouldn't want to be a party to it."

At the Bass Creek, just off what is now Lagoon Pond Road and once upon a time used to be Chicken Alley, there is the boatyard that he established, and there the shed in which, for years, the aromatic shavings of promise have heralded the creation of fleet new craft to sail the Sound. Waiting for a warmer tomorrow, the shrouded vessels in the yard, silent and anonymous, are without the life and grace that water will give them. At the roadside, a little boy feeds bread to the crossbred mallards and black ducks that snatch and gobble eagerly.

In some important ways, I suppose, the boatyard is a monument to what was and is no more; some would argue that numbers alone have made this change imperative. A young island woman to whom I talked about this said, "It's not government regulation that's to blame. It's just that one shop on the shore of a pond wouldn't hurt but ten would change the whole picture."

4. The Harbor

VINEYARD Haven was the island's port of call in the days of heavy vessel traffic; my father was responsible for recording the marine comings and goings, not only for the *Gazette* but for the federal government. Even when I was very young, it was my task to assist him in the routine matters, to board the tugs at the dock, count the barges in the lower harbor, and hail the coasting-schooner crews in their yawl boats.

So we produced the weekly grist: Put in for harbor, schooner *Thomas Lawrence*, light, bound east; tug *Prudence*, with three loaded barges for Boston; and tug *Lehigh*, with two light, bound to the westward.

The figures were impressive; in 1934, the port logged 35 steamers, 176 barges, 89 tugs, 64 schooners, 291 yachts, and 55 fishermen, for a total of 710. It is worth noting that these figures went up or down depending on weather conditions; the more gales held up coastwise traffic, the higher the commercial figures rose.

Because it is comforting to believe in the permanence of things — and implicitly, of ourselves — it is proportionately disquieting to be reminded that whole ways of life, their personalities and symbols, drop like fine ash through the sieve of time and disappear. The whole of this process is accomplished with a finality no less clinical and complete because it is gradual. For a while, as an era slides out sideways into history, there is a lingering aura that deludes and reassures; it is like the smell of everlasting spring on a windless day — a fragrance gone once the breeze rises. Yet the wood of yesterday crumbles, its iron rusts into uselessness, even as the illusion of continuity persists, and eventually, the whole business is, incredibly, in the past tense.

But I remember, for I have lived long enough to see these vessels and their people and idioms drop out of sight because of change. There was a time when it never occurred to me that anything as prosaic as economics could make anything as poetic as a ship come or go, but one learns, one faces, the truth of the sailorman's lament:

> *It's the twilight of an era*
> *Preface to a clanking dawn —*
> *The belching stack is here to stay,*
> *And the silent coaster's gone.*

As did Stephen Vincent Benét, I fell in love with American names, the "sharp names that never get fat," and that is what I think of first when I recall all the towboats I have scrambled aboard.

It was something to see them when the wind hauled out to the eastward and blew great guns and they snuggled in, three and four abreast on three sides of the dock, black smokestacks against a sky of slate-gray rags, waiting for a better day. Then I would stand there on the caplog and roll their names on my tongue: *Valley Forge, Cheektowaga, Honeybrook, Tamaqua, Catawissa, Wyoming* — a lonely yet pleasurable litany, with only the wind's howl through the knotholes of the freight shed for response.

The presence of the big steel tugs, rail to rail, and heaving easily in the surge, transformed that storm-bleak place. They made it a piece of a world I had never seen, with strange speech from the mouths of strangers; bare-armed, tattooed cooks, pink from the galley heat; buffalo humps of bow fenders, brass cuspidors on the rope mats in the wheelhouses, and the steady *swish ka-pow, swish ka-pow* of quiet pumps. I think they did not see many boys, these people, and they found my pencil and paper interesting and amusing. Why did I want to know where they were going? What did I do with the information? How old was I?

Some talked more than others. "How you like living in a cemetery with lights?" hollered the Philadelphia mate, because he had been waiting for a shift of wind for two days and we didn't have a barroom in town. I grinned, because I had never thought of Vineyard Haven as being like that and he said, "O.K., you come aboard and have a piece of hot bread with butter and sugar onto it." I did and we went from the galley across the windy, wet deck, up the steel ladder to the pilothouse, I clutching pencil, paper, and bread, to meet the captain.

He was a short, rosy-cheeked Scandinavian, as solid and shiny as the binnacle beside him. We discussed swimming very briefly. I said I swam in the harbor in summer, having begun the learning process with an automobile inner tube, which a friend of mine punctured while I was over my head, forcing me to learn to swim immediately. The towboat skipper thought that was amusing and he added, "Vere I coom vrom, ve svam bare-ass-ed." He chuckled, the mate laughed, and I ate my bread and thought about that.

I thought of the tugs and their people as being friendly, because they shared the sea with us and understood what that meant. Early one March in the thirties, Captain Zeb Tilton, master of the coasting schooner *Alice Wentworth* of Vineyard Haven, had been waiting five weeks to get through the ice to

Nantucket with a couple of big storage tanks. When the situation finally eased, he and his mate spent several more days heating water in the cabin, trying to melt snow and ice that had run into the schooner's centerboard casing and frozen the board solidly in place so that it could not be lowered. It was discouraging work and they were not getting anywhere when the master of the big tug *Catawissa* found out what they were up to. "Bring the schooner alongside us with the yawl boat," he suggested to Zeb. "We'll free your centerboard." And they did; the towboat engineer ran a steam hose aboard the *Wentworth*, thawed out the casing, and the schooner was on her way in no time. That was the kind of thing one expected from people who shared the sea, whether islanders or not.

Down in the lower harbor lay the tugboats' tows, usually one to three barges apiece, those eastbound and loaded with coal lying deep. A few were square-bowed box barges and once in a while, you might find an old mastless schooner winding up her days as a barge, but mostly, they were built for the purpose, bluff-bowed and massive in their parts. Even when a barge was driven ashore in a storm, it took forever for wind and weather to get at her planks, timbers, and fastenings and reduce her; to the last, so hard and heavy as to defy a beachcomber, she insisted on preserving her identity. Barge crews lived in a little house aft and if there was a woman aboard, you could always tell, because there would be curtains on the cabin window and very likely a potted geranium on the sill.

When the weather got to moderating, the tugs would begin whistle-talking to their tows before daybreak about getting under way. From the dockside, the deep *whoomp! whoomp!*; offshore, the responding *wheep! wheep!*, much lighter-toned; until finally, they decided how it was to be accomplished, and by the time I got up, they had gone their watery way, all the black-stacked hens, with their clumsy chickens strung out far behind.

One of the most sobering experiences I ever had afloat occurred when my father and I were sailing a small catboat somewhere west of Paul's Point in Vineyard Sound and fog came in thick, very quickly, great dripping rolls that blotted out everything. When the whistles began blowing around us, we tried to reconstruct what had been in sight — an east-bound tow, a steamer, a fisherman, and what else? — and match the sounds, which, as always, tended to be confusing. The tow had been closest; unfortunately, because of the angle of vision and the fact that we had not been paying that much attention to it, we were not certain how many barges the tug had — two, certainly.

I was forward, peering and blowing; the air was light and we were ghosting, making no noise except for the ripple of water at the bow. From the whistles, we concluded that the towboat had two barges and that all three vessels were now to starboard of us and well clear; nothing else was close enough to worry about anyway.

Then it happened. A barge whistle sounded to port, very close at hand. I do not believe she had blown before. Now we knew that the tug was towing three barges; we were some-where between the second and third, and the latter was near enough to call for action on our part if we could decide, blind, what that was.

Before we could make a move, there was a new sound of water, the black, dripping catenary of the towing hawser broke out of the fog just ahead of us — not touchable but far too close — and as we came about, deathly slow in the light air, there was the great bulk of the barge sliding by, dark, silent, and enormous. It seemed a long time before her stern showed, then there was a little wake, then nothing, and she was gone into the mist as if she had never been at all. I saw no one on deck; I am sure no one on the barge saw us. Had we fouled the tow and been rolled under, I do not know whether we could have attracted anyone's attention or how long it would have taken them to get to us if they could have found us. There was so little time before danger was at hand that I did not even get below for the life jackets and my father could not swim a stroke.

I was shaken. It seemed to me that I had not breathed for at least two or three minutes. We remained silent until the whistles, now diminishing, reassured us that we were all clear. Finally, my father said, "Godfrey!" And a while later, he said, "I don't think you need to say anything about this to your mother."

As the towboats were casual and familiar, the down-east, deepwater schooners possessed both magic and majesty, even those that had lost their shape from hard work.

These big vessels hailed variously from Lunenberg, Parrsboro, Portland, Calais, and Boston. Many brought lumber westward from the down-east ports and picked up a load of coal in Norfolk or Hampton Roads. Occasionally, they made trips to the Caribbean, to South America, or to Africa; they trafficked in wood pulp, cement, and lime, and sometimes brought back salt from Turks Island. Fifty years ago, the skipper of a four-master gave me a green bottle of Saint Lucia double-distilled bay rum from Castries, in the British West Indies. "This is great stuff," he said. "You can put it on your face after you shave, put it on your hair to make it lay down, gargle with it if you got a sore throat, use it to help a earache, and some drink it, I hear, but I don't." To this hour, the half-inch that remains in the bottle (because I cannot bear to end completely this unlikely link to so much that is long gone) has a scent that stirs in the mind the imagery of coconuts, copra, and a copper sun.

Long ago, there was a rare Sunday in April when three of the big windjammers, eastbound from New York with coal, came racing into Vineyard Sound before the blast of a stiff northwesterly in the best tradition of the palmy days of coasting when no man would allow another vessel to pass him without making a supreme effort to prevent it. Masters of the vessels, the *Rebecca Douglas* and the *Lucy Evelyn*, both three-masters, and the *Lillian Kerr*, four-master, had decided to anchor at Vineyard Haven to wait for the sea to subside before venturing across Nantucket Shoals. This was because one licking sea washing over the bulwarks could sluice overboard a ton or more of the coal on deck, and there might be many such seas before the shoals were passed.

Their black-waisted hulls had a glint of green below and showed an occasional flash of red copper bottom in the bright sunshine as they snored and plunged on their way in a welter of foam from the breaking following seas that spattered the blue Sound with racing whitecaps. All their lower sails were straining stiff as boards, with lifting booms; their burdened topmasts swayed, although the four-sticker carried her fore-topsail only, probably because of the stiffness of the breeze.

The course lay in about mid-Sound, the wind drew over the port quarter and that was about as good a sailing point for the vessels as they could have had, although the following sea caused them to plunge heavily as they ran before it. Broad off Nobska, the schooners hauled by the wind for the slant that would take them into the harbor. Holding for the harbor, hove down under pressure of sail, they now revealed a clear streak of copper along each weather side; white foam billowed and rose beneath the old-fashioned clipper bows.

Far into the harbor, leading the fleet, came the *Douglas*,

pointing into the wind as though a witch held her wheel. Then came the *Kerr*, rounding to more slowly and remaining farther out, the better to get under way when the weather was better. And close on her windward quarter foamed the *Lucy Evelyn*, so all three came to anchor almost simultaneously.

The weather bluff of the high bows smashed against the sea as they headed into the wind. Sails thundered and slatted as they were emptied. The big schooners eased leisurely ahead now, with anchors lowering slowly from the catheads, until all way was stopped. All the while, the jibs fell with the slat of canvas and the rasp and rattle of sliding hanks along the wire stays. Then, three great splashes as the anchors struck the water, a prolonged rumble of chain cable running through the iron hawsepipes, and the vessels swung on the tide, their lower sails being lowered and furled, one by one, almost as in an ancient ritual.

Many of the deep-legged coasters were family vessels. The *Laura Annie Barnes*, a four-master that grounded on Tuckernuck Shoals when she missed stays and went to pieces in a northeast gale, was home for Captain James L. Publicover and his three sons for twenty years. Every member of her crew played at least one musical instrument. On a January day in the mid-thirties, when all hands had gathered around for a session of sewing ripped sails aboard the vessel, they were entertained by a daughter (or daughter-in-law) who read aloud from "Victorious Troy, or the Hurrying Angel," which was then John Masefield's latest story of men against the sea.

On one Christmas Day aboard the *Douglas*, her captain, Burtus Wasson, had aboard with him four sons, two of whom were also licensed captains. James sailed as mate, Alvin, Harold, and Paul as members of the crew, while Paul's young wife presided over the galley and cared for her year-old son, who was as good a sailor as the rest of the family. The Wassons attracted widespread attention along the coast. They sailed together for years; during the Depression, they continued to carry cargo, and because they pooled their efforts and divided the returns, they made the schooner yield a livelihood for all.

When the schooners and barges lay at anchor waiting out the weather, Chaplain Austin Tower of the Boston Seamen's Friends Society, who presided over the bethel at the head of the steamboat dock, would go down the harbor to hail them and take off anybody who wanted to go ashore. His principal errand was to inquire after the men's welfare, offer help if needed, make available the facilities of the bethel reading room, and invite them to an evening of worship and entertainment.

I went with Chaplain Tower a number of times, initially, in the *Helen May*, a launch with a house enclosing most of her length; she brought ashore thousands of seamen over a period of nearly forty years. "Jump Spark" Jim West, who ran a furniture shop on the Beach Road, had a drawing of her — the product of unleashed imagination — in which she was leaping over mountainous seas. The fact is that she did do some peculiar things when the going was dusty but I always assumed she had been lengthened several feet as an afterthought, and this sometimes produces hysteria of the metacenter.

In 1930, the society had a new launch built, the thirty-six-foot *Madison Edwards*, named for Mr. Tower's father-in-law, who founded the bethel and served it for more than a half-century. She was high-headed and ruggedly built and did an easy ten knots, but it still took her a week to come down from Maine because of one of the longest March northwesterlies in years, which produced snow, heavy seas, and icing. The dedication of the boat, a few weeks later, was a better beginning for her.

Because it was all so long ago, it is essential to understand that as the port was fundamental to the town, so this church of the port (of no denomination) and its seagoing pastor were fundamental to the people, no matter what their persuasion. So it was that a large gathering came for the formal presentation of the *Madison Edwards* and to honor the man for whom she was named. This was because nothing about the bethel or the purpose it served was quite like anything else anywhere. I always thought of it as relatable to that episode in the book of Matthew in which Jesus is walking by the Sea of Galilee and comes upon James and John, in the boat with Zebedee, their father, mending their nets: "and He called to them. And they straightway left the boat and their father, and followed Him." I found these things relatable because the bethel was of the sea, the man who ran it could box the compass, steer a course, and tie a clove hitch; he shared a boat with the working seafarer, and comfortably.

Typically, the dedication ceremony was closer to this world than the next. The bethel piano was carried out on the lawn; the new launch, gay with whipping pennants, lay in its berth nearby. Dock workmen listened while Mildred Renear and Annie Gonyon (a pupil of Lillian [Norton] Nordica) sang. A quahaugger, shirt sleeves rolled to the forearm and bull rake hung over the stern, touched up his skiff on a flat on the other side of the wharf, while the speakers remembered Madison Edwards, humanitarian and friend of the sailor. The times being as they were, among members of the audience were the masters of two coasting schooners lying in the lower harbor.

I did not then appreciate the ageless and traditional lone-

liness of men ashore from ships but I have seen them fill the
bethel of an evening, with their ruddy faces and pale wrists
just below the shirt cuff, heavy in their creaking, wooden
chairs, and their voices like careless wind in the winter as
Mrs. Tower played "Pull for the Shore, Sailor, Pull for the
Shore." And then, very likely, my father would recite some
of his verse, standing there, waggling a forefinger, and beginning, "Oh, the devil he chafes the ratlines through / And
he heaves the seas aboard / But the Lord he strengthens the
seaman's grip / And he runs the lifelines through the ship /
A-keeping his watch and ward . . ."

And when it was all over, those men would applaud heavily
with their great hands, slowly and heavily, great hands worn
hard taming the slat of canvas in a gale, forever coping with
roll and pitch, net, cable, and hawser. Finally, they would
return to their darkened ships and to the night and to the sea.

"Return" to the sea is the proper verb in this context. What
harbor, water, and sea represent to an islander constitutes the
other half of life. The landsman stares at the sea, the seaman
is more likely to be staring at the land. The islander, being
necessarily amphibious, has it both ways and knows that if you
would find a new world within an old one, you need only look
at it from the opposite direction.

Consider how the island looks from the sea, therefore. It
is early morning; there is a crystal quality to hour and season,
and the land lies as if it were in another dimension. I know
who lives in those houses and even in houses that cannot be
seen for trees. I know who is up at this hour and where bound,
and whose dog waits for his breakfast, yet, at this distance,
the familiarity of yesterday blurs. Especially is this true because there is no noise at this hour, because the pale light of
morning smooths harsh lines, and the land seems new and

timeless. It could be any year, any country, expressed in any idiom.

There is no intrusive punctuation in this morning poem — no crying child, no backfire, no slamming door, no ranting over cold eggs or unpaid rent — the island is basically itself, a matter of pleasant outlines awaiting Bartholomew Gosnold's arrival. It is as it was, an attractive composite of sand, pines, boulders, shrubs, vines, headlands, hills, and hollows. From this distance, one holds the land in perspective, can see what its shapes mean, how it folds and unfolds, and in what manner it confronts the water that alters its architecture perpetually. The pace of the island's own leisurely clock now becomes apparent; from this viewpoint, one can think in terms of the time required to create a grain of sand.

In the west, there still are the laggard masses of night but the breeze that came with the day has a certain insistence, and gradually, the clouds whiten, puff like popcorn, are blown like enormous leaky pillows down over the sharp-clean horizon, and then the whole sky is magnificently empty. In watching the machinery of the blue bowl overhead, there is both peace and adventure.

This vessel in which I oversee the universe, this microcosm of the moment, independent of the continents within its eighteen feet from stem to transom, is a catboat, the only one in the harbor with an overhanging stern. Her name is *Rip*, not in the sense of tide rip, but for Rip Van Winkle. She was built in the late 1800s for Joseph Jefferson, the actor, who once played the role of Washington Irving's hero and perhaps paid for the boat with the money that his interpretation of Rip earned for him. The boat leaks more than I wish; I always have a feeling that she "works" like a wicker basket when under way, but her lines are clean and she is fast, and I have great respect for her because she has lived from one century into the next.

Now, we will drop the mooring, one of the most final of human gestures and as fundamental as cutting the umbilical cord. This boat is no longer bound to the earth; the human creature in her is no more secure than his judgment is sound — our destinies are linked more closely than those of husband and wife, and we need each other in order to survive. Hear the agreeable creak of leather in the gaff jaws as the peak of the mainsail nods; ease the sheet and the brightly varnished blocks chuckle; the wake ripples the sea's glass surface darkly and *Rip* makes her easy way from green water to blue.

In those years of the *Rip*, the island and its people were sea-oriented, sociologically as well as economically. The salt water around them not only provided bread and shoes, it also created important headlines and generated excitement. Consider a handful of events in the last half of 1930:

A four-stacker, the former navy destroyer *Downes*, taken over by the Coast Guard for picketing and trailing of the off-shore rum fleet, came in to the dock at Vineyard Haven for water. Her skipper was then–Lieutenant Commander Edward H. Smith, widely respected for his work in oceanography and a recent recipient of a Ph.D. from Harvard. But what was most important at that moment of docking was that Commander Smith was a native Vineyarder.

"Unchanged and totally devoid of self-importance, Eddie comes home and enters into the spirit of things at just the point where he last left them," my father wrote.

It is because of this that the rare visits of his ship are the signal for a general letting down of business while the town's population gravitates toward the dock.

He remains always the same boy who played about the streets
at home. He hails his former schoolmates with the same whole-
hearted friendliness. . . . He evinces the same respect for the
grizzled coasting and fishing skippers as he did when a boy and
that is why the town turns out to greet Eddie and his ship. . . .

On the same day, the Edgartown schooner *B. T. Hillman*
came in after two weeks on Georges Bank with 112 swordfish
"lying cold in the ice," the biggest trip of any vessel in the
fleet thus far that season.

"On the way in," a crew member of the schooner related,

the weather was fine and all hands cheerful once more after a
good wash and a shave. It was most noon and everyone had their
ears caught for the mess whistle when it finally came, and the
cook came with it, blowing for all he was worth. All hands
gathered and took their places when the surprise was sprung.

John Salvadore, as spokesman for the crew, made the presentation of a crown to no other than our honorable captain, H. O.
Hillman. "Captain Hillman," he said, "on behalf of the members
of your crew, it gives me great honor to present to you this crown,
which I know you will cherish. It places you as the official king
of the New England swordfishing fleet for the year 1930. Through
your good judgment and skill, you have landed the biggest trip
of the fleet up to date."

Captain Hillman arose with words of thanks and praise to his
loyal crew. He placed the crown on his head and it was just a fit.
Chief Steward Harden Paul, a wonderful cook, then laid a
spread fit for a king: a swordfish dinner with all the fixings, two
kinds of pie, lemon meringue and mince, frosted cake, tea, coffee,
bread and butter, and cigars afterward.

As we approached the Cape Cod Canal, all hands settled down
to enjoy the scenery, which was beautiful after being at sea for
two weeks, half the time in fog. Chief Engineer Waters would

go down every now and then and throw a barrel or two of oil at the engine so as to keep her rolling along smoothly on her trip to Boston. When the vessel arrived at the Fish Pier, the captain and his men were greeted by a host of friends. . . .

A month later, the steamer *Kershaw* was blown up and that, too, was memorable in its way.

Two years before, there had been in and about town a fellow much given to wearing tweeds whom local rumrunners suspected of being a "dollar-a-year" federal informer. Whatever he did, he was up and about at unearthly hours, and on the night of May 30, 1928, he woke everyone in our house by throwing pebbles at our upstairs windows and shouting hoarsely for my father, who was, among other things, a correspondent for the Associated Press, United Press, and International News Service.

The fellow in tweeds said he had been sitting in his car at East Chop watching two steamers, one bound east and the other west. Abruptly, both sets of lights stopped moving, he thought he heard a noise that he described as "deep and hollow," then one set of lights assumed a sharp angle and soon disappeared. He believed the ships had collided and that it might well be a major news story.

The vessels had, in fact, collided, despite the fact that it was a bright moonlit night. One was the Merchants and Miners Line steamer *Kershaw*, loaded with office supplies, machinery, paint, rugs, shoes, and barreled goods; the second ship was the *President Garfield* of the Dollar Line. The *Kershaw* went to the bottom with a loss of twelve lives. Only one body was recovered and there was some doubt as to whether it was that of a member of the *Kershaw*'s crew. Divers were never able to find a trace of the other victims.

Because the sunken hulk was a menace to navigation,

several tons of dynamite eventually were placed aboard to blow her up. A salvage vessel, some Coast Guard craft, and the steamer *Azalea* of the Lighthouse Service were on hand when the explosion was scheduled, to make certain that the area was clear of all other traffic. The time of the dynamiting had been made public in advance and a fairly large number of people and cars were gathered on the shoreline.

Precisely at 6:45 P.M., the charge was touched off, ripping up the placid water of Vineyard Sound over a quarter-mile area and sending a cone of water four hundred to five hundred feet into the air. This cone, white as milk, was both beautiful and awesome; it hung in the air no more than seconds and as it fell back, the outer edges of this mountain of water rose in their turn, presenting a startling contrast in color. The cloud of water that rose the second time was almost black and appeared to be filled with wreckage and ooze from the bottom of the Sound. When this water fell, nothing was left to mark the scene of the explosion but a heavy cloud of smoke and an area that was slick and smooth with oil. Ashore, there was a slight jar felt in Vineyard Haven and East Chop but boats fairly close to the scene experienced no wave or disturbance and people in some of them picked up fish, mostly scup and sea bass, that had been killed by the dynamiting.

A couple of other things of moment happened that year. The boat line sold the *Uncatena* that had brought us to the Vineyard. So the last of the side-wheelers, now so outmoded that she had become small, queer, and old-fashioned, was gone and the whole era of walking beam and paddles ended. I was glad to have known a little of it. I was also comforted by the notion that there was no going back for us now; we were Vineyarders irrevocably.

The other matter also involved change. On November 14, the *Gazette* noted editorially:

Another instance of attempted plundering of summer homes during the absence of their owners in the winter season reminds the Vineyard that summer property is not so safe as it used to be.

All thoughtful persons must look upon such a passing of our old-time integrity and security with concern and sorrow. Until now, the island towns had been spared the necessity of doing police duty about closed summer homes, except in a casual way. Summer resorts of the mainland have suffered greatly from winter mischief and plundering but the Vineyard has not shared their unfortunate and expensive experience. It begins to look as if the island were now fallen from this historic state of grace.

I do not think of island "mischief," in whatever season, without remembering the wreck of the fishing schooner *Etta M. Burns*, a rumrunner that ran ashore in 1927, about three miles east of Squibnocket Point. Something like five years later, the boys of our Sunday school class, including my friends Arnie and Ozzie Fischer, were spending a weekend at H. N. Hinckley's camp at South Beach. What happened, I suggest, is of sociological interest in even the most casual study of island life-styles because it reaffirms what some public officials will tell you even today: There appear to be patterns of limitation in the kinds of misbehavior in which most Vineyarders will engage. Over the years, there has not been a lot of violent crime, there have been only a handful of murders in the island's long history, and there does seem to persist — at least among the residents — some kind of special social consciousness possibly related to their very insularity.

On that spring day in 1932, we set out in the early morning, Arnie and I and a dozen others, to walk the beach westward. Earth and sky were benign; here, all was dominated by the orchestration of the sea. Offshore, the great surgings (I thought of them as having last been seen by someone who spoke Spanish, before they started their rolling voyage across the Atlantic) were still anonymous, no more than wet dark lines of warning, as they approached the land. But at that point where the depth commanded, they rose, legion after legion, assuming form and identity; there began to emerge from them, if one could hear it, the first voice of the symphony, the high hiss and swish of powerful motion. Once started, they shaped quickly, not in the manner of regimentation but of fierce individuality — as no two snowflakes are alike, no two waves are alike, and watch the rogue seas, for they do not bear even family resemblance.

Heading for the beach now, the speed and size of these tons of uplifting water became apparent quickly. They assumed new tones and dimensions. At the base, dark and swirling; at the crest, translucent and wavering, like an animal quivering before the strike; and uppermost of all, the frothy white lace, half of it airborne. If one could have heard them, there were middle-range voices now, not only those of landbound water tumbling and spraying, but those as well of acres of shells, stones, pebbles, beneath these seas that were rolled, tossed, flung, and ground by the ocean's charging columns.

The last was the best and briefest, the bass voice of the symphony, as the wave thundered upon the hard-wet sand, dissipating itself in a final mighty explosion of sound as its predecessors had been doing for centuries. And when it had done so, whatever comprised it flowed shapelessly back off the shore, reduced by its onslaught to trickling and small foaming as if it had never possessed the power to shatter ships and kill men.

That was what we watched on that day.

Finally, we came upon the wreck of the *Burns*. I remember to this day how massive, how lonely, how starkly tragic the vessel's remains were, the only work of man — and a shattered work at that — rising above the empty miles of sand.

Not much of it was left, a chunk of one side, yet in the curve of the weather-silvered plank, there was still a hint of the grace that had made her go, once upon a time. The piece of wreckage, poised aloft like a half-cupped hand, was higher than our heads by far; its inner and outer planking, with heavy ribs between, made a natural chimney.

I cannot remember who gathered the kindling of driftwood, who placed it, jammed in a jagged hole at the base of the hulk, or who lighted the match. But I can remember the beautiful and somewhat frightening dance of the first flames in the bright sunlight. The old schooner did not burn easily or quickly in the beginning, but suddenly what we had done was out of control. As if something within her, sensing the end of the end, had taken a great and terrible last breath (Cheyne-Stokes, I thought, because I had seen one man die in bed and I had never forgotten what he did and what they called it), the draft roared up between hull and sheathing. Fire, in fierce and writhing sheets, twisted like gold, dancing out of the top of the wreck. Within moments, a column of black smoke — scar against the fair sky — began to wind a quarter-mile high.

The fundamental of this incident is that, as one of us put it, even though we had not harmed anyone or much of anything, we knew we were going to "catch hell" from a variety of people. Yet we stayed on the scene, knowing we had an obligation to put out the fire if we could; we formed a largely useless bucket brigade, running back and forth to the sea with rusty tin cans found in the dunes until we were breathless — and until some inconvenienced and annoyed townsmen came up over the dunes with proper equipment and doused the flames.

Today, Arnold M. Fischer and his wife Priscilla live on 131 acres at Flat Point, which stretches out toward Tisbury Great

Pond between Pear Tree Cove and Tiah's Cove. Mr. Fischer
and his late father, Albert, bought this land in 1939; the
rambling farmhouse and the property had belonged to James
and Prudence Look. The place once was a stronghold of the
"great pond people," and years ago, mainland gunners used
to come here to stay during the season.

Arnie, a comfortably big man, ruddy-cheeked and soft-
spoken, is a farmer, a graduate of Stockbridge, the state agricultural school. He is an island native; his mother's people
were Vineyarders for generations, and he was graduated from
Tisbury High School. He is West Tisbury's first and only
fire chief, having held this position since the selectmen appointed him in 1949. He was one of the original forces in the
move to unify island fire fighters into a cooperative body and
establish a mutual aid system.

He was a strong supporter of the successful effort to create
a Dukes County communications center at the Martha's Vineyard airport and was very active in the establishment of an
island regional high school. Prominent in West Tisbury town
affairs for many years, he served as a school committee member for twenty-one of them. As an agriculturalist, he was
awarded the Dukes County soil conservation district certificate
of merit for carrying out a progressive soil and water conservation plan on his farm.

It says much about how he and Priscilla live that the dinner
I have just eaten here this evening, from pork to beans to
fruit, all came from their land and was a result of their efforts.
In the kitchen in this old house, where wine from their own
grapes is made, a mother cat sleeps in a basket with her kittens.

"Fifty years ago," Arnie says, "people were closer. You
knew your neighbors more and would help each other. Today,
you don't know everybody anymore. Even as fire chief, and
I've been here forty years, I wonder, 'Where do all these

people live?' There were one hundred fifty voters when I moved here and now there are nine hundred. Originally, I paid one hundred sixteen dollars in taxes and it is now over three thousand.

"Still, people coming in are fitting into the town better than they did ten years ago. It took five years for me to feel at home; people were not that friendly. But people aren't as happy as they used to be; there was more smiling, they stopped to talk.

"When people went to the county fair years ago, they sat and visited," he says. "Today, they get mobs of people and they don't visit because there are so many strangers. No matter what the weather is, you get a good crowd; they like fiddlers, singing, woodchoppers; they go to look at things, not to socialize."

Priscilla first came to the Vineyard in the late thirties. She was a student at Framingham State Teachers College and worked summers as a waitress at Havenside in Vineyard Haven, a very genteel hotel that catered to older families staying several weeks. She married Arnie in 1945; they had four daughters and a son.

When she returned to teaching in 1952, she was the only teacher for the first four grades and there were twenty-two children in the West Tisbury school, one of whom was her oldest daughter. During her twenty-four-year tenure as teacher and teaching principal in the West Tisbury school system, she had all of her five children as pupils.

"Now," she says, "there are twenty-two kids in one grade and one hundred sixty-five in kindergarten through eight, including kids from Chilmark and Gay Head. You couldn't get to know them all."

She recalls that school began in the early years with a Bible reading, a prayer, and a poem, and she thinks that was "a good way to start. It was a quieting influence, a sort of serious thing. We would repeat the Golden Rule fairly often and you could get some other good ideas across in that time."

She believes that making little girls wear dresses and insisting that little boys look neat also helps in the development of a serious attitude toward school. "I remember how I had to iron my four daughters' dresses at night," she says, "and I was tired and probably didn't like to but I think that 'dress up' had an influence on the kids' behavior. When you are in sloppy clothes, you act a little sloppy, but when they discontinued the dress code at the high school, there was nothing we could do but discontinue it, too."

Homeward bound on West Tisbury's Old County Road, I think of Priscilla saying, "The town has grown so; there are so many more people." On this road, I can remember when there was hardly more than one house — Sam Thompson's, I think — and now, again and again, the new roads (or are they streets, I wonder?) wind out of sight to where new people live in new houses, many of them.

And last year, Arnie turned down a one-million-dollar offer from a Boston developer who wanted his land. "If you work forty-odd years," Arnie said, "you want to enjoy it yourself."

5. The Gathering Places

IT seems to me that we do not talk with each other as we used to. This may be due to the massive noise pollution we have created, which, for many hours of day or night, creates an intrusive background that discourages conversation. Maybe there are so many other things to do, including those that merely waste time, that a lot of people give talking low priority. Perhaps we are less articulate than we used to be — where are the storytellers of fifty years ago? Where, for that matter, are those whose individualism was sufficient to inspire the stories?

In any event, once, on Martha's Vineyard, there were gathering places where men talked; each site had its own following and this was an ancient custom that prevailed at least through the 1930s. My father, writing about George G. Gifford's store, at the junction of two of the roads that lead into West Tisbury village from down-island, called it "as much a part of the Vineyard scene as some of the rocks and hills." He recalled that "here, on winter nights when the wind howled along the road like a lonely dog and the dead leaves rustled in windrows under the big trees outside, a row of blanketed horses stood at the hitching post and inside, a circle of men smoked their pipes and talked of all things under the sun around a red-hot stove."

Some of the gathering places meant much to summer residents as well as year-rounders. One of the former, commenting on the death of William H. Mayhew, who had been an Edgartown businessman for many years, recalled, "He and his store both fascinated me and my father also. I do not believe that father and I ever went into town without going up to Will Mayhew's and buying something and I think father made many purchases for the fun of talking to Mr. Mayhew. The round stove in the back of the office with the sandbox in front of it was always attractive and it was easy to see that in the long winter, there was a good deal of interesting talk around the stove, when the city folks had been disposed of."

In later years, these gathering places ranged from the porch of Carl Reed's store at Menemsha to John Conroy's fish market in Vineyard Haven, to Manuel Swartz Roberts's boat-building shop in Edgartown. Those who gathered talked about things both large and small. They were not gossip mills; if people were discussed, it was usually in anecdotal vein. In a sense, the places were a linsey-woolsey version of the English eighteenth-century coffeehouses; they offered not elegance of speech or thought but did provide an intimate experience as wit, fancy, and shrewd observation were applied to the facets of everyday life. I have spent many hours listening in these places; I do not recall a single instance of obscene language and profanity was rare.

In Vineyard Haven, some gathered regularly at Cromwell's Winchester store, which sold guns and ammunition, among other things. Even when Big Ben was aboard, and he was the proprietor, Captain Hartie Bodfish tended to moderate the discussion by virtue of seniority and experience. Hartie was lean, hawk-nosed, and quick (he yanked his plug of pipe tobacco and jackknife out of his hip pockets as if he were drawing a pair of six guns); he had a laugh like gravel swirled in a tin bucket and a thousand stories about bowhead whaling

beyond the Arctic Circle. It was he who related that somewhere north and east of Icy Cape the ship's cook found a
dry riverbed full of smooth round stones, put one in the
galley oven, and hatched a dinosaur. "We didn't get too much
chance to look at it," said Captain Bodfish when somebody
asked him to describe it, "because when it broke out of that
shell, it was ugly and growing fast and we had to hit it with
an ax for fear it would take over the ship."

What did they talk about in these gathering places?

Well, in 1933, for example, you might have expected them
to talk about the national banking holiday and they did, but
not exactly as you might have expected; islanders tended to
have a special kind of attitude toward money. Bear in mind
that the year before, motivated by the general economic
depression, Judge Herbert M. Chase, owner of the Wesley
House in Oak Bluffs, had written an unusual letter to his old
guest-friends.

Those who during the past ten years had stayed at the
hotel for at least a week and who desired to make a reservation for a week he invited to come and name their own rate.
"We have full confidence in your sense of sportsmanship and
fair play," he wrote, "and know that in determining your
rate, you will keep in mind both your present financial con-
venience and what is due in fairness to us. Let us eliminate
this atmosphere of dread and doubt and return to normalcy."

Suddenly shut out of their banks without warning a year
later, islanders proceeded to cooperate in the same friendly
fashion. Ready cash on the Vineyard was circulated as much
as possible and sending cash off-island was looked upon as
something akin to betrayal since the limited supply could not
be increased until the banks opened. There was no uneasiness
about the safety of deposits; the public was interested, cheerful, and disposed to take a humorous point of view.

It was appreciated that Stephen C. Luce, Jr., then cashier of the Martha's Vineyard National Bank, and one of the two bankers involved in keeping island business affairs going, was among the many who got caught with a small amount of cash in his pocket. At the time of the holiday, he found himself with eleven dollars in small change. All the rest of his funds were locked in the vault. His car developed muffler trouble, which cost him exactly eleven dollars to have fixed. They talked about this in the gathering places and it was referred to publicly as the "scrap irony of fate."

Checks on island banks were accepted freely. Gas stations, groceries, barbershops, movies, and all sorts of businesses encouraged the public to buy as usual. Credit was offered liberally to old and new patrons. Merchants generally urged their customers to use their charge accounts. So when Leo Pepin, manager of the First National chainstore in Vineyard Haven, received orders from the mainland that nothing but a strictly cash business should be done, he protested to his superiors — who apparently did not understand Vineyarders. The order was modified.

The dragger *Nellie*, out of Point Judith, sailed into Edgartown, where her skipper, a fellow named Jones, was well known; he was unaware of the bank holiday. Following his usual custom, he asked George F. Daly in the Edgartown drugstore to cash his check because he wanted to buy food for the galley and go to sea again. Unfortunately, the check was on a Connecticut bank, but Mr. Daly rounded up grocer Frank Connors, who agreed, on Daly's recommendation, to accept the captain's check for the amount of the purchase. The *Nellie*, well supplied, sailed without delay.

By helpful coincidence during the time of the holiday, the *Vineyard Gazette* had opened certain of its columns free of charge for barter ads "as a depression method for Vineyarders to swap or exchange articles and services." For the old-timers, it was nothing new, and younger islanders found it helpful, especially during the cash shortage. John H. Macdonald said, "I will do furniture and automobile upholstery. Work in exchange. What do you have to offer?" Brickman's of Vineyard Haven: "Shoe repair or merchandise, for a kitchen range in good repair." Leonard's Service Station, Oak Bluffs: "Exchange auto oil for gallon glass jugs." Mrs. Arthur O. Watkins, West Tisbury: "Exchange a half-ton of coal for the plowing and harrowing of a small back lot."

In short, as islanders discussed among themselves, they emerged from the bank holiday with a reaffirmation of what they had known before it began. Their banks were sound; deposits exceeded withdrawals for the first several hours of resumed operation. Their people were sound to the point where Vineyard community confidence could not be shaken by national events. Both small businessmen and consumers kept their heads. They had nothing but scorn for "the big fellows on the mainland scurrying to save their own skins by putting a ban on credit, rejecting checks, and demanding cash or money order," as the *Gazette* commented. "If anything," the island newspaper added, "it would be this kind of behavior on the part of those big corporations in a position to know the condition and prospects of the country that could strike panic in the hearts of the public."

Islanders, as they observed in retrospect in the gathering places, never had thought it likely that the nation was about to come a cropper. And it hadn't, demonstrating just once more that Vineyarders were practicing no more than simple prudence in ignoring the mainland's frequent crises.

In the places where they gathered, they also talked about President Franklin D. Roosevelt, but again, not necessarily in the way you might expect, considering that the Vineyard was traditionally Republican. Pilot Lewis Smith was generally so unconcerned with national matters that he once growled, "What do I care for a coal strike?" when informed that John L. Lewis's union workers might walk out of the mines. But Lewis, Cy Sears, Harry "Poker" Norton, Ernest Mayhew at Menemsha, and trap fisherman Norman Benson at Lambert's Cove, among many others who went down to the sea, were interested in learning that Mr. Roosevelt was a sailor. It would be too much to suggest that the ancient mariners of the day took a man's measure wholly by his ability in seamanship, yet if he could sail and speak a boatman's language, they were at least inclined to find him more understandable, perhaps even more trustworthy. I know of at least one Vineyarder who voted for FDR (it was the only Democratic vote he ever cast and he cursed himself forever after for having done so) solely on the basis of this reasoning.

So salty Vineyarders (and some not so salty) were titillated in varying degrees to learn that Roosevelt's schooner *Amberjack* was in the area in the summer of 1933.

Amberjack came out of Woods Hole bound for Nantucket. Charles Ellis, assistant lightkeeper at West Chop, spotted her as she stood for the chop. At the reservation flagstaff, he dipped the colors — the President's first Vineyard greeting — and the destroyer escorting the Roosevelt yacht twisted the tail of its siren in return. The word spread quickly and islanders showed up on the headlands for a glimpse of the schooner.

It was a day for weather, a lowery time with a sky full of dark clouds rolling and eerie light spots. Even the water was rippled dark and streaked with spray; against this somber background, the little schooner leaned and scudded, her mainsail single-reefed, her forefoot flinging foam. On the headlands, they watched her, thinking with approval, "The Old Man's carting canvas." They did not know that the President was at the wheel and giving the orders, yet it pleased them to think so.

Then the first squall struck. Wind whistled along the bluff, bringing with it a torrent of rain and thickening the mist that hung over the sea. It was no surprise to the seawise watchers when *Amberjack* hauled on the wind and headed for Edgartown; any one of them would have done the same, with the weather worsening.

At Edgartown, the lower streets and wharves were well sprinkled with spectators coming and going, despite the gray and rainy afternoon and temperatures low enough so that islanders who stood at wharf's end gazing at the white schooner anchored under Tower Hill had to stamp their feet and move about to keep from shivering. There wasn't much to see, but no President had visited the Vineyard since Grover Cleveland and it was something to stand on the caplog and realize that in yonder vessel's cabin was the most important individual in the country and one of the most important in the world, whether or not you had voted for him.

Boats sped from shore through the squalls and a launch from the destroyer circled in ceaseless patrol about the *Amberjack*. Newspaper representatives scurried back and forth. Telephone and telegraph wires, much in demand, notified the nation that the President had come to anchor.

Actually, islanders did not stay long to watch but, in the gathering places, including Manuel Swartz Roberts's boat shop, they did remark on a couple of things. First, some who had gone out to look at the schooner noticed that before he went below, the President, clad in dripping oilskins, looked over *Amberjack*'s gear and rigging. Everything was, in fact, properly snug on deck — sails neatly stopped, sheets and halliards coiled down. That struck them as speaking well of the man because they would have done the same.

The other matter was the security factor. As for the gray launch that kept moving around *Amberjack* in circles of varying diameters, those who watched commented on the gasoline that was being burned and some felt that the sailors in the destroyer's boat must be uncomfortable and perhaps even dizzy. What the gatherers were saying really was that all this show of protection was unnecessary; the President, they were certain, was perfectly safe on Martha's Vineyard or in its neighboring waters. What is more, they noted, with the common sense of natives, protection for Mr. Roosevelt was not as complete as those who set it up thought.

Two destroyers blocked the entrance to the harbor but no one in officialdom had thought of the opening in the South Beach, so the presidential party was exposed completely on the Katama Bay side, which led to the Atlantic and then directly to the rest of the great nations, some friendly and some not so. No one had thought this important, yet the gatherers thought the navy should have considered it important because at high water, a boat drawing as much as four feet could have gotten through this opening.

Anyway, nobody with malice aforethought *did* show up and some interested viewers compared the presidential visit to the time when the *Graf Zeppelin* flew low over the island on its first homeward-bound trip a few years earlier. Both were uncommon glimpses of something important. And even though Mr. Roosevelt did not come ashore during his visit, he was making an impact on the Vineyard and that, too, was something to talk about.

One of the President's responses to the Depression, the Civilian Conservation Corps, established a camp in the state forest on the Great Plain; the 106th Company was two hundred men strong and of the first group of fifteen islanders enlisted, I had gone to school or worked with nine. Pay was thirty dollars a month and all islanders who enlisted were guaranteed that they would remain on the Vineyard for their tour of duty, which was a considerable incentive.

Fifteen hundred pounds of salt pork, as well as coal, beef, butter, eggs, corn, beans, flour, and prunes, were sent to the island by the federal government for distribution among the needy. Allotments of clothing, blankets, and bed linen were on the way; more government-generated money and work for the unemployed was the order of the day. Federal orders instructed local welfare boards to disregard all previous limitations of men and money and to present new and additional projects for civil work in short order.

Francis P. Luce, Tisbury selectman and director of the civil works program in that town, sent his compliments to President Roosevelt in acknowledgment of the "great good accomplished by federal relief to the unemployed." Mr. Luce found that every man in town needing a job, seventy-five all told, had been supplied with work. He sent a photograph of them, together with the board of selectmen and the town office force, to the President.

As was noted in the gathering places, everyone was not so enthusiastic about the socioeconomic trends. "Now that we are all expected to spend money like drunken sailors, whether we believe in it or not," observed James E. Chadwick of Edgartown, "and now that the federal government is throwing money right and left with no other order than to spend it, why not look around and see if there are not ways and places to lay out money so that some real benefit will be received?"

Al Tuckerman, who had lent me my first musical instrument, offered an amendment to the Townsend Plan, which proposed to provide older citizens with a weekly government check. "Adopt Dr. Ostler's idea of a few decades back," he commented, "and chloroform all people of sixty or over. Then we won't need to appropriate any money for old-age pensions." The author of the *Gazette*'s About Town column added, "Various substantial citizens find merit in this suggestion."

But more often, gatherers did not talk about politics, government, or such timely things; they talked about island matters because they considered them more important and more lasting. The prevalence of being island-oriented was persistent; although this is an extreme example, consider that in December, 1933, Mrs. Elsie Randolph of Oak Bluffs visited New Bedford. It was the first time she had left the Vineyard in thirty years. When she had last been on the mainland, Roosevelt was President, but it was Theodore. The Wright brothers had just made their first airplane flight but not everyone knew about it yet, and when people talked about the war, they referred to the war with Spain.

The anecdote was favorite grist in the gathering places. Usually, it involved real people and ordinary events; sometimes it was humorous, sometimes it reinforced generally accepted ancient beliefs. Consider these examples:

Captain Zeb Tilton was working aboard his schooner, the *Alice S. Wentworth*, which was lying at the dock, when he was approached by a staff officer of the Wayside Army, who was soliciting funds. "What can I do for you?" said Zeb, as he straightened up and replied to the officer's greeting.

"You can give me fifty cents," replied the solicitor.

"Why should I give you fifty cents?"

"It's for the Lord," was the answer.

"How old are you?" inquired Captain Zeb.

"Thirty."

"Well," said Zeb, "I'm sixty-nine. You'd better give me fifty cents for the Lord. I'll see Him first."

Then there was the matter of the old *Helen May*, replaced by the *Madison Edwards* as the Boston Seamen's Friends Society's vessel. The *Helen May* was sold and moored back of the Vineyard Haven breakwater. Something like a half-dozen times, she broke adrift and, in each instance, headed directly for her old berth at the bethel. "There are many men of intelligence and education in Tisbury who explain the antics of this boat in the terse expression, 'She wants to go home,'" wrote the *Gazette* correspondent. "As they say, 'There is far more to any boat than mere wood and iron.'"

Captain Francis J. Marshall probably had more consecutive years in side-wheel steamers on the Vineyard line than any other man. He commanded the *Monohansett*, *River Queen*, and *Island Home*, and was skipper of the *Uncatena*, the first steel ship of the line, from the time she was new until she was retired. Short, broad-shouldered, with a mustache that turned white over the years, he was a quiet figure of great dignity.

Nothing serious ever happened to any vessel that he commanded. The one incident often told about this man who wasted no words and made no false motions concerned the time when his steamer ran into a wharf. It happened because the engine was on dead center and failed to respond to bridge signals.

As the vessel went ahead and those in the wheelhouse were powerless to stop her, the pilot said to the skipper, "What are we going to do?"

"I am going to hold on like this," replied Captain Marshall calmly, and he braced himself for the impact.

Islanders were close to nature in a practical way; birds and beasts figured much in their lives and in their talk. There were not many bird-watchers and few conservationists as such, yet most did not abuse nature because they relied upon it for food and fuel. They were much interested in what went on in the world of nature.

Mechanics at Dukes County Garage heard the honking of a goose one morning. It sounded close and they ran out through the open door to see where it was coming from. The honking was being made by Dolph Manning's Rhode Island Red rooster, which had been kept in a poultry yard a few fathoms from the nearby beach for several months. It had abandoned *cut-cut-kadakut* and *cock-a-doodle-doo* and although it remained in prime condition and presided over the flock of pullets in a normal manner, it continued to arch its neck, spread its tail, and honk. Older Vineyarders, although mildly amused, were not surprised, for they believed that the influence of salt water upon barnyard fowl was generally degenerative and some of them said they could recall similar peculiar occurrences.

Elmer Chadwick had a cat named Dixie that lived in his blacksmith shop. She had a litter of kittens and he left her one, which was more or less customary, but apparently not adequate. Feeling additionally maternal, she went in search of remedy and returned from her search proudly bearing a large and sulky meadow mole, one of those fat fellows with claws like paddles. Chad promptly named him Oswald.

Oswald did not take kindly to the family life Dixie wished him to share. He did not view with favor the nest in the old stove that Dixie had fixed up for her babies. But for some time, his resistance was in vain. Dixie watched him as closely as if he had been a mouse instead of her adopted child and every time he made a dash for liberty, she grabbed him, gently, but with no thought of compromise. Eventually, of course, she had to catnap. Oswald fled — well, scrambled — below ground level, to freedom.

Gordon E. Spofford was the state game warden. Between tasks, he spent a great deal of time keeping his automobile shiny. On the particular occasion, he had purchased a huge can of polish, washed his car, poured on the polish, and rubbed and burnished until the surface of the car glistened — in the words of an observer — "like the sun at noonday shining on a red nose, or even more so."

Soon after, Mr. Spofford went on patrol and left his car parked in a field. When he returned, he was astonished to see, even at some distance, that the enamel on his automobile did not glisten anymore. At the rear of the vehicle, he discovered the explanation: two large, limpid-eyed oxen, one on each side, with tongues the size of snowshoes, as he described them later. They had licked off every particle of the polish and, even as he watched them, were investigating every crevice to secure whatever drop they might have missed.

More then than now, for whatever reasons, humor bubbled just beneath the surface; it was gentle, often imaginative, and country-style, and it did not run short despite toothaches, unpaid coal bills, or other dour circumstance.

Charlie Dunbar was an insurance salesman and a volunteer fireman. On the day when a West Chop forest fire broke out, he dropped all business as usual to roll to the blaze. It was his task to take the wheel of one of the pieces of apparatus and he "stepped on her," as they used to say, until, according to Donald Tilton, a lumber dealer, who was part of the fire crew and riding beside Charlie, "the telegraph poles went by like fence pickets."

Donald saw fit to expostulate. "Take it a trifle easier, Charlie," he said, "I'm not carrying any too much insurance."

Dunbar held the accelerator to the floor, kept one hand on

the wheel, reached in his jacket pocket, and drew out a policy application. "No better time than now to sign up for more," he yelled above the roar of the motor.

Captain Chester Robinson was a man of dignity, precise language, and common sense, and the lack of the last he could not abide in others. His discourse, even on fairly ordinary subjects, was lively and thoughtful. One day, he was talking about what had happened to hardtack: "There was a time," he said, "when I used to pay ten cents a pound for pilot biscuits that were wholesome, well flavored, well made, and properly baked. They were food that a workingman could live on.

"Now, you get a package of white-livered, anemic-looking disks that appear to have been stirred up in foggy weather, with plenty of the fog hove in. They are pallid, filled with wind, soft, and bilious in appearance. What is more, they cost four times what real hardtack used to.

"Indeed," he said, "the country has gone to hell."

Once, I was in Cromwell's store listening to the gatherers, and during a lull in the conversation, Captain Robinson turned to me and said he had observed me riding my bicycle on Main Street and he thought the seat was too high. I have no idea what got him onto that subject. Being young, I thought of him as Zeus-like, but I was not prepared to surrender my prerogatives; it was, after all, my bicycle seat. So, in defense, I began my explanation, "You see, Captain Robinson —" at which point he interrupted me.

"Young man," he said, "the expression 'you see' is much used these days by people who do not understand what they are saying. I see everything that you see. I have seen everything that you have seen and far more. I know everything that you know and I know more. I shall understand whatever it is that you are going to say. Probably I shall know what you are going to say before you say it. You do not have to say, 'You see, Captain Robinson' to me. I see very well."

I have never used the expression since.

The elaborate fabrication, often at the expense of the un-initiated, was frequently on the gatherers' agenda. Like chowder, it was looked upon as good the first time but constantly improved thereafter, with each re-serving to the appreciative. As an example, Frank Swift once suggested to a novice that the latter had "stretched the molecules" and weakened the barrel of his new shotgun by firing at objects that were too far away.

Captain Robinson once told a newly arrived mainland reporter with a Midwest background a yarn concerning the Nantucket Lightship, landfall of many ships inbound from Europe.

There had occurred on a given night a good solid blow from the northeast, accompanied by heavy rain. On the following morning, the newspaperman was paddling along Main Street and encountered Chester Robinson. "Ah, Captain Robinson," he said, "I am making my morning checks for the newspaper. Did the storm last night do any damage of which you are aware?"

Chester paused a minute, looking at the young man seriously. "You haven't heard?"

"Heard what, sir?"

"Well, the short of it is that this blow has been going on offshore for several days. What it amounted to was that nobody could get to the Nantucket Lightship to provide them with supplies. The sea and wind were just terrible. Finally, the lightship crew got down to where they had no food at all and they up-anchored and went drift fishing to keep from starving to death.

"It was blowing like the devil all the time and I under-

stand now that the Coast Guard has finally located the lightship off the Jersey coast. Everybody's still alive and well,
thanks to the fish they caught, and I guess now a cutter will
help them get back on station as soon as the weather lets up
a little."

The young man took notes furiously, thanked Captain
Robinson, and ran for a telephone. Someone on the mainland
newspaper who suspected that, to mariners, moving the Nantucket Lightship might be something like moving the Green-
wich meridian must have intervened, for the young man's
story never appeared in print. But the incident was told and
retold many times on the Vineyard.

Sometimes, natives were the butts of gatherers' jokes. Cy
Sears showed up at Conroy's fish market one day with a pair
of hip boots that leaked above the knee. One of the fre-
quenters present recommended brushing on some kind of
black roofing compound and letting it dry, which Mr. Sears
did. Later, he wore the repaired boots to the fish market and
took his chair next to the hot stove to talk with his friends
for an hour or so, during which time he sat with his legs
crossed.

When he tried to get up to leave, he discovered that his
boots were stuck together because the heat had softened the
compound. He could not uncross his legs or get them out of
the boots. His colleagues loaded him into a wheelbarrow,
largely against his wishes, and this characteristically quiet
and dignified, middle-aged man fumed as they wheeled him
leisurely up Union Street to Main — through the center
of town — to Church Street, where he lived. As the proces-
sion creaked by Lane's block and the post office, where there
were the usual number of bystanders, some of them assumed
— because those in charge of the wheelbarrow made no effort
to explain the situation — that Mr. Sears had been drinking

at midday and was unable to walk home. Cy was doubly furious because he was a teetotaler and my father wrote a story about the affair that was published in the *Gazette*.

But it says something about the nature of the people and the times — and their ability to separate truth from triviality — that when Cy's wife died, my father went to his house, obtained information for the obituary, and sat with Cy all that night, because he was alone. And they remained not only neighbors but friends for long after the boots were forgotten.

The matter of sea serpents was something else for the gathering places on occasion; some joked about them and some did not. My father did not and I did not either, principally because I was with him when he interviewed two commercial fishermen who sighted an unusual marine creature. What they had to say about it was much discussed by the gatherers, both facetiously and seriously, because as Rod Cleveland, who fished out of catboat and No Mans Land boat all his life, remarked of the sea's depths, "I've got some idea what's down there because I've hauled enough of it up but I sure as hell wouldn't want to go down to find out how much I don't know."

In this instance, Captain Fred Caldwell of Fairhaven and his mate, George Roche, were otter trawling out of Menemsha Creek. One day early in July, they were bound in from back of Gay Head and just after turning the bell buoy in the Devil's Bridge area, they came across floating lumber. They slowed down and started picking up loose boards and timber. At that point, they noticed something thrashing in the water and steered for it to investigate.

It is helpful to understand that Captain Caldwell had followed the sea all his life and Roche had been in fishing vessels for a dozen years. Further, when my father talked with them at Menemsha, they spoke not only earnestly but as if they had been or were under stress; their descriptions of what happened and what they saw coincided in every detail, even though at times, both men were talking simultaneously.

Roche, who was on the bow, saw the creature first and shouted to Caldwell to keep away. The skipper, not understanding, held on his course, with the result that the boat came squarely alongside the big sea lizard, which thrust out one hind leg and pushed itself clear of the vessel. Whatever it was, was heading to sea, moving very slowly so that both men had ample opportunity to study its appearance.

"Our boat is fifty-two feet long," Caldwell said. "This thing was several feet longer, sixty feet anyway. I didn't know what was going to happen. If it had started to fight, I hate to think.

"It was shaped like an alligator, only the head was more rounded, with the jaws swelling out from the joints and curving in toward the front. The mouth seemed to open clear back to the joint, but you couldn't see any teeth.

"The general shape of the head was like a cow's and it was almost four feet long. There were big nostrils and ears shaped something like a cow's and something like a pig's. The eyes showed a great deal of white and were the size of a medium plate, about eight inches. The body was perfectly smooth, with its greatest width at the shoulders, tapering somewhat toward the rear.

"The forelegs were shaped exactly like a man's arms, with five toes on each paw. The hind legs were much longer in proportion, with the middle joint, or knee, bending backward like that of a person. They also had five toes on each foot.

"The tail was of slightly darker color and carried a ridge along its upper surface that gave it a triangular appearance. It was the size of a barrel where it joined the body, tapering to the size of a man's leg or smaller. On the extreme end was a triangular fin or something similar that seemed to be composed of a horny substance and showed signs of being worn and broken. Almost four feet of this tail appeared above the water as the thing swam and it was constantly thrashed about. The swimming was all done with the forelegs, which moved like a person's limbs."

Both men spoke excitedly. Both said they had never seen anything like it before and never wanted to see anything like it again. And there were a couple of footnotes.

A few days before, there had occurred the unexplained loss of a Woods Hole fisherman out of his boat while he was hauling pots near Quick's Hole. The boat was found steaming slowly with no one aboard; there was a lobster pot buoy jammed between two bait barrels and the line trailing over the stern, parted, as if from strain. There was no sign of the fisherman and no indication as to what manner of disaster had overtaken him.

Also, it was recalled that seventy years before, an Edgartown packet captain, whose "truthfulness and aversion to exaggeration" were vouched for by the editor of the *Gazette*, had reported the sighting of a monster between Gay Head and Newport. It was described as about seventy feet long, with a head shaped like that of a horse and as big as a barrel; it also had foreflippers or -limbs, the captain said.

My grandfather William, who had no imagination at all and little storytelling ability, once said that he saw a sea serpent on the South Side while mowing salt hay. He described what he saw as "more like a snake than a lizard." He was not aware that the creature had limbs but admitted that being at sea level himself, he might not have been able to see them. All he did see was the monster's head and portions of its back; he said it was "big" and the sight unnerved him enough so that he ceased his mowing and went home. That probably would have been sometime between 1890 and 1900, between Chilmark Pond and Tisbury Great Pond, very likely in the Quansoo area, where the family owned property.

I first heard the story when I was very small and concluded that it was only fair to believe it because I would, after all, have believed the sea serpent if it said it saw my grandfather.

If it was difficult in the gathering places to establish the reliability of sea-serpent sightings — and it was — some matters were more easily disposed of. A fellow who was responsible for distributing some of the free federal-government food on the island told Big Ben Cromwell that he just couldn't get needy Republicans (and most Vineyarders *were* Republicans) to come to his storefront operation to pick it up because they did not want to be considered beholden to FDR.

"I assume Republicans get hungry like anybody else," said Big Ben. "Open up your place after dark and they can sneak in."

Which I assume the fellow did because the food was, after all, ultimately given away. Political historians may also conclude one day that this marked one of the earliest moves toward new Democratic strength on the island.

This may well be so, because Vineyard life for certain numbers of people was difficult then. "I wouldn't want to live as many of my neighbors and my own parents did forty or fifty years ago," says Elmer W. Athearn of West Tisbury. "It was a hand-to-mouth existence for many and considerable hardship for some, even though most people got along and life did seem more relaxed."

Simon Athearn was one of the proprietors of Tisbury in the seventeenth century and there have been Vineyard Athearns ever since. Elmer was two years ahead of me at Tisbury High School. He was a gifted student and was graduated in 1931, at the age of sixteen. In the family tradition (the Athearns of earlier years used to play and make violins, one of which was mistaken for an Amati, from which it probably was copied), he has always been musical and a competent bandsman. Except for two years of preparatory school (the Beacon School in Wellesley Hills), a summer working in a boys' camp, and five years of army service during World War II, he has spent his life on the Vineyard. He is now retired, after a career with the Cape and Vineyard Electric Company.

"On the street where I live," he says, "from the West Tisbury Congregational Church to the Chilmark line, there are about twenty-one houses, of which seven are occupied by families with at least one native-born member. Of those seven, I believe every one has an off-island-born spouse. When I was growing up, there were about fourteen houses in the same area and all but four were occupied by entirely native families. I suspect this is fairly typical of the whole island although, of course, the proportion of natives in the new development areas is still lower.

"I try not to take the standard old-timer's attitude that everything is going to hell and that everything was better when I was a boy, but sometimes I wonder. Certainly things were simpler in our youth. I think people then put more emphasis on appearances and tended to act and expect others to act in what was considered a proper manner. I can't see why that is bad but it seems to be considered so by many today. Doing one's 'own thing' seems to be the way to go now and I daresay it contributes to the general disorder.

"Still, what changes there have been have been gradual enough so that I still feel at home and I'm sure some of the changes have been improvements. You win some and you lose some. Almost everyone has plumbing, electricity, a washer, television, and a car now — none of which (except for a Model T) were enjoyed by my family when I was young."

Within the context of Mr. Athearn's comment about plumbing, electricity, and so on, it is relevant to remember that, whatever the gathering places may have contributed to the Vineyard's idiom and anecdote, they derived some of their vitality from the unemployed and the underemployed — who had nowhere else to go and nothing else to do, even in the best part of the day.

6. The Summer People

"SUMMER people," especially on an island, which has only a certain amount of room, constitute a unique sociological phenomenon. The fundamental is not whether they are good or bad, well behaved or otherwise, little or largely seen abroad in the villages — and all of these matters vary according to the individuals and the era — but, rather, what kind of psychological impact their presence has upon the native. This is something over which the average summer visitor may have some control, but not much.

I remember standing next to a meat cutter in an island grocery on a bright July morning. He was chopping up stew beef on the butcher's block and facing the front screen doors of the store. Through the doors came an absolutely handsome woman of about forty, a summer visitor. Her coiffure was flawless, her clear skin bronzed, and her figure utterly exciting. She paused at the entrance to study a wire rack of cantaloupes, standing easily, with legs apart. Because she wore little under her light skirt, her splendidly proportioned legs, clear to the thighs, were silhouetted.

The meat cutter looked and finally took his eyes away as if it were a great effort. Then he looked down at his hairy, stubby-fingered, red hands, greasy from beef fat, and he said, largely to no one, "I am going home and kick my wife down the stairs."

If you peruse the columns of the *Vineyard Gazette* for the

more than fifty years from 1925 to the present, and I have, you will discover that periodically, often in letters and sometimes in editorials, the sensitivity of the native–summer person relationship surfaces. It is a hot-and-cold thing but not nearly so simple as some would have it; it involves far more than natives who want the visitor's dollar without the visitor. This is not fair to either natives or visitors. What is more, as some of those interviewed herein have suggested, both the kinds of visitors and their relationship to the natives have changed over the years. But whether then or now, one is concerned with an extraordinary juxtaposition of life-styles; if the differences between these once were greater, the abrasiveness was lessened because there was less contact. If the differences today are fewer, sheer weight of numbers and increased frequency of contact have introduced new elements into what is essentially an effort to balance a social equation. The effort may be more intense but it is not new.

In a page-one verse on July 31, 1925, the *Vineyard Gazette* urged summer guests to linger longer in the fall:

> *Why leave our isle on Labor Day at first approach*
> *of fall*
> *And miss the charm of autumn gay you haven't*
> *seen at all*
> *When from the hills the sweet wind blows and all the*
> *woodlands blaze*
> *With coloring no painter knows on Indian summer days.*

However, on November 29, 1929, a *Gazette* editorial observed:

Considering the great influx of visitors during the summer, the dozens of parked cars along Main Street and crowds at all times of day, the accelerated pace of vacationing young people, considering these, to mention a few superficial aspects of the summer side of island life, it is strange that all this should so soon be wrapped away in forgetfulness like a discarded garment. . . .

We doubt if summer people realize how completely they pass out of island life and how little they are missed. Life on Martha's Vineyard, one readily perceives who lives here, is complete in winter as in summer. Those who never come here except during the fleeting warm months can hardly picture the island settled down comfortably about its business in winter. . . .

It is now the summer which, in retrospect, seems dull. After all, so many things belonging to the island itself were held in a state of suspended animation while the summer people had their day. Now we are ourselves again and life is rich in the stimuli of work and enjoyment.

Four visitors and a native responded to the editorial. Mary L. Gough questioned whether it was in good taste and added, "It certainly does not help advertise the island to summer visitors, who, contrary to your assertion that 'they are not missed,' really keep the permanent population going from one summer to the next. I daresay they would be missed if they did not return next summer."

H. K. Fowler found it "extremely rude and discourteous" to the summer visitors. Florence B. Washburn concluded that "so many of us realize that all the 'natives' want of us is our money." Nelson C. Hinckley, treasurer of H. N. Hinckley and Sons, builders and contractors in Vineyard Haven, said, "We cannot help but question the common sense of the one responsible for this gross misrepresentation of the feeling of our best citizens toward the majority of our summer guests."

The editor responded, with particular attention to the phrase "how little they are missed," and commented:

To tell the truth, the reference, which is perhaps justly questioned as to its taste, was prompted by a desire to make summer people miss the Vineyard. How better to do this than to let them know that we are self-reliant and resourceful enough in work and leisure not to miss them? To face the prospect of their failure to return in the summer is, putting it mildly, a horse of another color. We are sure that there is too general an impression that Martha's Vineyard is lonely in the winter. It isn't. It isn't that, or dull or idle, but the antithesis of each of these things.

Undoubtedly, the exchange did not alter anybody's opinion about anything, but then, it really wasn't supposed to. Some natives like summer residents and some do not. Some summer residents are more likable than others. These are truisms. But what the editorial revealed in its forthrightness, tasteful or not, was the strain of summer upon the native population: the need to earn much of a year's income in a few weeks, the reliance upon good weather, the faster pace, the crowded roads and stores, the increased noise levels, the daily exposure to the affluent, and the need to work while surrounded by people at play — all these made the once-quiet autumn welcome. In the era of the Labor Day exodus, one could almost hear the island sigh with relief as the steamers left loaded and the streets lay newly empty. This was far less a matter of liking or disliking the visitors — in those days, most islanders were not well acquainted with any or many summer people — than it was of the need for a rest.

Over a period of about ten impressionable years, roughly from the ages of eleven to twenty-one, I came in contact with summer visitors as a group solely because I provided them with goods or services. At that time, I believe this kind of relationship was less common for islanders than it is now because the Vineyard was less dependent upon the visitors' dollar and there were other kinds of jobs available, including more fishing and farming.

My first impressions were fragmentary, gained at Menemsha, where I went lobstering with David Butler a few times. On days when I was working aboard David's boat at the dock, I would look up suddenly to discover four or five tourists peering down at me with friendly curiosity. The women, standing close together in the sunshine, their colorful dresses blowing, reminded me of a bed of flowers. So the first thing I thought about summer visitors was that they dressed up; they always did in those days. I think I concluded that they probably dressed like that all the time and that the women, at least, did not do any work. I could not reconcile being dressed like that with, for example, the fact that my mother scrubbed the kitchen linoleum on her hands and knees. Most Vineyarders whom I knew dressed up for church, weddings, funerals, and lodge meetings, and to go to New Bedford for eyeglasses, and that was about it.

Occasionally, staring down at me in my khaki pants and boots, the visitors would ask a question. I sensed that they were interested in knowing what went on aboard a lobster boat. The idea of responding appealed to me because I was pleased to know something that an adult did not. I developed a short spiel, describing how a lobster pot works. I also took the cover off the launch's well and with a dip net scooped out whatever was in there — an occasional crab, eel, fish, or lobster — and talked to them about it. They always thanked me, and once a woman offered me a quarter, which I declined because I did not think of my lecturing as being a commercial venture. I was simply talking to people because I wanted to talk to them.

David was not a talker; he was gentle and kind, but he was

not much of a mixer, either, and perhaps this had something to do with his reaction. He was usually at work in the boathouse, boiling lobsters or working on gear, so he did not discover immediately that I was lecturing to the visitors. But one morning, when all the flower ladies and their husbands had departed, there he was, and I knew he had been standing behind them while I talked.

"My," he said, "you certainly have the gift of gab." And he went back into the boathouse, leaving me feeling uncomfortable. I concluded that I had overstepped some kind of traditional boundary in which he believed. I had gone beyond an economic relationship with the summer people in attempting to establish a social relationship, even though of the most limited nature. David was not impressed and I did not give the caplog talk anymore, sensing that the closer I came to the summer people, the farther apart he and I were likely to be, and I did not wish this, because I liked him. "Don't put on airs," he said once.

There were deep and complex roots to this sort of feeling among some islanders; it was a tacit acceptance of associating with one's "own kind." The men whom one could find along the waterfront on any given day were open with each other. Whether they talked little or at length, they stood at ease in their samenesses, sharing common idioms and values. Each man knew where the others had come from; they all used canned evaporated milk in their coffee, generally favored galluses over belts, and if asked about tomorrow's weather, probably would agree on what it would be, because they proceeded from the same premises, based on the same kinds of experience.

Except for one man. Even as a child, I sensed this difference when he approached them. Their easiness became less easy; there was no coolness in their greeting, but it was no more than that, it was no invitation to join them, and whatever they were talking about hung suspended until he had passed by.

I could not understand why this was. The man in question was intelligent and a good boatman, although he did not fish for a living or do any other work of which I was aware.

So I asked my father about him. "Over the years," my father said, "there have been a certain number of Vineyard males who thought it would be a good idea to marry a summer person. Most have not succeeded, in part, at least, because some summer people, probably wisely, have not encouraged their daughters to go out with islanders.

"This fellow bought the right clothes, went to the right places, did the right things, and did indeed marry a summer person. As a result, he has money, but I have had a feeling for years that he is lonesome, because he doesn't really fit anywhere anymore. I don't know how he gets along with summer people but the natives don't know what to say to him because now he leads a life they don't know anything about. Or maybe are even jealous of."

I had reason to think about this later. At one point, I had a summer job with Cronig's Market. On a Saturday morning, I sat on the tailgate of the store's Model T truck; it was shortly after 7:00 A.M. and we were bound for West Chop to make the milk and cream deliveries. Up front, Henry Pacheco was driving and singing with spirit; the words, whatever they were, were whisked away in the wind. We went down a sandy road toward the harbor, halted before a place where roses would hang over a white fence soon enough. I jumped off the truck, carrying a pint or quart of this and that, and ran into a customer's kitchen.

She was just down from the mainland, opening her house for the season, and she was radiant with the joy of returning to the island. I do not know that she was really pretty and yet I found her so because of the animation, the vitality that she brought to the moment. I put the cold beaded bottles of milk and cream on her counter, listening to the excited spring hunger in her voice. Had I ever seen a sky so gloriously blue? Did I know that the herring gulls cry *kee-ow, kee-ow?* And then she said impulsively, "Can you take just a minute to come see my new cesspool?"

Now if this seems strange to you, that probably is because you have never had a new cesspool. I know of no experience in life that gives quite such a wonderful sense of fresh start. So I hollered to Henry that I would be right out and I stepped out back with her and surveyed the nearly completed cesspool, its sturdy iron cover lying nearby. It was a good job and that was no surprise because I knew who had built it. When he had built ours, he was down in the hole and I was on top watching; he knew just how to do it.

"It's great," I said to her. And then I suppose because I was conscious of her womanliness and wished to make a favorable impression, I added, "Your cesspool reminds me of Dante's *Inferno.*"

She was surprised and amused. "Why on earth —?"

"There are pictures in *Inferno* of tortured spirits trying to crawl out of holes and from under heavy covers."

"How do you know about Dante's *Inferno?*"

I knew about it because blond Lena McCoy, my French teacher, a vital force in first revealing to me what lay beyond the island's perimeters, had lent me an enormous volume of the work, with steel engravings, to look at. I found the text so heavy that I gave up on it but the illustrations were so indelibly awful that I had already decided not to be a sinner.

"One of my teachers loaned me a copy," I said.

I made deliveries to the woman's house for the next couple

of weeks and we talked about what subjects I was taking, what my father did for a living, and what I thought I wanted to do. One morning, she stood in her kitchen, holding the half-pint of cream I had just brought in, and she said: "I think you deserve advantages. If you would consider coming to New York during the school year, I will see that you get an excellent education, I will make a room in my apartment available to you, and I will pay all of your expenses. In part, I am doing this because I have no son of my own. Do think about it and if you are interested — and if your parents are willing — I will discuss the arrangements with them."

I found the prospect overwhelming. I spent the next several working hours forgetting my duties and falling over things. Later that day, I told my father about it.

"How old are you?" he asked sharply.

"Thirteen."

"How old is this woman?"

"Older than you are."

"All right," he said, "let us assume then that this is a platonic proposition, even though that may be the worst mistake since General John Bankhead Magruder tried to take Crew House Hill. Whatever it is, it requires a lot of thought. Apparently, she has money. More money than I have."

"Aren't you going to say that I can't go?" I asked.

He thought about it. "No. This could mean a lot to you. It could change your whole life. And I guess your mother and I could go along with it because we want what's best for you. It wouldn't be easy, but I guess we could do it."

So I sat on the back steps and looked at the pear tree and the quince tree and the dusty miller planted inside the automobile tires on top of the two elm stumps. My tiger cat jumped on my shoulders and lay across the back of my neck and went to sleep, which she usually did while I was doing

Martha's Vineyard

my homework. She smelled of salmon and I said so to her. She purred one burst in acknowledgment and did not move.

Part of me wanted to go to New York but because part did not, I was irritated that my father had not said I couldn't go. "Do you want me to go?" I hollered through the screen door. "You have to decide," he said.

I got to thinking about David Butler and the man who was lonesome and I decided not to go to New York, no matter what it might mean to me, because I thought that if I made it there, it would mean that I was no longer the same person and I would then discover who and what I had left behind irrevocably — possibly including my father and mother. I did not think that you could be a summer person and an islander simultaneously because there was too much difference between them.

The next day, or perhaps the day after, I had to deliver milk and cream to the woman's kitchen again. I felt upset enough about having to face her that I had considered quitting my job, but I needed the money for my school clothes in the fall. I hoped perhaps she would be absent, but she was not; she was arranging a vase of flowers on the counter.

I put down the milk and cream and stood there long enough that she knew I wanted to say something. I thought it was going to be the hardest thing I had ever done in my life and I could not even think how to begin. She lifted the burden from me.

She folded her hands on the counter, in what I thought was a most composed manner, and she said quietly, "I believe you have decided not to come with me to the city."

"That's right," I said, feeling both clumsy and cruel.

"Was this your parents' decision?"

"No."

"That makes me feel better," she said, "and you do not

have to explain. I think I knew from the beginning that you probably would prefer to stay here. I cannot put myself in your place but if I were, I might feel the same, I do not know."

She resumed arranging the flowers. "But you must know that I meant every word of it," she said, "that I wish a good life for you — and you must not feel uncomfortable for one moment when you come into this kitchen."

Then she ordered another half-pint of cream, which, as I think about it, was no more than a gesture to relieve the great heaviness of the moment. We never discussed more than the weather after that, and the next summer, the house was rented by someone else.

Eventually, my personal consideration of the summer people became even more complex, principally because I was more aware of economic inequities. I worked a few summers for Smith, Bodfish and Swift Company in Vineyard Haven, an S. S. Pierce store, and one day delivered a grocery order to the home of an obviously wealthy professional person. His wife insisted on showing me her new electric refrigerator, which had just arrived. It gleamed and sparkled, it had every latest device, and I had to listen to a detailed explanation of all of them, especially because she was a valuable customer.

At home, we had a wooden, zinc-lined icebox. Something like every other day, Henry Burgess, who drove an ice truck for Harry Peakes, would come by, steel-pick a chunk the right size, and dump it into our kitchen box. It was my job to empty the ice pan underneath. Periodically, I would forget it until it was so full that it was impossible to carry without slopping water all over the kitchen floor — which I then had to swab up. It was not only a dull chore, it was a daily irritation.

What is more, our icebox was too small to hold much and it

did not keep things very cold anyway, and the metal interior smelled unappetizing, no matter how often it was scrubbed. I could not visualize that we would ever have an electric refrigerator because it was so far down the list of priorities. We did not own our home, had no furnace or storm windows, and charged our groceries from one week to the next, always paying for something already eaten.

So I stood there listening to the woman praise her electric refrigerator, conscious of my dirty apron — clean ones went to senior employees — and I could feel anger smolder within me. Not because she had a new refrigerator but because I thought she ought to have sense enough to know that not everybody did and that many never would.

Yachting offered one of the most visible signs of affluence, enabling the island native to contrast his circumstances and those of summer people. Of all the yachting, the most awesome and massive contrast of life-styles was offered by the arrival of the New York Yacht Club fleet. From beginning to end, it was to those of us who stood outside it a glimpse of glitter and pageantry so incomprehensible that it might as well have come not only from another world but from another century that we had not yet entered.

There was a breathtaking sense of majesty, of elegance, of something extraordinary about to happen, long before the yachts arrived. I remember especially one year when the fleet sailed from Mattapoisett to Vineyard Haven and its more than one hundred sail and power craft constituted the biggest cruise fleet following World War I.

The first movements of the fleet were observed from the cliffs at Gay Head at about one in the afternoon, when the lofty mastheads of the J boats, the four America's Cup contenders, could be seen over the high land of Nashawena as they beat down Buzzards Bay in a light southerly that shifted a point or two from east to west every few minutes. Even at a great distance, they were a unique sight; even in reality, there was an unreality about them, especially if, in addition to simply observing their great grace, you were aware of their cost and dimensions.

Enterprise, for example, cost $630,000, excluding "extras." Its mast, comprising two shells of duralumin, was 162 feet from keel to truck; it had to support the weight of more than a ton of canvas with wind in it. Its "Park Avenue" boom weighed a ton and a quarter; in its center section, it was wide enough for two men to walk abreast, and the foot of the mainsail slid to leeward on transverse rails and thus constantly assumed the correct aerodynamic curve.

By contrast, our brand-new Tisbury school housing eight grades and the high school was dedicated in this same year, 1930. It cost $185,000. The total recommended budget for the town of Edgartown for the same year was $95,570. And in February of that year, Congressman Charles L. Gifford of Cotuit told the U.S. House of Representatives: "Missouri may need flood relief, Florida may need fruit fly relief, but the people of New Bedford, Massachusetts, may need food relief unless conditions are changed very soon."

The breeze freshened a little from the southwest as the afternoon advanced and the fleet began to make better time, entering Vineyard Sound about three o'clock and slacking sheets for the run to West Chop. Along the West Chop road, there were massed hundreds of cars. Main Street in Vineyard Haven was jammed with them, and there were hundreds of spectators along the shore and harbor front awaiting the finish of the race. Cruising from one vantage point to another with their binoculars at the ready were fifteen or twenty representatives of the largest metropolitan newspapers on the Atlantic seaboard, each busy calculating time and tides, and not the least among them my venerable friend William U. Swan, the dean of such writers, in his customary blue jacket, gray flannels, and sneakers.

Already, several of the larger sailing craft and power cruisers had entered the harbor, among them the big three-masters *Atlantic* and *Guinevere* and the brigantine *Illegria*. A great fleet of small craft sailed back and forth around the Chop, a seaplane soared overhead, and at 4:30, the gun was fired for the first craft to finish, the graceful schooner *Lynx*. After her came schooners, sloops, yawls, and ketches of all sizes, all catching a stiff breeze off the land that tautened their canvas and showed them off to splendid advantage. The wind had backed slightly and nearly every boat had to tack across the finish line, giving the spectators an opportunity to see the maneuver executed at close range.

Virtually every craft of this class had appeared and the flagship *Nourmahal* had joined them when the first of the contenders appeared, lying down to it as she caught the land breeze, and identified at once as *Enterprise* by her silver metal mast. She tacked and slid across the line and the gun boomed, a puff of white smoke rising. Close astern came *Weetamoe*, dousing a jib as she neared the line and keeping off to pass astern of the committee boat to indicate her withdrawal from the race (she had crowded *Whirlwind* at the start). The old defenders *Resolute* and *Vanitie* came in, their glory moment diminished by the performance of the new boats, but their beauty as striking as ever.

At anchor, the business of caring for the great fleet began, with launches and tenders purring back and forth. Scores of white-uniformed sailors besieged the restaurants and ice cream bars, while truckloads of groceries were hustled aboard yachts and tenders as fast as they could be handled. With the coming of darkness, strings of colored lights decorated the yachts and cast a gleam over the anchorage; beneath the velvet of night, soft puddles of light; the punctuations of light, commas and colons; the geometry of light, circles and ellipses; the romantic mysteries of light, bobbing and swaying; and somewhere, light laughter and music playing. The launches came and went, purring through the night.

Besides this splendid sight and spirit of celebration, the yachts and their people transformed island life in other ways. From 1930 on, E. Issokson, the tailor at the corner of Main and Union, tried to have little of his ordinary stitching and fitting of garment work on hand when the yacht fleet arrived. In both 1930 and 1933, the big sloop *Weetamoe* split a jib — it was a thirty-foot rent the second time as she and *Vanitie* were footing down the offshore side of Middle Ground Shoal — and Issokson, adaptable and competent landsman that he was, literally filled his small shop with the massive canvas and worked through the night hours to patch the sail so that the J boat could have it for the next morning's departure.

I saw the shopful of jib, where normally there would be nothing more romantic than workingmen's pants. The jib was like all the rest of the world of which it was a symbol: if you were not part of it, you could not understand it.

Smith, Bodfish and Swift Company prided itself on staying open "all evening" Fridays and Saturdays and especially when the yacht fleet was in. For hours, we filled the visiting yachtsmen's orders, stowed them in cartons, and trucked them to the dock. In those golden days, a pork roast was 29 cents a pound and coffee, 47 cents a pound, but an income of $2,000 a year was a lot of money, and I wondered what the yachtsmen's grocery bills amounted to.

It was, of course, all relative. Not too long ago, my father said, "Certainly things are better today than they used to be. When steak was twenty-five cents a pound, I didn't have twenty-five cents. Now, steak is two-fifty a pound and I have it whenever I want to." But in those days, when the Martha's Vineyard Shipbuilding Company was advertising for sale a 26-foot motor sailer for $1,400, I knew that a good many people on the island did not earn that much in a year.

Handling the yachtsmen's groceries, I experienced a kind of pleasure of the senses because they implied good, perhaps even grand, living. The very colors and containers were seductive: winged nymph on the White Rock bottle, yellow globes of pâté de foie gras, red and green capers, gay in glass; orange marmalade in black-lettered British crocks, tiny cans of smoked clams with foreign labels, and golden biscuits in tins. Paring the limp leaves of iceberg lettuce each grocery morning, freshening yesterday's heads with a water spray, I wondered what it could be like to take all these things for granted.

Looking at the yachts as I paddled about the harbor or delivered lamb chops to the varnished, polished-brass tenders, listening to the men in yachting caps speaking casually about things of which I had never heard, I wondered what of all that I was looking at I would be able to afford . . . sometime.

Eliminate the boats, sleek, polished, spotless, and their brass binnacles, bright cordage, and snowy canvas.

Eliminate the initialed glasses, china with the yacht club crest, monogrammed flatware, silver pitchers with tea and ice, and bottles of whatever from wherever that sparkled and gurgled.

Eliminate the bronzed women whose ever-composed faces were never damp in the heat of the sun.

Of all this, I could not buy one spoon, one coil of rope; I could not buy one moment of their lives . . . not then, and presumably, not ever.

At noon the next day, long after the yacht fleet had set its acres of white canvas, hosed the mud off its spotless anchors, and departed, I went to the beach. There in the swash were two grapefruit rinds, an empty Haig and Haig pinch bottle, and a condom with a red fish's head. I assumed that you could not buy a condom like that anywhere on Martha's Vineyard. It was hard to believe that only last night the harbor had been full of lights and had looked like a floating city.

"The city has gone back to the city," I said, and picked up the pinch bottle because I had never seen one before and I liked running my fingers over its concavities.

On ordinary summer mornings at Smith, Bodfish and Swift we filled orders. It was customary for our representatives — always senior, knowledgeable employees — to visit the kitchens of summer residents six mornings a week before 10:00 A.M., to take their orders for the day. We would procure for them even articles that we did not sell, such as drugstore items. By eleven, these outside representatives were back at the store. Under their jurisdiction (they selected every cut of meat, tapped every melon, and polished the apples on their sleeves), we filled the orders and the delivery trucks rolled soon thereafter.

Usually, I worked for Fred Smith, who was assigned to East Chop. I remember him fondly; he had a neatly trimmed gray mustache and liked to go trout fishing. Mr. Smith would stand at the counter with his order pads in neat rows, occasionally sticking his pencil into his mouth to make it write blacker. "Four pounds kidney beans," he would say, and I would go to the bin, shovel the fat, shiny beans with an aluminum scoop, fill a brown paper bag, weigh it, and fasten it with a strip of sticky brown tape. "Pound of salt pork to go with," Mr. Smith would say, "and make sure there's a good streak of lean."

When we had stowed all the East Chop orders in cartons, a fellow from the mainland named Franklin and I would

load them in the truck. He supervised the loading carefully
— he was the driver and I the delivery boy — because obviously, the orders delivered earliest had to be near the back
or on top; we often carried large loads with two layers of
orders, carefully stacked to protect whatever was breakable.
Each order had a slip on it bearing the customer's name and
a list of the items; I do not know now how they arranged to
pay the store but they did not give any money to truck drivers
or delivery boys.

One day, after Mr. Smith had put up all his orders and
gone somewhere, Franklin said to me, "Here's another order
we have to fill. Mr. Smith must have forgotten it." I looked
at the pad and it said "G. O. Grubb," so I said, "O.K., you
tell me what you want and I'll get it."

So Franklin sang out, "One-pound can R. and R. boned
chicken." And I fetched it. Then he said, "Half-pound mild
cheese." And I got that. After that, he asked for a quart of
milk. Then he said, "And a apple pie. Get one of them that
come in this morning." So I got that, too. Following which,
we put the order on the truck and sped off to make our
deliveries.

That day, I rode up front because we had loaded tailgate
and all, and even if there had been room aft, my feet would
have dragged. Opposite Dukes County Garage, Franklin
whistled at a girl he knew, she blew him a kiss, and he said,
"Hot damn!" and out the Beach Road we went, summer wind
in our faces, and the little engine thundering under the
wooden floorboards.

About an hour and a half later, we had delivered all but
one order. I looked at it. "G. O. Grubb," I said, "and I don't
know where the house is, do you? I've never been there
before."

"Um, yes," said Franklin and he drove along a road edged

with pines and stopped where there was no house at all. Then he reached under the truck seat and hauled out a picnic package that the store sold; it contained paper cups, plates, knives, forks, and spoons. " 'G. O. Grubb,' " he said, "stands for 'Get Our Grubb,' because we have been workin' since early this morning and now it is the middle of the afternoon.

"Take a plate," he said, and began to open the can of chicken.

I could feel the saliva flowing but I said, "Why aren't they going to know at the store that you took this stuff?" He speared a big chunk of chicken onto his plate. "I didn't turn in no copy of the slip, that's why." He ate the chicken, took a swig of milk, and said: "That pie and cheese is going to hit the spot."

As almost always at such times, thoughts of my father and Henry Ritter and Sunday school came to mind unbidden. Without much conviction, I said, "Franklin, this is stealing."

Between bites, he took my plate, put some chicken on it, and handed it to me. "Now then," he said, "you got a plate of chicken. Where'd you get it?"

"You gave it to me," I said dubiously.

"Right," he said. "I give it to you. You didn't steal nothin'. Now eat it or I'll think you don't like me." He laughed and cut into the golden crust and the juicy apples.

I ate, gradually with gusto. Franklin led me into sin because I was weak. And hungry. He and I ate all the chicken, all the cheese, the whole pie, and drank all the milk. The meal was eminently satisfying.

For all of the next week, it seemed to me that Bert Smith, who, with his brother Art, owned the grocery business, looked at me strangely over the top of his glasses. I could not stand it. Finally, I figured out how much half the stolen food cost and left the money at the cashier's counter when nobody was looking. Actually, I paid for some of Franklin's, too, because he ate faster than I did.

Eating on the Vineyard always has had a certain special charm for the natives because, as Mrs. Poole recalled, it often involves personal harvesting, the return to nature to rediscover the bounty of the season. There is less of that pleasure now than there was.

"What fun it was to take a lard pail and roam almost anywhere to gather all kinds of berries," Mrs. Gale Huntington says. "But not only is there no lard pail now, there is no roaming either, for no-trespassing signs have put a stop to that. And what fun to fish almost everywhere and to go swimming in the surf at Squibnocket without having to be living in Chilmark and even then, having to have a pass to go there.

"Now, the farms are gone. Backyard gardens are gone. The fishing industry has dwindled. Many of the beautiful stone walls at the west end of the island are invisible, covered with brush. Villages are losing their identity; commercial sprawl is taking care of that."

Mrs. Huntington is the former Mildred Tilton; my father grew up with Vineyard Tiltons and so did I. Mildred was three years ahead of me at Tisbury High School; she and her family were neighbors and I played with her brothers. In high school, she was president of the student body, active in dramatics, a track star, captain of the girls' basketball team, editor of the school magazine, and on the honor roll consistently for four years. She is a graduate of Bridgewater State Teachers College, and has both fished and farmed with her husband. I renewed acquaintance with her and her husband not long ago after hearing them play and sing sea chanteys to a capacity audience at the Old Dartmouth Historical Society in New Bedford.

The Summer People

It was then that I remembered Alton Tilton's "Rolling Home" song (" 'Round Cape Horn one frosty morning, / And the sails were full of snow. / Wear your sheets and sway your halliards / Swing her off and let her go . . .") and realized for how many years, in both public and private roles, Mr. and Mrs. Huntington have symbolized the Vineyard, its spirit and its roots.

Gale is a graduate of Stetson University, obtained his master's in history from Boston University, has been a commercial fisherman, is a retired schoolteacher, and is well known as writer, archivist of the Dukes County Historical Society, gardener, square-dance fiddler, and violinist with a chamber music group. He has a long Vineyard family tradition and has done much to preserve island folk songs and ballads. At sixty-eight, he rowed a skiff from his home on Hine's Point, Vineyard Haven, around West Chop, up the North Shore to Menemsha, through the creek to Menemsha Pond, and on to his boat landing at Quitsa, a total distance of at least fifteen miles.

"I wish someone would do a survey to determine how many off-islanders have either bought or built a home here or winterized the one they already owned," Mrs. Huntington says. "It must amount to several hundred. More are coming, and fast. Many retirees are fine people; they are as opposed to ugly buildings and razing of the beautiful old ones as I am. But some newcomers strike me as having the feeling 'this is mine'; there is a drive to own and control land and beaches.

"Who would ever believe that there is no place to park on Main Street at any time of year unless you are lucky enough to meet someone pulling out? Or that you train yourself to take your keys out of the car whenever you leave it? Or that you lock your house?

"The island has lost much of its uniqueness and continues to lose. So I am bitter and selfish, too, I guess. Neither trait is healthy but I can't seem to overcome them."

Gale, who feels that "the regional high school is quite enough," that no more regionalization of the island systems is desirable, and that boys and girls got a sounder fundamental education in the three down-island high schools than they do now, adds, "I could go on and on, but Mil has already said it."

It is something of a footnote to Mrs. Huntington's comment that the big old house just back of Smith, Bodfish, Swift Company in which she grew up, the house where my father stayed when my sister Jo's scarlet fever quarantined the rest of our family, has been obliterated by the wrecker and the bulldozer. As with the little schooner under the sand in which I roasted potatoes, if you did not know that it was there once, you would never suspect it now.

7. The Heroines and Heroes

ONCE upon a June when I was twenty, a day as brightly beautiful as a bell and a song, my mother lay with her eyes closed in a bed at the Martha's Vineyard Hospital and I had to look particularly to make certain that she breathed. "The poor thing needs the air," said the nurse, as she removed flowers from the room. I thought of saying that flowers do not consume oxygen but that did not seem to matter and besides, their smell was cloying.

So I whispered good-bye but she did not answer and I left without making any noise. Then I walked along the road, with broken white shells beside, and went to the beach, this being what islanders do more often than not when everything is too much. I shoved the skiff overboard, rowed out to the catboat at the mooring, opened the cabin door, and hauled out some lumber with which I was making an engine cover for the old Hartford one-lunger. I drilled a couple of holes and put in the screws, thinking, "I am building my mother's coffin."

After I had worked for an hour or two, I heard somebody calling my name and I shoved my head up out of the cockpit. It was Walter Booker, a neighbor, who worked at the Cape and Vineyard electric plant. He was waving at me from the town dock.

I got into the skiff and rowed toward him, knowing all the way in, with my back to him, what I would see in his face when I turned around, knowing all the way in what he wanted with me. It seemed to me that someone else pulled the oars, because I had no wish to do so; that they made no noise, neither blades dripping nor looms rubbing against rowlock, because I did not wish to hear them or concede that it was I propelling myself to an encounter from which I would have preferred to flee.

When I got alongside the dock, Mr. Booker leaned down. His face was red and his mouth worked at the corners. I sat there in the sunshine, hearing the lap of water under the skiff's stern but feeling detached from my mind and body, as if I had left them to avoid what they were going to feel when they were struck with the words. His voice came from so far away that I expected it to echo: "Your mother's gone." I believe he said it twice and I thought that strange because I was very close to him, but it seems to me now that he just wanted to be quite sure I understood, perhaps because he had never before had to deliver the message that somebody was dead.

Evangeline Ritter invited me for lunch in the garden that day. As I think of it, she was often there when people needed help; not summoned, just there. I do not know what we had to eat but once, during the meal, she put her hand on my arm, saying, "You don't have to hurry so. There is no hurry." And of course there was not; haste would just get you more quickly to those scarring rituals, those interminable rituals that immediately follow death — and I did not wish to get to them at all. In a vague way, it occurred to me that I was going to wear black-and-white saddle shoes to my mother's funeral because I had no others and it seemed inappropriate to bother my father with such a detail. I was comforted by the fact that church pews tend to conceal; I did not think that anyone other than members of the immediate family would be able to see my feet.

I put down my fork and listened to Evangeline. "I went to

see your mother shortly before she went to the hospital," the Duchess said. "She and I used to walk a lot when she was well, down toward West Chop and Tashmoo. Once, she picked a holly sprig and some boxberries and pinned them to her coat; she was pleased, and I thought it was an expression of something within her that few knew about.

"She kept some things of yours in a drawer in that table in the front room. She showed them to me. I remember especially two spelling-bee medals and a published poem about a river that won a prize for you at school. Can you remember how the poem began?"

Yes, of course. "City river, / Oozing its greasy way (wind in the bottle neck wailing) / Through the slabstone verticals / Of humanity . . ."

That was as far as I got. I excused myself quickly, hearing Evangeline say, as I started across the lawn, gradually running, "Your mother was very proud of you; she —" I went into the Ritter house, to her bathroom, and threw up.

When I came back through her living room, I thought, "This woman, this duchess of a woman, is the only person I know poor enough in dollars to burn paper in her seventeenth-century fireplace and rich enough in spirit to make you believe it is birch logs." I returned to the garden, feeling empty of everything, kissed her hand, and left. "Come back when you will," she said, regally, womanly, with the white linen and the summer shadows, "but come back."

Shortly thereafter, "Aunt" Hattie Tilton, Mil Huntington's grandmother, came to help us keep house. Any consideration of Vineyard heroines and heroes might just as well start with Hattie and the Tiltons because several of that family possessed the ingredients of the heroic figures of those times. I once mentioned to Dr. Milton Mazer, founder and director of the Martha's Vineyard Mental Health Center, that there were important distinctions between those figures and contemporary island celebrities, the nearest thing now left. He suggested that the old heroic figures were not only natives, but "doers." That is so, but what set them apart was not only what they accomplished, often extraordinary, but an uncommon attitude.

What they *did*, Tiltons or otherwise, retains respectable proportions even when viewed from the worldly-wise perspective of our own age, and the examples are numerous.

Captain and Mrs. John S. Reynolds were married when he was twenty-four and she, seventeen. Immediately following their wedding, husband and wife went to sea on the bark *Mattapoisett*, of which he was master; they went a-whaling for two years. On other voyages, they sailed most of the world's oceans, cruised the Bering Sea, ventured along the Alaska coast, doubled Cape Horn three times, and made port at scores of the outposts of civilization, including those of the South Seas. A number of Vineyarders, male and female, did approximately the same thing.

At twenty, Captain Everett A. Poole captured and killed a five-hundred-pound swordfish with his hands.

Blacksmith Prentiss C. Bodfish, a man of great, rawboned strength, was captain of a hook-and-ladder truck in Tisbury at the age of eighty-one and was usually the first of the volunteer crew to board the vehicle, night or day, in answer to an alarm.

Solomon McLeod Attaquin, as member of a lifeboat crew, rowed four hours in fierce weather to reach a steamer stranded across Vineyard Sound. He and his mates lowered ninety-seven people in slings and boatswain's chairs down the side of the vessel into the tossing lifeboat and transferred them to a revenue cutter standing by. Not a life was lost.

Such stories abound in Vineyard history but fully as interesting as the extraordinary efforts and the brave deeds are the underlying factors: what the people involved were, and why. A portrait of Hattie Tilton, even though admittedly broadbrush, provides some insight into this.

Hattie came to help us, to cook, wash, and iron, not only because my father paid her something (not much, I am sure) but because she knew him as a North Road boy, his children were motherless, and because she possessed a kind of strength and common sense that enabled her to know what she could contribute to our household in the way of stability, after all the cooking, washing, and ironing was done.

This understanding of life and death, common to many of the older Vineyarders, derived in part from the crucible of their upbringing that required living at the frontiers of daily experience. If you are going to have chicken for dinner, somebody has to grab its feet and chop its head off. If something breaks — hame, hoe handle, or mixing spoon — somebody has to locate tools, screws, twine, or whatever, and make it workable again. And if you want something — quilt, pudding, or hen house — you have to find the time, provide the effort, and make it.

Some Vineyard heroes and heroines had money; most did not. But the important thing is that money was less used in those days even by those who possessed it, because they were able to do most things for themselves. This quality produced not only self-sufficiency but an extraordinary kind of quiet capability that did not falter even in crises.

I emphasize "quiet." Apart from one or two Vineyarders who succumbed to the enthusiasms of tourists and the mainland press, I do not know of any island heroes or heroines who ever considered that they were heroic at all, or who would have come to personal grips with the term without embarrassment or annoyance. Whatever they lived and hoped for, it was not adulation.

Hattie was a short woman, pink-cheeked and positive, and when she first walked into our kitchen from the backyard (older Vineyard natives never used the front door), I suddenly felt at peace for the first time in days. And hungry, which goes with it after stress, I suppose. Without words, she personified the resilience of the enduring human creature and had no need to say, "This, too, shall pass away." Some might have wasted time commiserating; she put on an apron and began slicing potatoes and onions for a chicken chowder, a Vineyard specialty to which my aunt Anna had introduced me long before. Smelling its steaming broth, watching its buttery eyes floating merrily, I understood that tomorrow would be better, perhaps even better than ever.

Hattie possessed that practical old-style attribute, the ability to converse animatedly, anecdotes and all, without ever so much as missing a beat in her work, whatever it was. "I grew up on No Mans Land," she would say, swishing a hot sadiron deftly between the buttons of a shirt, "and my father couldn't afford to send my sister and me and my brothers to the mainland or the Vineyard for schooling. The town of Chilmark refused to establish a school on No Mans until my father agreed to pay half of a teacher's salary and to provide a room for the school and heat it.

"School was held only for three months of the year [swish, swish went the sadiron] but we did learn reading, writing, arithmetic, and geography. Not many of us had the advantage of going to high school. I didn't. But my girlhood on No Mans was a very happy one. Everyone there was always willing to lend a hand to anyone who needed help."

No Mans Land is the little island just south of the Vineyard. In the years when Hattie grew up there, a few families were permanent residents, a number more were seasonal, drawn there by the fishery. A fleet of roughly fifty boats fished from the island at the peak of activity. Spring and fall were the codfishing seasons; the vessels fished on the area ledges and the catch was salted and cured for exporting. In summer, the residents set lobster pots and cruised for swordfish.

Religious services were held occasionally and there was a store with very limited stock in staples. Traffic with the mainland was sketchy and most of the supplies for the island were brought in the smacks that came for lobsters and fish, for the No Mans Landers did not often make the trip. If the store ran out of supplies, and it did occasionally, especially in periods of hard weather, the people of the island shared their beans, bacon, or whatever. There was no doctor on No Mans, and sometimes suffering and even tragedy resulted, for during the winter, there were many days when a boat could not leave the shore. "It was better," Hattie once observed, "if you had to be sick or get hurt, to do it in good weather." She made a point of noting that No Mans Landers, who always worked hard and sometimes dangerously, were especially careful to avoid accidents, knowing that a relatively simple injury in isolation can be serious. I quoted to her the old navy adage: "One hand for the ship, one hand for yourself" in sloppy weather, and she nodded.

No Mans life was the ultimate distillation of what it is like to live on an island because it was even smaller and more tightly knit than the Vineyard. There was no cover for the introvert and while there was no denying the individual's need for self-sufficiency, the obligation to relate to the community, to share its daily grief, joy, or burdens, to "pull your oar," as the No Mans Landers said, was unspoken because it was undeniable. The result was that the people of No Mans

Land, sharing a few acres of windswept outpost with the pattering coot in the deep swells of fall and the fork-tailed tern sweeping the summer rips, achieved an extraordinary sense of fellowship and a love for island that nothing could diminish. Their little houses, gale-scarred yet stubbornly rooted against the weather that roared in from the north, were symbols of their own tenacious spirit.

What No Mans was is important because it shaped in fundamental ways what Hattie became, as a woman. Since No Mans *is* smaller and its people were fewer in number, it is easier to understand from the lesson of this place what island living instills in people, how it shapes their values and, in so doing, implicitly creates their heroes and heroines. The Vineyard is no more than an extension of the No Mans Land proposition.

Whatever did Hattie do in her long life that was heroic, in terms of being an islander? I am aware of three facets of the woman that seem to me to delineate what she was and to emphasize those characteristics that Vineyarders traditionally have looked upon as exemplary.

In order to appreciate the first, it is essential to understand the nature of a yearly No Mans ritual, a sailing race in those open, double-ended, lap-straked little boats named after the island, in which its people performed their sea work, in fair weather or foul. The boats were part of the men; the men were part of the boats. The event was, of course, more than just a race. It was a celebration, occurring at the end of the fall codfishing season. It was a time of work done, crop secured, and chowder shared, and although its Yankee principals did not know or care, the race had root kinship with the harvest festival of the *Iliad* and every similar observance down the centuries. This meeting of little boats in contest was

a check mark on the calendar of the seasons, the end of a cycle, and it was generally sailed in weather blustery to bitter.

Personally, it was something else as well, also profoundly related to history. As the thirteenth-century tiltyard joust at Saint James's, London, comprised an exhibition of practical skills, so the No Mans race was a demonstration of those talents essential for survival. A No Mans Land adult, especially male, who could not handle an engineless boat in most situations suffered an important loss of both personal and economic security. That is why those members of a seabound, seagoing society were sailors by instinct, from childhood.

When Hattie was sixteen — she was then Hattie Butler, described by her contemporaries long afterward as "the belle of No Mans Land" — she chose to enter that year's race.

"Were you the first female ever to do so?" I asked one day while she was putting together a bowl of corned beef hash.

"I might have been," she conceded. "I never knew another."

"What did the men say about it?"

Chop, chop went the bright knife down through the onions. "Oh, they joked some because I was the only girl racing but I guess they thought it was good sport."

Of No Mans Land boats in heavy weather, they always used to say, "one to sail and one to bail" — that is, to bail out the seawater that came flying in sheets, green, cold, and solid, over the bow. This particular race day dawned with a half-gale of wind smoking in from the northeast and skimming the froth off the sea tops; intermittently, the slate-gray sky spat snow, at times heavy enough so that it was hard to see through.

It was a simple event; into the wind and away from the wind, yet designed to test all of the qualities of boats and skippers. The thrash to windward was wet all the way and lumpy as well; the run to leeward, lifting on the roller-coaster crests that sped the boats homeward, was drier, but the hand at the helm had to be a sure one because the following seas came rolling right up to the hip pockets of whoever was at the tiller. Hattie won; she cleaned out the fleet.

In so doing, she aroused the admiration of a big blond codfisherman and mate of a coasting schooner named Welcome Tilton, one of the racing skippers whom she defeated.

When Hattie and Welcome observed their fiftieth wedding anniversary in 1936, my father wrote a few lines about the race:

> *He led the fleet of fishers on the ledges out at sea*
> *He held on last of any when they ran to make a lee;*
> *But when they met for racing after filling every flake*
> *'Twas Hattie took the trophy, Welcome trailing in*
> *her wake.*

The second thing that I remember about Hattie — and it concerns a quality possessed by many Vineyard women who also were heroic in their own right — was the manner in which she accepted the dangers of the sea, even while the men of her family made their livings upon it. It is simple enough to say that this kind of self-discipline — it is in no sense stoicism — is traditional and expected of those whose kin are sailors, but that is not much comfort to the woman who waits ashore when the ragged clouds come down the wind masthead high, there is white water even in the harbor, and still no sign of the single-masted dragger rolling her wet way home. And the waiting gets no easier simply because you have done it countless times before.

Earl Wade's mother, who lost both her father and son at sea, observed shortly before Earl sailed for the last time: "Out there is God's sea, smiling, threatening, or raging, according to its mood, but always capable of drawing men away from their homes, their fireplaces, and their women. It has always been so and it will always be, here or somewhere." That is about the way it is, and was with Hattie.

I saw Hattie not long after she lost her grandson, Leslie "Kaiser Bill" Tilton, with whom I grew up and played for years. He and his mate, Joe Thomas of Edgartown, were dragging off East Chop when their vessel went to the bottom. The best guess was that they were towing their gear from the derrick-boom, the towing chock broke or the cable slipped out, and that the boat swung broadside to the current and tripped. Searchers found fish boxes and other loose gear adrift off the Chop that day, probably from Leslie's boat, and they found his body, but there never was a sign of Thomas or of the vessel.

I told Hattie I was sorry about Leslie and asked her how she was, meaning that I hoped she was weathering it. She looked at me with those kind eyes that had seen and reflected almost everything in the human experience. Then she replied stoutly, Vineyard-style, "So's to be about."

Finally, demonstrating that heroines retain their exceptional characteristics regardless of the years, Hattie was moved to take a stand in the sometimes acrimonious regional high school controversy that divided her town, in some instances, not only neighbor against neighbor, but relative against relative. My father and I, holding differing views, eventually agreed not to discuss the subject. Many town residents, for a variety of sensitive reasons, chose not to commit themselves publicly.

But Hattie said, "I think it is very sad that Vineyard Haven has voted down the regional school. I say this because I know that I would have profited so much in my lifetime if I could only have had a better education. I still, at my age, read to try to improve myself to make up for some of the education I missed when I was a girl.

"Today, it is necessary to learn so many more things; particularly this is true for the boys and girls who are going to stay, live, and work on the Vineyard. I do hope that the people of Vineyard Haven will forget all their selfish reasons, change their minds, and vote for the school for our young people."

She was eighty-six at the time. The town did, in fact, eventually vote for the school and I have to believe that some may have been moved to do so because of what they knew Hattie to be and what she had to say at a moment when it mattered.

Although, as Dr. Mazer suggested, most of the Vineyard heroes and heroines were natives, not all were, and this may surprise some residents who have arrived on the island more lately.

I was talking with a professional woman who, with her husband, has lived on the island several years; both are active in community affairs. "How long does it take to be accepted here?" she asked, almost in exasperation. "We pay taxes, we attend town meeting, we interest ourselves in the hopes and problems of our fellow townspeople and yet I know, even though it is primarily unspoken, that we are looked upon, not only as off-islanders, but as meddlers. Some, perhaps even many, natives still feel that by exercising our rights as citizens here, by sharing their concern about what happens to the Vineyard, we are encroaching upon their exclusive rights and privileges. Will that change — ever?"

The life of "Doc" Lane, Vineyard hero, offers a reply that I hope will be encouraging to her and to all those who ask the same question. He was not a native but he possessed those attributes and attitudes that mattered to the natives, and once they discovered this, they were with him — or vice versa.

Charles F. Lane, M.D., was a Maine farm boy who became, although he would have been reluctant to admit or believe it, a Vineyard institution. As a young man on the mainland, he told my father, he worked as a carpenter. Something, undoubtedly some of the same astuteness that made him outstanding in later years, attracted the attention of a physician friend, who lent him medical books. Lane spent much of his spare time reading them, prepared himself for college, and after prodigious effort (which he always minimized), was graduated.

His first job was in the office and drugstore of a Vineyard doctor. He used to recall, with amusement by that time, that he discovered immediately it was a long and discouraging task to gain the confidence of the island people and to serve them as he wished to. They wanted the physician they were used to, they assumed age knew more than youth, and they did not want an apprentice to minister to them because that implied that they were not very ill or not very important.

In the beginning, there were no telephones. The roads, as with the North Road even in later years, were an ordeal, washboarded with ridges and ruts when frozen or soupy and half afloat in mud during the thaws of spring. In winter, heavy drifts frequently blocked the main routes and, equally bad, the long and winding private driveways that led into many of the farms.

But Doc, more than six feet tall, with a spare frame as tough as steel springs, quick, surefooted, and charged with endless energy, was equal to all of it. He got around in a horse and buggy; he chose his horses for speed, and the old-timers always said that nobody ever drove as fast as he or dared to. Somebody was discussing this with my grandfather William, who was not much of a traveler or given to extravagant phrase; evidently, grandfather had been to North Tisbury, or Middletown, as the older people called the place, to pick up a pair of shoes that had been sent up from Vineyard Haven. While he was at the store, Doc Lane came flying past, horse at a gallop, on his way to a patient. "He goes some," said my grandfather, sitting beside the kitchen stove and stroking the bony head of his skinny tiger cat, Josephine. "When he went by, I expected to see his behind afire."

Few *had* to drive as fast as Doc did. When he left his office on a call, he never knew how long it would take him to get there or what he would find when he arrived. Many times, perhaps even mostly in the beginning, he got word of someone in need second- or even thirdhand. Often, much time had elapsed since whoever required help had started the message on its way, by horse or even on foot. And he had to carry with him what almost amounted to hospital equipment of the day.

The first thing islanders learned about him was that neither weather nor bad roads would stop him. If his horses could not wade or wallow through the snow, water, or mud, he left his team at the nearest house he could get to and walked, lugging a heavy medicine case in each hand. Had he not been a person of extreme vigor and unusual strength, such a schedule might well have broken him. As it was, he triumphed over fatigue as if doing so were no more than a matter of mental discipline, and he seemed never to be ill himself.

After he became as much a part of the Vineyard scene (and as enduring) as the scrub oak on the Great Plain, up-islanders liked to say that Doc Lane gave them the telephone, in addition to all else. Initially, the post offices were connected by phone, and residents living along the single line of the Southern Massachusetts Company were given the opportunity to subscribe. Other roads were unaccommodated and the doctor was one of the foremost in asking for additional phone service. He knew better than most that communication delays were a major obstacle in his effort to tip the balance of circumstance in favor of life.

Eventually, Lane established his own telephone company and set the first line of poles on several of the up-island roads. In time, his service extended over three towns and his lines paralleled those of the Southern Massachusetts. It was a common sight to see this lanky fellow dressed in dignified doctor's garb — no one else on the island looked like him because he wore a tall silk hat and a long ulster — buckle on a pair of lineman's climbing irons and run up a pole like a squirrel to make repairs to the wires. He maintained his own equipment up to the time when he sold his phone service to Southern Massachusetts.

After a half-century of medical practice on the Vineyard, he retired, and that is how I remember him, with gray hair and beard, in and about the Main Street block that bore his name. He was still handy enough to tack on a shingle, build a piece of fence, and he kept some poultry. When these had young, passersby often stopped to watch this scholarly-appearing man sitting on a box in the chicken yard while yellow, white, and mottled chicks climbed and fluttered to his head and shoulders, gently pecking at his cheeks as he talked to them, for he cared for all creatures as he cared for mankind.

Those who knew him well said that his buggy seat was "hard as a piece of the nether millstone" (which is right out of the Book of Job) when he began island practice but that it grew softer with the years because he stuffed it with bills for medical service that he chose never to collect. When Doc Lane was an old man, my father, half facetiously, asked him about that. The doctor's face lighted with mild amusement; he did not reply, but shook his head as if in disbelief, and went on scattering grain for his clucking Rhode Island Reds.

There is a worthy footnote to the consideration of the heroic on Martha's Vineyard, not solely because of the hero's accomplishments but as well because of a profound question raised by his passing that has broader application.

The *Manxman* was a 112-foot cruising yawl owned by E. W. Clucas; she was the largest of her kind in the world and had been converted from a Class J sloop. I am among those privileged to have seen Captain Sam Norton, Vineyarder, bring her into Edgartown harbor under sail and with the wind ahead.

It was something uncommon to see Sam and *Manxman* coming in past the lighthouse, he with an eye on the Methodist Church tower, knowing exactly how it should bear, and she, with everything drawing, driving like an express train, her great mast towering. He would bring her in between the town dock and Chappaquiddick Point and come about, magnificent spread of canvas thundering, with neither time nor room for as much as an instant of imprecision. In seconds, *Manxman* was about and away, bound for the inner harbor like a lean, clean saber, and at the dock caplog, elbow-to-elbow spectators would chuckle and applaud, saying, "That's Sam!"

When Sam died at the age of sixty-one, the *Gazette* commented, "There is an irreplaceable type of man and, with changing conditions, as one generation yields to another, the breed of man changes until there are none left who have the combination of aptitudes, resources, strength, forthrightness and so on, which was once familiar." Referring specifically to Sam's ability to sail *Manxman* into Edgartown, the editor asked in conclusion: "Where is there another man who could do that?"

With reference to all of the island's heroines and heroes, its splendid "doers," are there really still men and women who could do the things they did — and which, being what they were, they regarded as unheroic? Is there somewhere another Evangeline Ritter, who also was a heroine in a way particularly hers?

I suppose I am given some hope that the answer is yes, because Dionis Coffin Riggs comes to mind; she lives in West Tisbury and, being modest, probably would not thank me for suggesting that she possesses heroic qualities. Yet Mrs. Riggs is a poet of consequence; what she preserves of the island in words might otherwise drop through the sieve of time unnoticed, and although she writes of life as it is (and was), she actually writes from a larger-than-life viewpoint that is heroic, surmounting the moment, the day. The products of this relatively timeless perspective, truth and beauty, are, among other things, comforting to those who hope that the island will continue to produce and attract extraordinary people.

Simon Athearn and James Allen were among the seventeenth-century proprietors of Tisbury. That is how long Mrs. Riggs's family and mine have been on friendly terms. At one point (1934), her husband, Sidney Noyes Riggs, and my father produced *Vineyard Poems and Prints*, a volume of wonderfully executed Riggs block prints and Allen verse. She was born in Edgartown and is a descendant of several other early island families, including the Butlers, Cleavelands, and Mayhews; she still resides in the ancestral home.

"The word *insular*," she says, "is a misnomer. People who live on hills and plains are much more insulated. The oceans bring people together; the oceans take people places; here on the Vineyard, we have been great travelers; those who *did* travel, traveled far.

"Some changes have come about as an outgrowth of public desire. As the plane became more important, we had to have an airport. We went from sailing ships to the steamer *Mono-*

hansett to modern ferries. We also went outward in experience
and interest. Mother used to sing us a lullaby in Edgartown
until the steamship whistled. The candy store proprietor used
to say, 'Put the corned beef on when the steamboat whistles.'
We were governed by the steamer's whistle and it was an
evening's entertainment to go down to see the boat come in.

"Many islanders then never went off-island. I never went
off until I was seven or eight years old. Once, I stood on
Brandy Brow and saw a puff of smoke on the mainland that
I thought was a train. The train was a wonder to me — and
now our high school teams play everywhere. The island now
reflects more accurately what goes on on the mainland than
it did.

"I do not think there is greater peace of mind than there
was fifty years ago," she says. "Many of the young people, however — and there is an influx of young people here — are not
interested in the acquisition of material things. There is lots
of new blood and that is good. Many youngsters are interested
in conservation and some want to bring back island farms and
that is good, too. Some disagree, but I say that if Vineyarders
come back from college and become carpenters and farmers,
there is nothing wrong with it."

To reveal something of what Mrs. Riggs is, where she has
come from, and what kinds of things she notices and remembers about the Vineyard, there is this poem:

> *Hot sun cursed*
> *the thin small leaves of scrub oak.*
> *Under sparse shelter*
> *blueberries*
> *grew;*
> *Little star noses*
> *on powdery faces.*

Martha's Vineyard

I hold them in my hand
I could hear the berries soft thudding into Aunt
    Henrietta's pail.

"They're thick here,
Little one" and I moved
through bushes as high as trees
to a path where berries
grew green, red, blue
all on one stem. With a delicate stroke
Aunt Henrietta skimmed off
the ripe ones. Mine
fell into the pail
with a hard little clatter.
I picked out the green, the red
pieces of leaves, dead sticks.
The berries that clung to my thumb were sweet.

8. The Seasons

SOME measure the Vineyard year by what people do, reckoning the months and their characteristics in terms of college students, day-trippers, busloads of tourists, summer renters, bass derby fishermen, and deer hunters, as well as those occasional arrivals who come to the island intent upon observing the sixty festivals of ancient Athens or Guy Fawkes Day.

My own preference is to consider the island's seasons in terms of nature and of creatures other than people, simply because I like to get as close as possible to the earth's axles to find out what is really going on.

Late one afternoon in the first days of the year that I choose to think about, an otter entered the dooryard of a Vineyard resident. This is a good way of being reminded of what really goes on in January because I do not know many places where otters make house calls.

If otters are not among your acquaintances, they are colored an agreeable chestnut, have broad, flat heads, and tend to be long of body and short of leg. Some might say that what this particular otter did was not remarkable; I say that the fact he was there at all was remarkable and what is more, he was right at home, and that was remarkable, too. He made a short but perceptive tour of what would be a flower garden in spring and found a spot in it that, for reasons beyond human ken, was more otterish than others. Here, he abandoned dignity and rolled over, clawed webbed feet in the air.

In due course, he rose, and poured himself over the fence and out of sight. "Poured" in this context is not of my invention but an otter would agree with its accuracy.

Mid-February was something else. On the south beaches, the wild ducks lay dead and dying by the score, perhaps even by the hundred, as they had for at least ten days. Rendered helpless by gummy floating oil, they came to the shore, perhaps forewarned by some instinct of their fate or maybe simply weakened, and there, in such slight shelter as they could find in the low beach hills, they were dying miserably.

Forty dead ducks lay in one heap on a Tuesday morning, dozens of others were strewn along the shore within a space of four hundred to six hundred yards, while flocks of fifty or more walked painfully across the beach or fluttered feebly toward the water when approached. They were all oiled, all doomed to a lingering last illness, and a wretched death.

Nearly all of the ducks were eiders, handsome seafowl, the snowy-backed males with their jet-black crowns lying beside the brown, barred females. They had been spotted by the fatal oil as they swam together a couple of miles off the land; now, the few living birds crouched in the shelter of the beach banks, waiting to die.

It was a wicked sight to look upon and each day had added to the horror of the situation. A mile and a half off Squibnocket Bight, thousands of other eiders were on their winter bedding ground. There they lay, coming inshore periodically to feed on fish and shellfish; they fancied themselves secure, even as the film of black sticky bilge pumpings drifted down upon them in the current.

So I remember Ida, who made that winter season different

from all others. You will pardon the fact that her name is a poor pun and frightfully obvious, because those were simpler days, long before anybody had sniffed glue and people used to laugh at things like, "I'm a little stiff from Bowling." It was before there were laws against pumping ship bilges into the clean sea that my friend and I, trudging the long, empty Squibnocket Beach, halted in the midst of this terrible scene of death and dying before one female eider (Ida, of course), a creature soiled and sick from the gummy oil plastering her feathers.

She squatted on the sand, barely beyond the sea's reach, too weak to flee from us, the enemy, too near death to care whether man hastened it. We looked at her, feeling anger at the situation and hopelessness and compassion for her condition; head averted, she refused to look at us. I could not walk by her.

So we put her, unprotesting, upon burlap sacking on the back seat of the car, drove home, squirted gin and water in a medicine dropper down her throat ("She can't be any worse off," said my friend), washed her gently with warm water and soap, clipped the most soiled tips of her feathers so that she would not try to clean them, and made a bed of dry seaweed for her in a little house formerly inhabited by a wayward Belgian hare. I was not at all certain that anything we had done was helpful or correct, yet to do nothing would have been more than I could bear; it was bad enough to have turned our backs on all the others.

I did not sleep that night. Several times, I went to the bedroom window, squinting futilely into the deep shadows of the backyard, where Ida waged the battle that each of us must fight essentially alone. There was no sound out there, no movement, nothing but terrible and interminable silence; I thought, "Death makes no noise," and I could not bring myself to go out there in the dark to discover the truth, whatever it was. I thought of her dead, one big, funny foot outstretched and her soft head unmoving upon the seaweed and I could neither bear the image nor put it out of mind.

At daybreak, I ran out, bracing myself.

Behold, she stood, the wild sea rover. Her eyes were like jewels in the fresh morning; feet apart, chest out, and bill high, she made one demand of me, and I knew what it was. I shucked and hand-fed Ida a pint of clams, joyous at the arrogance of her reborn appetite, unmindful of the fact that she nipped me unmercifully and unintentionally.

That was the beginning of many meals of clams, of an occasional handful of corn, even of a slice of bread now and then. For six days, Ida ate and drank, regaining her strength. Eventually, she took to splashing about in a large pan of water and to feeding from the fingers of anyone who approached her. The little rabbit house and the wire pen surrounding it seemed to become increasingly smaller. I had to remember that she was accustomed to whole oceans to move in, that her life was never meant to be bounded by man-made horizons.

I cannot say that Ida and I became close. She was at home in the vast loneliness of the offshore swells. She would never have needed man if he had not created the need by befouling her world — and his, for that matter. She kept her distance from me; she was never to be confused with barnyard fowl. Thus, but for one thing, I might have had no more to remember about Ida than that first long night and the fact of her recovery. But for one thing . . .

There came the inevitable seventh day when we took her — she was now restless and struggling, her health reborn — to, as I remember, a brackish pond on George Eustis's place, and freed her at the shore.

I suppose sentimentally I had come to this moment hoping

for some kind of signal from her because bonds between mankind and other creatures arise unbidden and most unexpectedly, especially when matters of life and death are involved. Not that I expected her thanks, heaven knows, for I was man and man had nearly killed her. Yet because I was man, and conscious of the crime committed against her, I think I hoped for an instant of mute reassurance, the slightest suggestion that at least one creature forced to share this planet with us understood that all mankind was not bent on her destruction.

"You are a fool," I chided myself. "It is against both her interest and instinct to consider you a friend, even momentarily."

Still, when we let her go, she lunged for the water, strong again, paddled offshore, stretched her neck, and, in a moment, clambered into sluggish flight. I expected her to go directly to sea, low over the water. But she did not. Instead, she made one great circle over our heads as we stood at the pond edge before beating seaward; then, as we watched, the dot that was Ida became smaller and smaller until finally it blurred into the horizon's vastness and could no longer be perceived.

Of that last circle over our heads, my friend remarked, "She was just getting oriented." Perhaps, but I like to keep my own thoughts about why I think she did it, and as she completed the circle and departed for her destiny, I said to myself, "You may not remember me, Ida, but I shall not forget you. Go in peace."

And what of March? Well, this much, as my father was moved to observe:

> *Now hail drear winter's utter end*
> *One small sound through the misty night*
> *The song of farmer's, fisher's friend*
> *The pinkletink, shy, cheerful mite.*

What was exceptional at the particular time was that the pinkletinks' spring song was heard in full volume all through a warm night on March 18 and this was a full two weeks earlier than the first report of a year before. For the benefit of those who do not know, the appearance of this undeveloped tree frog, whose piping fills the night wherever there is a swamp, is generally heralded by the natives as marking the end of winter and winter weather. Some, to whom coasts and islands are no more than names, may find it beyond understanding that Vineyarders listen instinctively for these first pipings and experience a deep and private joy in the hearing of them.

Even coastal mainlanders may not appreciate the historic significance to the Vineyarder of the first call of the pinkletink. What it has meant traditionally in terms of season — as islanders listening at their open doors on the first misty night of lifting temperatures and dying wind hear the peepers — has been this: "The codfish have come!" If you live close to the weather, as islanders do, you know it is no more unlikely to relate cod and frogs than to relate salmon and peas, because when the earth turns, everything on it turns.

Today, one supposes, the codfish could come or not come, and thousands would be unaffected or even unaware, but once, the codfishery of the Vineyard supplied virtually the only source of cash income during nine months of the year. So in these years, when Vineyarders hear the pinkletinks and experience a feeling of well-being, even of anticipation, romantic geneticists (there must be some) might suggest that this is the working of an instinct inherited from older generations.

If you want to relate in a pleasant manner to those things and times that were, to understand more fully what this particular season meant to Vineyarders, the codfish does offer a gastronomical bridge of sorts. We are not talking about simply eating a fish; we are concerned with the reconstruction of a way of life and a related set of values that were fundamental to generations of islanders, even to the time of my growing up.

First of all, the weather was seldom comfortable when cod were taken. It was in either the raw chilliness of spring or the dead coldness of fall when the small boats anchored on gray water lifted by the swells that rolled in from offshore. Sometimes, a boat was large enough to have a cuddy where a fire was kept in a tiny stove and that meant hot coffee, to help keep the blood circulating. But many on the ledges were in open dories or No Mans Land boats that offered no shelter at all, and if there was food aboard, it was plain and cold.

It was a hard-earned living. The cruel wind found the back of the neck and the ears; the arms and legs grew weary and the fingers stiff; there were fathoms of line to be hauled repeatedly over wet gunwales, and there was little to uplift the spirit in the gray seas and slate sky. Yet as hard as it all was, there was a lasting satisfaction in the fishing:

Break the tough, rubbery conchs with a hammer. Slice the meat and pound it to make it tender. Fill the huge hooks with the conch slices, and lower the whole business to the kelp-grown boulders below where the cod swim slowly back and forth, feeding on mussels, crabs, and the like.

Now the bite of a cod is neither as sharp nor as lively as that of some other fish but it carries a certain authority. It is a slow but heavy pull and the old-fashioned fisherman provided himself with gear heavy enough so that he could "horse in" a fish of twenty to thirty pounds without playing it. He was, after all, not out there for the fun of it and the sooner the fish was off the hook, the sooner another could be caught.

Even so, there were fish so heavy that delicate handling was necessary; a large cod could be lifted aboard only with a gaff, a heavy hook on a wooden handle.

The fish are caught; what then? They must be dressed, and, in the old days, the dresser removed the head so as to include with the body the triangular piece of flesh that grows up on the back of the cod's head and neck. The fish was then eviscerated and split, the heavy part of the backbone being removed in the process with a curved splitting knife. This operation laid the cod flat; the peaks of the nape tended to give the laid-out fish the appearance of a shield.

As fast as the fish were split, they were dropped into the soaking tub full of salt water, where they remained at least until the splitting was done. When removed from the soaking, cod, in many instances, were kenched — this being a word of provincial English derivation — or salted dry in pens or tubs; a layer of salt was spread on the bottom and each layer of fish was buried in more salt. Some believe that cod will not take salt after four days standing in the kench; some allowed them to stand longer. Then they were removed from the salt, washed clean, and spread out to dry.

Cod should not be subjected to either hot sun or rain when drying; too much sun causes the meat to flake from the skin and rain, obviously, prevents drying. Much cod used to be spread under sheds; if in the open, it was laid skin side up or taken under cover when weather conditions were adverse. Slowly, the fish became dehydrated, and eventually were bundled or stacked for sale or home use.

Came the day when the family was to eat salt cod, and in my family, we ate a lot of it, some of which we caught and salted ourselves. First, the fish was skinned, and then soaked overnight, perhaps with the water changed before boiling. Once cooked and broken into flakes, the cod can be creamed

The Seasons

(white sauce, with hard-boiled-egg slices) and served with boiled potatoes, sprinkled with parsley and well-drained, crisp pork scraps. Or it can be mixed with mashed potatoes, chopped onions, and beaten eggs and made into fish cakes.

If you prefer fresh cod, you can bake either a whole fish or a couple of good-sized fillets. In either case, make a moist dressing of poultry seasoning, a couple of beaten eggs, chopped green pepper, minced onion, a dash of savory and oregano, and stuff the whole fish or place the stuffing between the fillets. Pour over all something like a half-cup of dry white wine and thirty minutes in a 450-degree F. oven ought to be about right. Some baste it along the way and serve it with white sauce; some don't think it needs either. You might want to sprinkle bacon bits on top along toward the end of cooking.

What the whole business amounts to is that eating (and thinking) in such a manner heightens the sense of the season. If you have caught and prepared your own fish, this is even more true because you now have, as your predecessors had, a realization of nature's bounty, an appreciation of the effort that brings food to table, and the satisfaction that comes from being reasonably self-sufficient.

Privately, I feel that if the fish is cod, the impact of eternal Vineyard truths is doubled, not because cod is the best fish there is, by any means, but because it is about as native as anything there is. Some things are synonymous with place, and I share Holman Francis Day's sentiments expressed in his "Cure for Homesickness":

> He pasted a sheet of postage stamps
> from snout clear down to tail,
> Put on a quick delivery stamp,
> and sent the cod by mail.

Clearly, if you want to understand the seasons, you not only have to get outdoors, you have to get outdoors and look at things and think what they mean. Consider this strip of weather-pounded Vineyard beach:

Here at the water's edge is not only an island clock, a calendar, but earth's very lifeline, that centuries-old demarcation between landborne and seaborne living things, and the particular province of the amphibious creatures that have linked the other two since time began, something like the equal sign in a mathematical equation.

Within the confines of this thin ribbon of world is the province of non-man and its first obvious characteristic is age. There is a rise and fall of tide here that not only means inundation each day, coupled with the deposit of offshore culch, living and dead, from the sea bottom, but a constant redrawing of the beach architecture as the water floods and smooths, withdraws and scours. Add to this the persistent waves' molding and shaping and estimate how long it takes to make a cupful of fine sand.

As well as the geological, there is creature age. This round shell the color of maple sugar is empty of life, but not long so. It is that of a young horseshoe crab, nature's superior version of the World War II "swimming" tank. With the fluted scallop and the box turtle, this stands as a masterpiece of design, so eminently successful in concept that it has not required major change in order to adjust to — and even flourish in — a world that has itself undergone revolutionary alterations, hot and cold, wet and dry. About the best man has to offer in this category is the Volkswagen and that is not even antebellum.

Or regard the feathers here, somewhat disheveled from the tumblings of weather, some damp, some sandy, yet still re-

vealing the splendid dynamic of line that accomplished soaring, diving into the fish-filled rip, and skimming the tops of the hissing rollers. Here is a sample of what makes the sanderling flash white as he chases the retreating waves; here, a calling card of the black-collared plover who cries *chi-we*, and there, the milky-spined, black-tipped wing feather of the herring gull. Beauty in all of these, beauty of such nature as is compatible, not only with the thermal current, but with all the lonely freedom of the upper air.

Some of the shells here are tidy halves, still with the color of occupancy, ecru, pale yellow, purple, and mottled pink; some are worn fragile white and smooth by the interminable comings and goings of sand and water. Their fragments dotting the relative sameness of the beach's grains are like coins from a careless hand, spendable but once and flung away forever, to become smaller and smaller, and finally disappear into the whole.

Most temporary of the life evidence within this thin road between wet and dry are the tracks, the signature of a passing, the clue to a confrontation, and a census of sorts as to what was here between one high water and the next.

Some of the prints are predictable — gull, sandpiper, and plover — but some are not, for here, at the edge of the most recent tidal mark, is the three-toed sign of a cock pheasant, which rockets across the marsh to the beach and back each day. Just beyond are the little footmarks of something else; if this were somewhere else, I might say a red fox had been here, but frankly, I do not know whether there are foxes on the island, and more likely, it was a cat that came this way.

Whatever it was, its prints remind one of the truism that things in this area of beach eat other things in it, but then, in what part of the world do they not? Moreover, in many instances, this is accomplished with such natural efficiency,

The Seasons

with such consummate grace, and it is so obviously inevitable, that it may well be the prey is no more than momentarily dismayed to discover which end of the daily seesaw it now is on.

True, it might be nice if nothing were eaten, not even codfish, although I am not at all sure about that. Yet man himself has not discovered how to create a fuelless perpetual-motion machine, and the world of which this sand strip is an infinitesimal item obviously is a massive engine of ancient beginnings; great effectiveness; formidable momentum; and insatiable appetite, without which, the first three would not have been possible.

The evidences of the full-cycle formula in this place — from life to death to life — are everywhere obvious. The little crabs scuttle busily; the big crab lies eyeless and still, plucked empty. When water washes across the flat, bubbles rise from a dozen holes; there is life below, and life making life. In the shallows, the fingerlings dart and shine. A tern strikes and rises, fish in bill, but the school is large; it re-forms and goes on, dark ripples marking its broadly twisting way. Something, perhaps whatever left the paw prints, reduced this once-gull to a pile of bones, yet the sky is full of gulls, crying and sweeping across the dome of weather.

In these days, perhaps always, but more so now, the man world is the enemy of this world. Some of the beach erosion is not natural, but man-caused; sometimes, there are man substances in the water that kill or cripple at various levels of the life chain, that produce such unnatural phenomena as eggs too thin-shelled to hatch, thus threatening existence of a species. Sometimes, the intrusive sounds, smells, and stains of man's society are more than this world can bear.

Yet the society and chemistry of this strip of beach go on, largely as they have gone on for longer than we know. Mostly, what happens here is unheard and unobserved by mankind; except for superficials, we know little about its relationships and direction. But even though we cannot accurately compute the strengths and proportions of what is happening here, the most casual consideration of it suggests that, while its fragility in part is obvious, there is within this natural machinery an energy that renders ours puny by comparison.

We can hurt this world of non-man and we are doing so, yet, undoubtedly, are hurting ourselves more by the doing. Twenty years ago, I interviewed Arthur Hadley II, author and editor, in Edgartown and, at one point, asked him what he thought lay ahead. "The evidence is all around us that species after species has failed," he observed. "After looking into the nuclear future, I take the Greek tragic view. I see no evidence that man has the built-in ability to survive the nuclear age. I think the idea of destroying all life is nonsense, but no magic keeps *us* alive."

Gull and quahaug, I hail thee, for in your fashion, you may be building temples more lasting than those of the sons and daughters of Adam, and that is something to ponder, standing here at the sea's edge, where the years are translated into water upon pebbles.

I walk to savor the seasons. Walking is, of course, for any-body — it is as good for lucidity as it is for the liver — but especially, walking is for writers. "I'll walk where my own nature would be leading," Emily Brontë declared; "it vexes me to choose another guide." I walk to savor this island; I was going to say "my island," but the Vineyard belongs to time, not to people. It is no more mine than it was my ancestor Benjamin's, even though, before he got through, he owned more of it than you could walk over in a long day.

I walk. Walking is a pace of passing that permits both ob-servation and reflection. Sometimes I halt before a single stone or bush and think upon its role, parts, origin, and remark for future reference what changing light does to its colors and how it fares in the weather. In reflecting upon the origins of things here, I think somewhat of my own. In terms of the whole, they are less than one blade of the grass that nourished my grandfather's sheep, but still, they are mine and they also are here.

Where I stand now is private property although many people pass over it, especially in summer. The low bank rises above a rocky beach where the sea washes among small boulders and gravel, the latter dark with discoloration and alive with small, blue-black mussels. Parted kelp and ribbons and fronds of seaweed are tangled among the stones; unlike many places along the island's North Shore, there is no hint here of a boat landing in the days when work craft ordinarily were hauled out on the beach.

Above the bank are rising land and distant hills, concealed for the most part by brush and low trees, a tangled growth through which passage would be difficult for either man or animal of any size. The roofs of a couple of houses rise above the growth but they are not near.

Yet there is something interesting here: barely perceptible indentations in the earth, very old wheel tracks, showing that once people came to this place, and frequently. The road, long since abandoned, was cut deeply into the sward at one time and the wild bushes of the black huckleberry take root here only with difficulty, revealing by stunted growth that the soil is hard and very likely salted from the drainings of many a seaweed heap years ago.

Because the tide is low, it is possible to learn that the shore here once extended farther seaward, and probably the bank as well; for in the water, completely covered at high tide, are fragments of wood sunk into sand between the rocks, black

and hardened, salted and seasoned by years of immersion. These are of oak, still sound, although the tops of the pieces have been chewed by gravel washing and all the flotsam that has surged along this beach in generations of storms. The wooden pieces are set in a circular pattern and rise no more than ten inches above the sand.

There is nothing mysterious about all this if you know that there once was a saltworks located here and that that is why a road to this beach was required even though there was no boat landing. The chunks of wood are what is left of the heavy staves of a casklike structure, a tank or vat, undoubtedly built by island coopers to hold salt water pumped from Vineyard Sound — by windmills if there was a breeze or by hand pumps if not.

The remains of this wooden tank, defying decay after who knows how many generations, is a monument of sorts to what

was. So am I, for that matter, for I bear in mind, walking this land, that once John Hammett, my maternal great-great-grandfather, came to the brickyard on this North Shore for bricks with which to build a barn, one of only three such on Martha's Vineyard. Although I am less durable than either brickyard or barn (something of both remains to this day), still I can stand here and reflect with the warmth of belonging upon the prudent works of John Hammett and wonder how he would regard the Vineyard of today.

Because my father's roots and recollections embraced both, he never could decide whether he preferred the North or South Shore. One day in July, fifteen years ago, he took down the powder horn from the bookcase in his office, handling it with the same kind of pleasure with which he pondered his forebears. (Well, most of them, anyway.) For at least the tenth time in as many years, he explained to me, "This horn was made by Davis Allen, who lived at Quansoo. He was born in 1779. He died at the age of fifteen. He was my grandfather's cousin."

A few days after that, moved, I think by the reflections stirred by the powder horn, he went to look once more at that part of the South Side that he regarded as ancestral. It happened to be a warm-weather month but he considered the land in all seasons and what it meant to those who lived there:

Smoother than prairie land, its vegetation wearing a summer coloring of greens and browns, Quenames, named originally for the Indian's eel-fishing place, is yet unexploited and lies much as the settlers found it three centuries ago.

The several hundred acres that comprise the original tract lie empty save for a half-dozen buildings which mark the home sites of the ancients and, until recent years, their descendants. The woods have not yet begun to encroach upon the tillage and pasturage as they have in so many places on the island but form a distant screen against the northerly winds of winter that sweep downward from the range of glacial kames in the north.

Bounded for two-thirds of its area by waters of Tisbury Great Pond, with the white sand dunes looming above the pond waters beyond, and echoing to the never-ending pounding of the ocean surf, the place has a quietness nevertheless that can be sensed for miles distant. There can be none among the older island inhabitants who look upon this scene without stifling a nostalgic sensation and longing for a past that is vanished.

This area, Quenames, Quansoo, and neighboring tracts, all connected by dry land and separated by coves which extend inland like long fingers, was the choicest real estate on the Vineyard three hundred years ago.

Times have changed. Fewer have farmed the land until today, a furrow is seldom turned. The farmhouses are empty for the greater part of the year, the fields unattended for the most part and the pastures empty of livestock. Yet Quenames lies unspoiled, a smiling land where the wild ducks nest in summer and fly in winter, where the marsh hay still waves in the sweet winds that drive across the low meadows and nature smiles, as only nature can where the pattern has not been disturbed.

Thus it is that older islanders sometimes stop on the peak of Abel's Hill and look down across the low country, seeing visions once more of the fruitfulness which once rewarded the efforts of the people who lived there. Those were the natives who declared that the emblem of the Great Pond was the hoe, which, properly and energetically employed, would provide sustenance for man in every month of the year:

> 'Twas thus Josiah Torrey Hancock spoke,
> "The hoe is useful every workin' day.
> In summer, 'tis the English ploughland needs
> Some stirrin' round the corn hills in the weeds.
> And when the weather cools, you draw your lots,
> And use the hoe to bed down neshaw pots.
> Then after that; before, if you prefer,
> A man possessed of strength enough to stir
> Can always dig a mess of clams, you know,
> I tell ye, there hain't nothin' beats the hoe!"

And somehow, it is still Quenames.

"It is still Quenames" — that is, albeit with more difficulty, one can still immerse oneself in the basic atmosphere of the Vineyard and its seasons, given appropriate time and site. Periodically, this is worth attempting, because, at least for me, it constitutes a refocusing; I reaffirm what it is that ties me to the island. People may change. Places may change. But the essence of the seasons remains. Some may say that sand, water, and trees are essentially the same, no matter where you find them. This is not so, for it does not take into account sand, water, and trees that are laden with associations.

Even in an atmosphere of change, those associations need no more than a nudge of encouragement to surface in the mind, their colors and dimensions still fresh. On a day not long ago in my father's house, I gave them such encouragement, finding it appropriate to do so because it was my birthday.

As an aside, I concede that my intellectual betters long ago concluded that the date of one's death is and ought to be more important than one's birth date. Presumably, the only way to escape such an eventuality would be to do absolutely nothing, either good or bad, between those two dates and that would be difficult indeed because the world persists in bumping into us on a daily basis, whether or not we bump into it.

However, we entertain a habit of recognizing our birthdays, grudgingly or otherwise (at eighty-five, my father said to me, "I do not know how in hell either you or I got to be so old"), and, as inevitable as sin, on the right date last year, I had one. So it came to pass that on a particular Tuesday when I was alone, I decided to give myself, as a birthday gift, a day without time. "Time," I thought, "has produced Vineyard change. If someone had been able to stop the clock, how might ability to appreciate the island seasons have been enhanced?"

So I stopped every clock in my father's house. Try it sometime, and having done so, stand there in the empty pocket of silence. For a moment, I wondered how I had dared to do such an unnatural thing as to sever my mathematical marriage to the world. Then it occurred to me that it was not unnatural at all, but simply unhuman, at least in terms of Western industrialized society.

If time is suspended, I thought, it ought to heighten the senses, which, more often than not, suffer because we attempt to cram what is between what was and what will be and emerge from all three with a pallid Pablum of experience. We do not, I think, give decent due to the senses. Proust concluded, "When from a long distant past nothing subsists, after the people are dead, after the things are broken and scattered, still, alone, more fragile, but with more vitality, more unsubstantial, more persistent, more faithful, the smell and taste of things remain poised a long time . . . and bear unfaltering, in the tiny and almost impalpable drop of their essence, the vast structure of recollection."

It is, of course, too much to say that "nothing subsists" of what the Vineyard seasons were. It is more accurate to conclude that it is more difficult to get at them, to feel what they mean. In part, this is because where you are tends to influence how you regard what is being experienced — a hilltop and a valley differ in more ways than those of contour — and accessibility of places is an important part of island change.

Once, up-island hilltops were clear and accessible to those who enjoyed hiking. It was possible to walk almost anywhere and in almost any part of the island. Old wagon roads crossed and recrossed every township; footpaths, twisting and narrow, appeared in many places, and no-trespassing signs were few. Now, there are not many places where a hiker can travel once he has left the highway. And many hilltops are so concealed that only the old-timers know they are there.

Some of the new inaccessibility is natural. Once, there were stands of wood in various places but there was very little jungle of briars and brush and the many brooks were open and flowing clear. These days, for better or worse, nature is reclaiming its own in many areas. The barriers of greenbriers and scrubby trees grow higher and more dense, miles of fine stone walls are buried beneath vegetation, once-open wooded areas are filling up with undergrowth. Pastures and meadows are overgrown, entire home sites, dooryards, and tillages have disappeared, and many of the trout pools and nesting places favored by black ducks are choked with mud and vegetation.

Once, accessibility was of so little concern as to be un-thought of. Wesley Martin and I hiked the North Shore years ago, a splendid, leisurely venture in which there was no one and nothing to deter our walking, looking, feeling, and smelling. The island, with all of its wind, water, and weather, was ours. The only sounds were those of the place itself and there was a magnificent loneliness along the miles of beach.

There is nothing like walking the shore for hours, with the sea forever just at hand, persistently rolling and washing, to remind one of what an island is and why, to reestablish in one's consciousness the perimeters of its sanctuary. We logged the landmarks. Makonikey Head, the vacant-eyed windows of its abandoned hotel and the last salt-washed bones of its wharf serving as monuments to a nineteenth-century dream that died. Paint Mill Brook, where my father and I found a doll-house that he had had in childhood, broken and dust-covered, in what was left of the mill. Jethro's Landing, where a cart path once led across the hill to the Sound so that the old people could haul seaweed and fish to their farms. Beck's Beach, named for Rebecca Skiff, whose house stood nearby, this being a landing place for trap dories. The past was every-where and the places so little changed from the past that it was possible to believe, momentarily, that a way of life had not actually disappeared at all.

It was possible to suppose that, in terms of season — sea, sky, and the creatures of nature — this particular date in every year the island ever had was not greatly different from the day on which we walked.

In those days, one could climb the cliffs at Gay Head and we did, with a feeling of challenge and conquering, the red spur among them. Something like forty years later, when it was gone — destroyed by forces of nature that might have been held in check but never were — the geologist Clifford

A. Kaye observed that the island had lost its most precious possession. He wrote:

> *Who cut off your feet, giant dying*
> *the sea? . . . Down*
> *down stretched, slumped*
> *upon the shore; feet puddled in blood; shoulders*
>   *withered, head severed;*
> *only a few tufts of hair to show.*

Not once during that entire walk of many hours did we ever see anyone else on the beach. I remember to this day the unbroken silence, the strange hollowness of our voices on those occasions when we spoke. The greatest value of the experience, as strong with me now as it was then, was that nothing — neither people, nor noise, nor encumbrances, whether born of man, nature, or time — got between us and the moment. All of what there was could be had for endless experiencing. There was a great, timeless rhythm about it — the only unusual thing that occurred was the discovery of a wooden case of skinned rabbits from Australia, washed upon the sand — and everything else was magnificently unbroken, universal, beyond measurable proportions, and reassuring in its sense of permanence.

The island seasons are not so easy to get to in such quantities these days. The sense of permanence is disturbed.

If I were to select just one symbol of the summers that were — and I could get past band concerts at Owen Park, with flower fragrance upon the warm air, the still and silent hulls in the black-glass harbor, half-shadow faces, and the spirited lightheartedness of horns rising to the stars — I would think about Ole Borgen.

He was born in Eidsbold, Norway, but even by 1930, he

had been on the Vineyard for a quarter-century. A former member of a Norwegian army cavalry regiment, he was fond of horses and adept at caring for them. After a turn at island farming, he bought the building at Middletown that had been a grocery and post office. There, he sold gasoline and automobile supplies when motor traffic was in its initial years.

But what I remember about him is his ice cream, which began, at least, as an incidental to his business.

The recollection has to be treated in perspective. Obtaining the ice cream required pedaling a single-speed bicycle with large tires at a leisurely pace from Vineyard Haven to North Tisbury and back, eventually. Sunday afternoon was usually the only practical time when this could be done, but Sunday was a good day for Ole's ice cream since he offered more flavors then (I think no more than four at most) in anticipation of families out for a drive. The ice cream did not cost much in today's terms but one had to save up for it and refrain from spending the money on something else, including ice cream that was much nearer.

So going to Ole's amounted to a journey, viewed in prospect with pleasure for several days and savored in the doing. This was so because traveling in general, on the Vineyard or elsewhere, was as much an experience as arriving at the destination; one appreciated the distinctions of each mile and gave them their due, for there was time to do so.

It was unthinkable to pass Tashmoo without wheeling the bicycle off the road, leaning it against tree or fence, and stopping to look. To this day, that clean sweep of water and trees, clear to the Sound, gladdens the spirit; to look upon it is not simply to derive joy from beauty but to gain reassurance. "Where there is a great spring," the Indians called this place, and thus its name; to know that the human eye has looked with pleasure upon the natural orderliness here for so long

offers the comfort of continuity and is the stuff of which durable recollections are made. Any hour was better for having halted here a moment.

And as often as not, even though it was farther, taking the Lambert's Cove Road proved irresistible. However many times one traveled it, this road remained a particular kind of sanctuary, a joy because it meandered as if time had been given a lower priority here. Once in a while, I would stop to see Allan Keniston; he had a pond full of perch that he let me fish in occasionally. I liked to hear him talk about what nature was doing — he always knew, whether it was a black duck's nest at the marsh edge or a lady's slipper in bloom in the woods. Finally, I would sometimes stop to say hello to Leroy Bosworth and pat his dog, and that was about the last stop before Ole's.

The place where the ice cream was served was unpretentious, a room of bare walls, bare floor, bare tables, and plain chairs. It borrowed nothing from the mainland ice-cream parlors of the Greeks, with their swishing overhead fans, glass bowls of bananas, marble counters, and homemade murals. Its product was ice cream, not atmosphere, a product served in a plain round dish with a paper liner.

It is not my intention to suggest that Ole's ice cream was better than any that can be purchased on the Vineyard today because I think that is not the case, although it may have been as good as the best now. But after some casual time on the road, some warm pedaling in the sun, an occasional interlude of thinking what flavor one would select, and finally arriving, so careless as to have only the one thing in mind, that first spoonful, thick and creamy and bearing, let us say, a chunk of fresh peach, would, as H. P. Ayer used to say of my mother's tomato-soup cake, "set a bone." I hated — I think that is not too strong a word — to see the bottom of the dish appear yet it never occurred to me to have a second order, even if I could have afforded it, because it would not have tasted like the first.

Slightly later in the year, I sometimes bicycled through North Tisbury and along the North Road to part of my grand-father's property that he referred to as "the lower place," this being where the old people had lived, long ago. There remained a little culch near the home site if one looked hard — a piece of china, a broken brick — but once, I found something else that had meaning, and, as I grew older, I revisited it until it came to be associated in my mind with fall on the Vineyard. This is how it was:

Here is a place in which I like to walk about at this season, knowing that winter is coming on, yet being still conscious of the tenacity with which the thinning fall, its brilliance quieting, continues to cling to each shortening day. The year's sun slides southerly; today is cool enough to require a jacket yet too winey warm in the early afternoon to button it.

I come here at this particular time for a reason. Before another year starts and while this one is resting, after all that it has done to and for everybody, it is useful to hold one's condition at arm's length and reexamine it. Ellery C. Norton used to teach the carpentry course at Tisbury High School. He once pointed out to me the potential for error in sawing six pieces of wood supposedly of equal length by measuring the last five against the one previously cut, rather than by applying the rule each time. "If you don't use the rule every time," he said, "and if you make a little error every time, when you get to the last piece, you've really got something you don't want at all."

So periodically, I like to think about time, how I relate to it, what I am doing with it, how much I have left of it, and this is a proper place for such thoughts. It is something like re-applying the rule before picking up the saw again.

You will remember that Shelley wrote of the shattered wreckage of an ancient statue in the desert, a time-blasted monument to a man's arrogance, the legend of which read: "My name is Ozymandias, king of kings: / Look on my works, ye Mighty, and despair!" And Shelley added, "Nothing beside remains. Round the decay / Of that colossal wreck, boundless and bare, / The lone and level sands stretch far away."

This place in which I walk — land of my ancestors and symbol of the beginning of time for me — possesses a similar reminder, but one better for the mood because, even though it signifies how much and how little we are, it is a monument to a better man than Ozymandias; for what this man built was not pretentious but useful.

In this open grove where the hidden crow scolds and the gray squirrel bounds, cheek full, across the leaf litter, there is what once was a farm wagon. For quite a long time, I have come to look at it, once a year. I do not know what man or woman drove it there or how long ago or why, or even what he or she was to me, if anything. But the slow disintegration of this cart, a process disturbing neither creature nor thing, is a tribute simultaneously to its builder and to nature's inexorable insistence upon reclaiming its own.

In the beginning, the wagon's wheels and body were something of an entity. The total structure was high enough to cast a shadow. But year by year, it has come closer to the earth, and now it lies in silvered pieces, its well-shaped oak bones, the dark-rusted quadrants of its disintegrating iron tires, scattered low. I am reminded of Marcel Marceau's birth-to-death pantomime, in which he rises to full-striding maturity and sinks slowly, ending essentially as he began.

Nor do I find anything depressing in all of this. In the wreckage of the wagon, it is still possible to find mortise and tenon so carefully contrived that, even at this distance since creation, they remain artfully wed, testimony to the craft and conscience of their maker. I wish he could know this. However, *I* know it and take vicarious pride in it, for this is man saying, "Put what you believe into what you make," and that is as much what the Vineyard has stood for as anything I can think of.

Of course, this is more than a diminishing wagon. Its deceptively casual ending signals that time produces change and time never stops. This cart is a compatible item in a whole scheme that is moving, not much in a day but considerably in a year. Over the wagon, there is a last-season's bird nest, still fairly substantial but full of holes and trailing dried grass. In the same tree, upside down, there is a black-capped chickadee in search of bugs for lunch. He scoots over the old nest without even saying, "Well, look here!" because yesterday is not part of his vocabulary.

I am glad it is part of mine and I am willing to understand the meaning of ashes in order to have roots. I am willing to be reminded that time is not limitless; I am more likely to make better use of it therefore. And I leave this place each fall knowing once more approximately what I amount to. As well as what I do not.

So we come to winter on the Vineyard, and there are many things one could say about that. But what I choose to consider is a Christmas once upon a time, being prompted to do so by the visit to my grandfather's place, for in my childhood, his was such a house as I am about to recall, and this particular incident occurred on the North Road, near where he lived.

At the Christmastime of which I speak, our ways on the Vineyard were plainer and simpler, of necessity. I am not preaching; I do not propose to suggest to you whether they were better or worse — they were some of both and make your own judgment as to how the balance lay. All I am saying is that life was different, being in every way closer to the bare bones.

The house of that time, as with my grandfather's, was a reflection, perhaps even a product, of those who lived there. It was small and all of the three rooms on the second floor had sloping ceilings. Of the four rooms downstairs, two were usually closed, and if one opened their doors, they were always cold and there was a smell of age and disuse. Beneath the house, there was a partial cellar with a dirt floor; it contained brown crocks of eggs, "put down" in water glass to preserve them.

The only running water came from the red, cast-iron pump at the sink; a piece of broomstick or some such lashed to the pump handle gave the woman of the house more leverage. Members of the family, and rare guests, washed at the sink in a basin that smelled perpetually of tin; the water drained through a short lead pipe in the side of the house and, over the years, made its way down the grassy slope to the marsh below. Hot water came from the teakettle, kerosene lamps provided the only illumination, and the privy was about sixty feet from the house, which was a long way on a January night.

The kitchen, being the only heated room in the house, was the center of everything. Here, one worked, ate, read, rested, and recovered from illness or injury. And the central comfort of the kitchen, as well as the mainspring of its business, was the wood-burning, black-iron stove. This instrument was as enduring as those who relied upon it; like them, it eventually became warped by work but it continued to thaw fingers, dry mittens, and coax the cinnamon promise from a bubbling, brown pie.

Apart from bubbling pies, the satisfaction of viewing a piece of land stubbornly cleared of stumps and stones, the relief of watching the right kind of rain fall at the right time, there was not much promise for most of those people. Principally, life was a matter of hard work, from childhood on until such time as bone, muscle, and heart decided, "No more, my friend."

Aging was more all-encompassing then; there were few jobs that permitted one to do a little something each day even though infirm. That kind of life offered no room for cosmetic activity; either you could chop wood, pitch hay, and make soap in the backyard or you could not. Age also meant staying home because it took so long to travel even short distances, and what is more, the horse was needed for more practical things than visiting. So with advanced years, the limited horizons of the homestead, often unbroken by any other dwelling, came to delineate the perimeters of the world.

In those times, one understood and accepted all this, there being no alternative. With the acceptance, the remembrance of what had been in other times, other years, came to mean a great deal, to be savored, day after dwindling day, even though it, too, had been of the simplest, plainest nature.

In short, then, we are concerned with a Christmastime in which the principals were aged, their hands and faces marked by a life of country work. Their microcosms were bounded by a hard-earned woodpile, a hand-scrubbed floor, and an iron pot, filled oftener with what was raised or caught than with what was purchased. Not much to show for a life of country work but that was the case more often than not, and those thus affected bore the strictures with an unshakable mixture of acceptance and dignity.

Which brings us to the matter of Hannah Tilton and "Aunt" Rebecca Manter, old countrywomen worn lean, women with long-lobed Yankee ears, generous-boned faces, and eyes in which there were reflections of grief, love, and above all, truth, as they had come to see it. These women lived in such houses as I have described; they had survived such days and nights as I have suggested.

Now, it was December and coming Christmas, and both of them had had Decembers enough to ponder the meaning of the day. Hannah was the wife of a farmer who had, despite a lifetime of working his rocky patch, barely made a living. It was too late to try anymore or for him to do much beyond sitting in the kitchen corner where he could reach the woodbox and feed the stove without getting out of his chair.

Rebecca's husband had been a miller but was now so old that it had been twenty years at least since he had made the stones turn in their grinding.

As for the two women, they had been too feeble to visit each other for a long time, and, having no younger kin who might have brought them together occasionally, they relived separately the pleasures of their mutual memories. They had been friends as schoolgirls, as brides, and as mothers. And what was there to remember in such a plain and simple life as they had had? If you have to ask, and you may, because our world is a long way from theirs, perhaps no amount of explanation would suffice. What is so earthshaking about holding a buttercup under somebody's chin to find out whether he or she likes butter?

Yet surely it is understandable that if there is little in one's world other than hard work and quickly fading romantic notions of princes and castles; if there is no automobile, radio, television, cinema, library, lecture hall, fraternal organization, or adult education program; if there is no travel, no change of occupation or scene, and no new faces, ever — then a friend from childhood who remembers the same thing in the same moment for the same reason, even with no word spoken, looms large.

So Christmas was at hand and Hannah saw that her husband had stored a few bushels of white field corn in a crib that he had made of poles and brush. And she knew that the old miller had not been able to plant a garden for years, even while she remembered how she and Rebecca used to enjoy hulled corn when they were young — a plain and simple food, a porridge called by the Indians "saupac."

Hannah selected a dozen perfect ears of corn, found someone to travel the mile and a half that she was too old to go herself, and gave them to Rebecca for a Christmas present.

I am informed by one who knew them well that both wept, the one in the giving, the other in the receiving, for those were plainer and simpler times when it was much easier to discover what the Vineyard and its people really were like, in whatever season.

George W. Goethals is one of many long associated with the Vineyard who share a different kind of concern about the island's seasons. "We've shifted from seasonal to monthly to weekly to weekend to day-trip population incursions," he says.

Mr. Goethals, grandson of the builder of the Panama Canal and first governor of the Zone (who was himself a citizen of Tisbury), has Vineyard roots spanning generations, including being a lineal descendant of the first Portuguese settler of Holmes Hole, which was named after a member of his family. In terms of firsthand experience with the island as a year-round resident, he attended the sixth, seventh, and eighth grades in Tisbury in the early 1930s and, after World War II, taught for three years in Edgartown High School.

He has taught at Harvard University in the Department of Psychology and Social Relations. His graduate and post-graduate training has been in academic and clinical psychology as well as social anthropology. He spends much time on the Vineyard and has retained his extensive personal and family connections with the island, including continuing ownership of property.

"Since the Chappaquiddick incident and production of the *Jaws* motion picture on the island, there has been a tremendous increase in day-trippers," he says.

"Another trend began in the late sixties. We used to keep our big house on Hatch Road open year around and go down for weekends at least once a month. The few boat reservations we ever made were for our exodus to the Vineyard in June and for getting off the island after Labor Day. Sometime in '69 or '70, in February, we arrived at the dock and found the place mobbed as if it were July. This was not a long weekend or some extended holiday. Since that time, we have had to make a reservation for any boat we have wanted to take to the Vineyard.

"There has been a phenomenal increase in the number of people coming from as far away as New York and New Jersey to spend time in the fall and spring for weekends. Closely related to this has been the pattern of shifting from renting for the season to renting for the week and month. More people are coming, staying for shorter periods, and paying larger amounts."

In contrast to the island's present widespread popularity, Mr. Goethals recalls that "I attended Phillips Academy, Andover, from 1934 to 1938. At that time it was a largely New England school; I would say that the student population was eighty percent New England. When I was asked where my home was and said I lived on Martha's Vineyard, I would draw a blank stare; one person in twenty had heard of it. In fact, I underwent a great deal of ridicule at school for coming from a place nobody had heard of."

With regard to island development, he says, "There is a flip side to the problem. In many instances, development has come about because people have been forced to sell part of their land in order to hold on to what is left for their children. It parallels to some extent what went on in the big estates in England before and after World War II. I don't think it's fair to take a value position on this, but land cannot pass from parent to child in the way it did in the 1920s because of the drift of public policy as regards assessment and taxation."

I shall never live on the ancestral Allen acreage on Martha's Vineyard.

9. The Benign Neglect

MOSTLY, we remember what we want to, but I would not have you think for a moment that everything on Martha's Vineyard used to be better than it now is. When I think of what the island and its people were, I tend to remember the screen comic Harold Lloyd, who was not a Vineyarder, but who nevertheless remains mistily enshrined as a symbol of the life and times.

It so happened that when Lloyd died in the spring of '71, I was on the Vineyard and, walking past the Capawock Theater on Main Street, where I first saw his pictures, I thought how much a part of my growing up he had been — more, for example, than my uncle Charles or several other close relatives. Lloyd was part of a pleasant pattern; I cannot remember one piece without remembering all.

On Saturday mornings in summer, we would go to the bend of the beach, wade off until we struck gluey mud, and dig quahaugs with our feet. When we had a bucketful, we would take them to John Conroy's fish market at the head of the wharf; its cement floor was always hosed down and cool to bare feet, its iced bins were full of mackerel, cod and haddock. Mr. Conroy would wipe his red hands on his apron, dump the quahaugs gently into a wooden measure, and pay us. Then we would count out enough for the afternoon movie and a candy bar or peanuts and at least a half hour before the show started, we would have filled the front row, ready to applaud when the lady piano player in the pit launched into "Over hill, over dale, we have hit the dusty trail / And those caissons go rolling along."

It is of significance, in terms of both our pace and our perspective, that this song of the "wagon soldiers" — extolling a way of war long since obliterated by history — remained, even for the young, synonymous with action and derring-do.

As likely as not, the movie would feature Harold Lloyd, with his horn-rimmed spectacles, in something like *A Soldier-Made Man* or *Dr. Jack*, and we laughed very easily and loudly in those days. As a matter of fact, sometimes we even laughed during the newsreel that preceded Mr. Lloyd. I am not certain at this distance whether that was simply anticipatory or whether the news was really funny. Assuredly, there was more good news then, and if anything bad did happen, it was always in Oppau, Swatow, or Smyrna, or some similar place to which we could never relate at all. There was a general assumption, among adults as well as the young, that nothing really bad was likely to happen in the United States because Americans were smart enough to prevent it and that people who got in trouble, in America or elsewhere, deserved it.

Harold Lloyd, on or off the screen, stood for those qualities that most believed were bound to bring success. He was described by a friend as "a darn fine boy, who does not like unwholesomeness of any kind." He had a reputation for completely "clean" humor, loved to play baseball, had been born poor, and when he married his demure leading lady, Mildred Davis, he had installed in his new home Dr. Charles W. Eliot's "Five Foot Shelf" of books. Mr. Lloyd once said that his film career paradoxically began because of "a whole dickens of a lot of hard luck at one time." His ultimate triumph confirmed the popular notions that most things in life really were black or white and that no circumstance — including race or poverty — could defeat an individual (well, a *man*, anyway) who earnestly wanted to "get there."

So there were those on the Vineyard, even as late as '71, who marked Mr. Lloyd's death and thought wistfully of what their world was like when he was at his professional peak. I do not know what Mr. Lloyd might have thought about all this but I think it fair to assume that he was more complex (and understood that life was also) than those to whom he was a symbol. It is instructive to remember that, in what he later referred to as "the proudest moment of my life," he began his professional career, not with light laughter at all, but as Little Abraham in *Tess of the D'Urbervilles*. And if you have forgotten the tenor of this work of Hardy, the reminder that it concerns itself in part with "that shabby corner of God's allotment where He let the nettles grow, and where all un-baptized infants, notorious drunkards, suicides, and others of the conjecturally damned are laid" will suggest another side of the man and of the world.

As Mr. Lloyd was more complex than we thought then, so was life on the Vineyard; it seemed simpler and better than it was because of what went unremedied, unnoticed, or undiscussed. In those days, there were more people who needed to go to doctors and dentists and did not because they did not have the money. There were more people who had to charge their winter's groceries. There were more people who would have gone short of meat if they had not gone rabbit hunting. There were more people whose houses needed major repairs. There were fewer people who had a high school edu-cation and even fewer than that who had education after high school.

In the same year in which Mr. Lloyd died, my father was seventy-nine, and he wrote to me from the Vineyard: "I thank all the gods that may be that I have lived long enough to see some of the old-time evils eliminated. Even if they have been replaced by other evils, those are not as bad. We progress, even if we do move slowly.

"Folks were damned poor. I know that old people who couldn't work died from lack of food and shelter and nobody gave the matter much thought."

Mr. Lloyd's popularity was certainly due in some measure, not to the fact that he was the happy, laughing symbol of a happy, laughing age, but to the fact that in lieu of Social Security, unemployment compensation, Aid to Families with Dependent Children, Old Age Assistance, low-income housing, food stamps, Alcoholics Anonymous, child-care centers, adoption agencies, and marriage counselors, many longed to be told, however unrealistically, that fairy-tale endings could occur. Somewhere. Sometime.

In retrospect, I am aware that the Vineyard shared with the nation, and probably much of the world, an attitude of "benign neglect" toward people and problems in need of attention. As my father observed of the elderly poor, "nobody gave the matter much thought." And there were other factors in our less-than-perfect island society, including some interest in bigotry.

On September 27, 1925, the New Bedford *Sunday Standard* published an interview with the Reverend Guy Willis Holmes, pastor of the Pleasant Street Methodist Church in that city.

The first three paragraphs of the thirty-eight-inch story stated:

The ideals of American citizenship expounded by the Ku Klux Klan and by the Reverend Guy Willis Holmes . . . are the same. So Mr. Holmes readily conceded after defining for The Standard his own conception of the good American citizen and the Klan's conception of the good American citizen as he understands it.

He had that agreement of sentiment in mind, Mr. Holmes said, when he commented after his latest "loyalty rally" that if there were any Klan members in this vicinity, he thought it very likely they were in attendance.

The Klan, Mr. Holmes said, asks from its members: 1. Supreme allegiance to the constituted authority of the United States. 2. Belief in and practice of race purity. 3. Belief in the principles of sacrifices and fellowship expounded by Jesus Christ.

The interview was prefaced by the following, set in italics:

"Speaking as a Klansman, I suppose?" queried the reporter as Mr. Holmes finished the interview which follows.
"The Klan is a psychological thing," returned Mr. Holmes. "People have asked me whether I am a Klansman. It is a question I can't answer yes or no and be sure that the inquirer will understand the psychology of my reply."
"Well, we'll assume you're a psychological Klansman," the reporter came back. Mr. Holmes just smiled.

In those years, the people of the Vineyard were closer to New Bedford than to any other mainland city. Much island shopping, both wholesale and retail, was done there. Island steamers still ran to and from New Bedford, which was the principal mainland terminal. New Bedford stores advertised in the *Gazette*, scheduling sales and shopping hours to suit Vineyard needs. The New Bedford *Standard*, with representatives on the Vineyard, was making a particular effort to reach island readers.

Thus, it is reasonable to assume that those who invited Mr. Holmes to speak on the Vineyard in December of that same year were aware of the *Standard*'s September interview with him.

In what "may have been the call of the Ku Klux Klan," according to the *Vineyard Gazette*, Holmes addressed an audience of men at the First Baptist Church parish house in Vineyard Haven. The *Gazette* reporter, who attended the supper and lecture, described the event as follows:

The talk and discussion, which occupied between two and three hours, took the form of a general discourse on the corruption in state and national politics, its cause and probable remedy. At least one cause, according to Mr. Holmes, is the employment of the Roman Catholic Church as a cat's-paw or tool by unscrupulous powers to accomplish their selfish and designing ends. He stated that this practice has continued for years and is rapidly becoming more of a menace to the safety and welfare of the country.

He further stated that people were departing from the Roman Catholic faith of their fathers by the hundreds, rather than submit to the dominating influence which he said controls the church. Many tales were related by Mr. Holmes illustrating the effect of this condition in the Catholic churches in this country and the possible remedies, which he declared must be and, in fact, is a strong organization of Protestants to combat the alleged evil forces.

Again and again, Mr. Holmes declared that his organization held nothing against a person of Catholic faith, nothing against the Catholic church, in fact, but he said, "the menace which threatens this country can only be overcome by the defeat of the projects which it has set this tool to accomplish."

The Ku Klux Klan was mentioned but once, when Mr. Holmes stated that he had been accused by the New Bedford papers of being a member of that order. "I will not say anything in answer to that accusation," he said, "but if there is an organization in existence which is going to make this country a better place to live in, by electing decent, honest men to public office, and making true American citizens of our aliens, if this organization has aimed at the goal of teaching every man to do his best to make this country the land God intended it to be, then I shall be ready and willing to give my utmost support."

In closing his address, Mr. Holmes stated, with a pronounced twinkle in his eye, that he would be glad to converse personally with anyone upon any subject that they [sic] cared to, provided that he himself was not forced to broach the subject.

Mr. Holmes has been asked to speak again in the near future and it is probable that the crowd will be larger another time, as his talk was enjoyed greatly by all present.

In the late fall of 1929, there was an incident concerning historic Indian rights on the Vineyard, an issue that has surfaced often in recent years but that in those days was heard of very little. Marshal Jeffers, described as a "Gay Head Indian and scion of the ruling tribe which inhabited the Vineyard when [Bartholomew] Gosnold first saw the Gay Head clay cliffs [1602]," applied to the Edgartown selectmen for a license to take scallops in the waters of that community. Ordinarily, such licenses were granted only to town residents but Jeffers based his eligibility on the grounds that he was a descendant of the once-governing tribe of the island.

In making their decision to grant a license to Jeffers, the selectmen were influenced by a case in the nearby mainland town of Dartmouth in which the right of Indians to fish regardless of local regulations as to residency and the like was upheld. The rights of Indians in this respect having been thus apparently established, Jeffers received his license.

Resentment among Edgartown scallopers followed this supposed encroachment of an out-of-town vessel, Indian or no Indian. It was represented to the selectmen that Jeffers had sacrificed his Indian privileges by becoming a citizen of Gay Head. The selectmen took the position that if any law could be shown to them under which Jeffers had thus lost his rights, they would revoke his permit.

There was talk among the fishermen that an incursion of Gay Headers into the Edgartown scallop industry was threatened, following the success of the first Indian applicant for a permit. The selectmen replied, however, that there was not more than one additional Indian to whom the same privileges would attach and that fears of an out-of-town invasion were groundless. They refused to revoke the license.

The matter was one of talk only for some time but when Jeffers arrived at the Edgartown waterfront on a given Saturday morning in November, he found his boat sunk at the pier. "Person or persons," reported the *Gazette*, "had removed the plug and allowed the craft to go to the bottom."

On occasion, not because it was the Vineyard specifically, but because that was the way things went in small towns of that time, a Main Street anecdote was the only public attention paid to a situation that in retrospect proved to have been a signal for help.

Although I knew the name of every dog in town, I do not know to this day the name of the man who lived in a shack on the Beach Road. That probably suggests the degree to which I, too, was caught up in the attitude of benign neglect that was part of the spirit of the age. Most people had names but some did not.

He was a shambling, largely unwashed fellow with a disorderly black beard that looked like a wind-blown bird's nest; he was probably in his sixties but I daresay he looked sixty when he was fifty. Principally, he wore overalls and sometimes rubbers even when the going was not wet, because there were holes in his shoe soles. He did not speak a lot and his voice was a cross between a growl and a grunt; sometimes small boys teased him yet I think I never heard him use profanity.

Everything about him was marginal and peripheral; he

almost did not make it, yet he did; he was almost not there, yet he was. I think I never saw him work and I do not know where his money came from, however little it was. There were at least two men in town for whom the grocers, especially Paul Bangs, saved produce that was slightly over the hill and this fellow was one who shared in the bruised peaches and rusty lettuce.

The place where he lived had a stove and a bed and not much else. Somebody had stowed boat gear there once but did no longer and he had moved in; in those days, there was a kind of informality about such things that probably would be unthinkable today. Perhaps the owner of the place did not object, did not know, had moved away, or was dead. I went by the shack once when the door was open and the interior gave an impression of clutter both valueless and hopeless.

Since everybody needs somebody, this man had a dog, and I never saw one without the other. Both man and beast gave the general impression of having been put together from a collection of incompatible parts, yet they were inseparable because neither had anyone else. I have said I knew the name of every dog in town; I did not know that dog's name, for the same reasons that I did not know his master's.

The shack on the Beach Road had neither paper under the shingles outside nor anything but exposed studs — no sheathing — on the inside. When fall came, the wind whistled through the cracks in the walls. So this fellow made the rounds of Main Street stores, picking up cardboard cartons that he could nail between the studs, two or three layers thick, for insulation. He discovered one kind of carton that seemed to him heavier and therefore superior; whether because he was naive or illiterate or both, he did not know what this carton had contained but he did know the letters of the brand name. He wanted more of the cartons, and thus was born the Main Street anecdote.

On the given day, at about two in the afternoon, when several female shoppers were in the store, this bearded fellow shuffled into Paul Bangs's market. He growled in a voice loud enough to be heard throughout the place: "Paul, you got any more of them K-O-T-E-X cartooms? They work just fine!" The women were embarrassed, so was Mr. Bangs, and within a couple of hours, most of the businessmen on the street had heard about it and were chuckling accordingly.

This fellow insulated his one-room shack so efficiently that one night after the persistent cold weather struck, the little iron laundry stove he used for heat consumed all the oxygen in the place. A couple of days later, they found both man and dog dead in bed, curled up snugly under the same blanket.

Like the horse trough and the sadiron, the bearded man was of another time. No one now, including the Board of Health, would permit him to live as he lived and certainly not where he lived, which was fairly close to the center of town. Today, I think somebody, learning that he was collecting cardboard boxes because he was cold, probably would do something to help him. As it was, he signaled in his own way, but there was not anyone who responded, because really, he was not anyone's responsibility — not in those days.

The Vineyard probably was no more reticent about facing and dealing with such problems than a lot of other places but the fact that they always involved someone whom you knew made them more painful, more shocking, and harder to deal with. These factors also made those in trouble more reluctant to seek help, even if there was some. By the time of adolescence, I was aware of a layer of island life that was obscured by the pattern of things as they seemed to be and that it was seldom or never discussed openly. Much of it was blurred by innuendo; much of it was enveloped in a haze of ignorance and misinformation.

The layer of life beneath the pattern probably never applied to large numbers but it involved people from several walks: the pale, silent young man from the good Vineyard family who, one was informed, never was able to take his place in society because of permanent damage due to excessive masturbation; the handsome businessman who died young, because of "too much womanizing," it was said; and the fellow in his forties, whose hands shook and who never had a steady job, who went off-island weekends for "treatment."

One understands now that the pale young man with the good Vineyard name was the result of something like a couple of centuries of insular breeding. As historian Gale Huntington wrote in 1966 of island families, they "intermarried and interbred to an astonishing and even abominable degree. Cousins, first cousins, and double cousins married cousins, first cousins, and double cousins generation after generation. This resulted eventually in such traits as deaf-mutism, dwarfism, and feeble-mindedness. Of course, no family wanted to take the blame."

The handsome businessman, who *did* "womanize" somewhat, actually died because he refused to have a prostate operation for fear that it would make him sterile. The neglected situation eventually became malignant.

And the fellow in his forties, locked into a cycle of failure, inhibition, and alcohol dependence, went off-island every weekend to get drunk because his family would not let him drink at home and he was embarrassed to do it in public since habitually, he drank until he passed out.

One understands that now; one did not then. Those were the days, the good old Harold Lloyd days, except that some people's days were better than others'. And some of the under-currents were deep and old and not readily comprehended unless you had known the Vineyard and Vineyarders for a long time.

Once, I was with my father and we were about to leave Manuel Swartz Roberts's boat shop in Edgartown. Near the door, there were two men, at least seventy years old, and my father spoke to them. Had they responded, as they did ordinarily to him, I would have paid no further attention. But they ignored him, because they were angry with each other and age was denying them all ordinary means of releasing that anger, fierce and terrible though it was.

Very old men, such as they were, cannot punch, grapple, pursue, or strike. They cannot even make threatening gestures, for what is threatening about arms withered to the bones? They cannot indulge in strings of cursing because the voice cracks, the spittle dries up, the breath grows short, and what comes out is hollow rattle, more ludicrous than anything else. So they shuffle, breathe heavily, the veins in their skinny necks pump; beak to beak, they try to glare through cloudy eyes, and they shake like strings plucked and vibrating soundlessly.

Finally, one of the men shoved his bony face out of his shirt collar like an old turtle and he croaked: "Caleb's Pond child!" His thin, dry lips made an ugly, crooked smile and he said again: "You goddam Caleb's Pond child!" And in the eyes of the man to whom he said that, there was hate in return, more ash than fire because of his years, but hate for all that.

My father nudged me along. Afterward, when we were in the car, I asked him what "Caleb's Pond child" meant.

"Among the older Vineyard people," he said, "it was accepted that one or more unwanted babies, children born out of wedlock, were drowned in Caleb's Pond, which is on the western end of Chappaquiddick. From that beginning, an illegitimate baby came to be known as a Caleb's Pond child. That old man was calling the other a bastard in terms that they both understood. What hurt especially, I am sure, is there may be an element of truth in it, and they both know it. Most people are now dead who knew anything about it but when that fellow who was called a bastard was born, there was talk that his mother had been cheating on his father, that she had been having an affair with a man who was boarding with them. Whatever the case was, the boarder left about as soon as it was obvious that she was pregnant."

It is anticlimactic but historically significant to note that when Marshal Jeffers found his boat sunk, he replaced the plug in the bottom, pumped her out, and went scalloping. Whatever the issues were in the controversy, they were diluted and dissolved in general disinterest, and whether there were racial overtones in the incident — something that surely would be asked today — was a question never raised publicly. As with the nation, the Vineyard of that time was unconcerned with racial problems, including those of its own Indians; it was unaware of the existence of any such problems. The notion that race — rather than any individual lack — might make it harder for some to get an education or a job had not yet surfaced. Neither was there any generally expressed awareness of the truism that some people, both on the island and elsewhere in America, were accepted with reservations and that some doors were shut to them. There were "good" Jews, "good" blacks, and "good" Indians; they were "good" because they knew when and where to stop pushing. And if race caused you to have problems in getting along, most would have agreed — privately, of course — that some races are smarter and more likable than others, and that was why you had the problems.

So in the public schools of that period, although certainly there was daily emphasis on "liberty and justice for all," there was felt no official need to wonder whether, in the national scene, there was automatically more liberty and justice for some than for others. Similarly, there was felt no need to wonder whether island pupils might have benefited from an examination of social inequities because some, after all, would sometime leave the island and have to face "the real world" on the mainland. Instead, we were brought up — as I have said — like kittens in a basket, right to the last day of high school, believing there were no great differences among us or in the way in which we would be accepted elsewhere.

I received a letter last year from a member of a minority with whom I attended Tisbury schools from the fourth grade through high school, in response to my request for his comments on this subject. "My growing-up days on the Vineyard were great. There were minor incidents . . . but on the whole, I was accepted by the group of my peers and by the community," he wrote. However, once away at college, he found he was not accepted, and this lack of acceptance forced him to change schools. "I was hurt," he said. "There is no question in my mind that I lived in a cocoon on the Vineyard."

In part, the cocoon was perpetuated by certain generally accepted simplisms, no more prevalent on the island than in most of America at that time. In the early twenties, for example, members of the Vineyard Haven Acanthus Club met and Miss Albina Lambert presented the paper of the afternoon, entitled "America's Treatment of Her Indians." The newspaper account stated that Miss Lambert "clearly explained what the United States had done for the race and apparently felt it was all that was possible in the way of education and

opportunities of all sorts, which had been freely and gener-
ously afforded in their territories and in special schools." So
much for the national picture.

However, I am aware that thirty-five years later, Gale
Huntington, editor emeritus of the Dukes County Historical
Society's *Intelligencer*, concluded, "Where the Indians were
concerned, the English [who settled the Vineyard] were
mainly interested in only two things. They were interested
in saving their souls by making Christians of them and they
were interested in taking all of their best lands away from
them. Both of these noble aims were accomplished in a re-
markably short period of time." So much for local history,
although few thought about such things as this even in the
early 1930s any more than they did about the differences
among us.

Which brings me to the matter of my classmate Meriam
Vanderhoop Hayson, with whom I was graduated from Tisbury High School in June, 1933.

His heritage was exceptional. His mother, Anna, was the
daughter of Edwin D. Vanderhoop, the first American Indian
to serve in the Massachusetts legislature. Her mother was the
first to embody in literary form the legends and traditions of
the Gay Head Indians.

Anna Vanderhoop, described by contemporaries as "un-
usually handsome and poised, yet warmly human," was graduated from the Moses Brown School in Providence and from
Hyannis State Teachers College; she taught school prior to
her marriage. She also served on several civic and community
bodies, including the Gay Head School Committee. She was
musically accomplished and for years sang with the choir at
the Grace Episcopal Church in Vineyard Haven. Her life
and personality reflected the distinction and refinement of her
parents; on one occasion, she presented a benefit recital, in-

cluding songs based on Indian themes, a program whose high quality was remembered for many years by those who heard it.

"Van's" father, Meriam C. Hayson, was born in Washington, D.C., and educated in schools there and at Harvard. During his Harvard career, he met Anna Vanderhoop, and they were married. When World War I developed, Mr. Hayson attended officers' training school, was commissioned a first lieutenant, and went overseas with the American Expeditionary Force, serving for about a year.

After the war, he was named postmaster at Gay Head, operated a country store there, held various positions of public trust, including that of town treasurer, and, with his wife, ran an inn known as the Totem Pole for nearly forty years. He was one of the pioneer agents for oil burners on the Vineyard when the great movement to change from coal to oil began in the 1930s. The *Gazette* described him as "long one of the leading citizens of the town of Gay Head. His personal qualities were outstanding. Not only was he a man of strikingly handsome appearance but he had a depth of understanding added to the technical training which equipped him for wide usefulness throughout his active life. He was regarded as one of the ablest spokesmen" for his town.

It is true that Van did not possess the handsomeness or grace of his parents yet he was both friendly and outgoing. Gay Head pupils were bused to Vineyard Haven for high school and I remember him as early as the fall of our freshman year, while we were still in the old school building on Church Street. After lunch and before the afternoon session, we played mumblety-peg once in a while, and when somebody brought gloves to school, we boxed a little in the cloakroom. He boxed like an awkward steam engine, not too accurately but with an animation, even a zest, that I recall as being characteristic of him.

I have acknowledged that, as high school students, for the most part we were encouraged to regard ourselves as splendidly the same and that, as a group, we were splendidly isolated. Perhaps in part this is why I thought of Van as being adjusted. Yet his school record also would seem to support this. A classmate remembers him as being "reasonably bright"; I was in several of his classes, including physics and chemistry — he had a propensity for the sciences — and he was a better-than-average achiever in both of those subjects.

In addition, I regarded him as being more well-rounded than many with whom I went to school. He was the only male sophomore to make the high school track team (he was a runner), and when a high school band was created, for the first time in Tisbury's history, he played the mellophone. I can remember no incident during band practice or performance when he seemed other than at home with the group.

Between June and November of 1933, something happened to Van, and without indulging in fruitless conjecture, it may be useful to cite certain things that occurred during that period.

It was customary for island high school graduating classes to take a trip late in the senior year, usually to either New York or Washington, D.C. Especially because class members worked from the freshman year on to earn money for this trip, there was great anticipation concerning it.

Vineyard school officials had come to understand from the experience of previous years that hotels in the capital that their classes might reasonably go to would not accept as guests students whom they did not consider white. Classes including such students automatically went to New York, as did our class, because school officials concluded that Washington hotels would not consider Van white.

The matter was handled discreetly. A newspaper account related that

Graduates of Tisbury High returned from their New York trip Tuesday night tired, but enthusiastic, and winding up the post-graduation trip with an impromptu vocal entertainment delivered from the hurricane deck of the steamer as she lay at the dock.

The party left the island on Saturday morning previous. Traveling by bus to New York City, and stopping at Hartford for dinner, the party registered at the Hotel Bristol on Saturday, and divided, some of the members going to Coney Island, others to the new Radio City. On Sunday morning, the Edgartown and Oak Bluffs students departed for Washington, and the Tisbury contingent remained in New York, visiting the Cathedral of St. John the Divine and then embarking on a sightseeing tour with stops that included Roxy's Theater, where they were invited backstage, the first party of students to be thus distinguished.

I have to wonder what Van thought when "the Edgartown and Oak Bluffs students departed for Washington, and the Tisbury contingent remained in New York."

Once we had arrived in New York, there was some inevitable pairing of boys and girls for the weekend of events. Van asked one of the girls in the class for a date and she declined. Having known her since childhood, I am inclined to believe that she did so sensitively, but the matter may have loomed large to both of them since the girl had never had many, if any, dates, and Van was in the same category. I can see now that the refusal might have caused him to ponder further.

Van chose to attend the University of Maine and was accepted there. Apparently it never occurred to anyone on the Vineyard who was involved that northern New England of the 1930s was almost exclusively a white society that had had little or no experience with minorities. Even twenty years later, I knew a woman living in New Hampshire who drove her two young daughters to Boston for a weekend because, in her words, "I thought before they got any older they ought to know that everybody isn't white."

On November 17, 1933, the *Vineyard Gazette* reported:

Meriam V. Hayson, son of Mr. and Mrs. M. C. Hayson of Gay Head, is expected home from the University of Maine this weekend. The youth is suffering from a nervous breakdown.

Young Hayson, who was graduated from Tisbury High last June narrowly escaped serious injury last Friday night when he fell twice, the first time near moving machinery in a power plant which he was inspecting in connection with his college course in electrical engineering. The second fall was into a few inches of water.

In 1981, I discussed this matter with a person who knew Van and who was familiar with the circumstances:

Q. Was Van having trouble with his studies at the university?

A. He was high-strung but he was making out. He was smart.

Q. Did he try to kill himself?

A. He said so.

Q. If he wanted to kill himself, why would he jump into "a few inches of water?"

A. It was dark. The place was a kind of flume or spillway and he couldn't see that there was only a couple of inches of water there.

Q. Was he the only nonwhite in his class at the university?

A. I think probably he was.

Q. Was he the only nonwhite attending the university?

A. I think very likely so.

Q. Is the line of reasoning I am suggesting in these last two questions valid in your opinion?

A. Yes, I think it is.

Q. Was there a race factor here?

A. Yes, I suppose there was to some degree. It wasn't so much what anybody said or did but what he felt, the consciousness of it.

Van Hayson died, a very young man, of whatever. Had he been born thirty years later, or grown up in less of a "cocoon" than Martha's Vineyard, or chosen a school where there were other minorities, I have to wonder whether this youth, described by those who knew him as "reasonably bright" and "smart," might have made it.

Finally, there was Ben Turner.

Next to the Capawock Theater, where I first saw the posters advertising Harold Lloyd's movies, there still stands the great linden tree, gently fluttering green magnificence. Beneath it in those days, orange-and-black striped umbrella over the chair, was the shoeshine stand of Ben Turner. Ben was black.

A shoeshine then was a nickel. "When I get through, you won't need a mirror," Ben would say. "You want to shave, you just look in your shoes."

Mostly, I shined my own shoes, but one day, I was going to a party and I climbed up into his chair, privately hoping that someone I knew would see me there. I told Ben why I was having my shoes shined. He was bent over my feet, brushing away, and he did not even raise his head but he said, "When I go to a party, there ain't nobody there but me." At the time, I thought he meant that he was the best dressed or the best looking, and I laughed, appreciatively.

Now, of course, I am aware that in that time, there were only two hundred Negroes out of an island population of approximately five thousand, that I never saw him dressed up, that he had no car and no money, and that he probably meant something much more literal. I think he meant that on rare occasions when he could afford it, he bought a pint of something, took it to the little one-room house where he lived, and drank it for such comfort as loneliness requires.

Still, those were the good old days, the good old Harold Lloyd days; only bad guys got shot bad, the rest were just flesh wounds, and girls hardly got shot at all. But because I remember them more or less as they really were, rather than simply as they appeared to be, I find reassuring a fairly recent published statement in the *Gazette*:

> *As island walls*
> *are raised stone upon stone*
> *so Martha's Vineyard Community Services*
> *has grown*
> *agency by agency,*
> *program by program,*
> *to bring aid to island residents.*

In terms of Vineyard history, this is a relatively new kind of concern for people and problems. Michael Wild speaks for another kind of relatively new concern.

Mr. Wild, thirty-nine, holds a degree in social ecology; he has lived on the Vineyard for more than a decade, on his family-owned property on Katama Plain in Edgartown. Since 1979, he has been executive director of the Martha's Vineyard Commission, a regional regulatory agency that is actively engaged in master planning, historic inventories, revitalization plans, and harbor development.

Controversies surrounding the commission (Edgartown and Tisbury have withdrawn) stem from the difficulties of adjusting the agency's regulatory authority with the existing and more traditional authority of the island's towns. Mr. Wild, although recognizing that the island is a diverse community and that there are different shades of enthusiasm and support for the commission's work, remains optimistic that the commission will prevail.

"In-migrants constitute a sizable percentage of the population," he says. "Initially, they arrive to take advantage of summer. They have heard of the island through both good and bad media projects, such as the Kennedy bridge or the purchase of land here by former Defense Secretary McNamara. These projections produce mystiques, extracurricular interest in this place. People come here to do things differently or to be left alone or for reasons probably not true. You can't produce on the mainland this thing about islands. A lot of these attitudes might be called fantasy but they have practically produced the in-migrant population of the last twenty-five years.

"The stamina figure of the in-migrant varies; for some, 'wintering over' was a major hurdle. The Vineyard's mode of life is schizophrenic; summer is an idyll, winter is a difficult passage. The islanders know it, but some want to know it in different ways. Sometimes the fantasy turns sour for lack of creative forums that are found in suburban areas.

"In terms of decision-making here, there arose the need for more professional people — teachers, hospital people, people in this commission. Look at some of the newer selectmen; these are young people and some are in-migrants.

"There are conflicts between groups; between the native islander and the summer people, between the native islander and the in-migrant. The native is saying he is the only one who should be making decisions. We are trying to produce a forum to see how it can be resolved. Some in-migrants are not yet active participants; they are busy working things out for themselves. I am sure they exert influence, such as taste in buying, even though they may not go to town meeting or run for office. They are a large enough group so that they could change things. They may be waiting for an issue."

There is islandwide concern as to where the Vineyard is going. There is not islandwide consensus as to where it ought to be going. Within this vacuum of opinion, there may, in fact, be found the as yet uncrystallized issue.

10. The War Years

AT least as early as the final months of 1940, the conflict in Europe was preoccupying some Vine-yarders enough to prompt the *Gazette* to complain that "nothing happens here anymore, it seems, which is not linked in gossip with the war and with the activities of Mr. Hitler." Underlying many of the rumors was the traditional feeling of the native that the Vineyard was a place apart, that both water and wisdom separated it from the mainland; since this was so, an enemy of the United States might well be inclined to consider the island an entity and to reflect upon its usefulness as such.

Some said that it would be worthwhile for a potential enemy of this nation to open all the island's South Side ponds to the ocean in order to provide hideaways for submarines. Others thought that foreign agents would attempt to develop three or four landing fields on the Vineyard and some who subscribed to this theory suggested that the recent revival of sheep raising was an obvious cover for such a project. One of his Vineyard constituents wrote a long letter to Congress-man Charles L. Gifford urging that the island be elaborately and heavily fortified at once.

The *Gazette* shook its editorial head: "It is fine for people to be patriotic but there is a limit to the stories they should cook up about their neighbors. What everyone does not seem to realize is that common sense holds true in time of war as well as in time of peace."

All, of course, was not rumor. U.S. Army engineers visited the island in December, 1940, and made a trip to Peaked Hill, just off Middle Road in Chilmark, the highest point, as part of a survey of possible observation sites "to be used in case of necessity." Within about six months, wheels were rolling on the slopes of the hill — wheels of a sort, that is, being the treads of bulldozers and tractors at work on a road up the south slope.

"This is work of a variety seldom before done on the island," my father wrote.

About 800 yards from the crest of this hill, the Middle Road winds about its foot, at an elevation slightly above sea level. The slope of the hill rises with abruptness from this level, lying in slight folds across the course of the road. In order to make it possible to climb the hill in ordinary vehicles, the building of a very zigzag way is necessary and even with these devious courses laid out, the grade is still a good 12 percent.

Benjamin C. Cromwell of Vineyard Haven is in charge of the working force and he agrees that the 2,000 feet of way contains not an inch that is not nasty going. Boulders weighing several tons dot the hillside, often with but a fraction of their bulk exposed. They must be excavated and removed, the last being the more simple process because such rocks can be rolled down the slopes for a quarter-mile once they are set in motion. In spots, the hillside lies virtually on end, necessitating much filling as well as cutting and an idea of what the excavation gang is experiencing may be gathered from the fact that the bulldozers travel at times so nearly on a perpendicular plane that all the water runs out of the radiators.

Off to the west a few hundred yards lies the famous Bolster and Pillow Rock, or Moshup's Bed. [Moshup was the giant god of legend who warned the Indians of the coming of the whites.

He hurled great rocks into Vineyard Sound, creating the Devil's Bridge off Gay Head. He dumped his pipe ashes into Vineyard Sound; they were carried to the eastward, lodged on shoals, and formed Nantucket.] Moshup was supposed to have been a pretty rough and ready old chap himself but even in his palmiest days, he failed to upset the landscape as these roaring mechanical monsters are able to do.

Upsetting the landscape was the least of what was about to happen on the island. Strangers in U.S. military uniforms were about to be introduced to Martha's Vineyard and its people, an extraordinary infusion of different ways, words, and thought. The rumblings of the outside world and the responses of the nation were coming closer rapidly.

In August of '41, Menemsha residents rubbed their eyes in amazement at the sight of two U.S. cruisers, the *Augusta* and *Tuscaloosa*, accompanied by five destroyers, that loomed above the horizon shortly after noontime, steamed to within a mile of the beach, and anchored. Shortly afterward, five planes were catapulted from the decks of the cruisers, droned over Menemsha Village and Bight for a half hour, returned to the moorings, landed in the water, and were hoisted aboard the ships again. A few inquisitive civilians boarded catboats and launches and ventured offshore to circle the cruisers. Returning, they said that instead of obtaining information, they provided it. Sailors aboard the ships had asked them what state they were in.

In the same month, "off limits" signs were posted on the state reservation and it became known that troops would be landed at Paul's Point and that permission had been obtained from property owners to allow passage of the soldiers across the island to the reservation for maneuvers. The observation station at Peaked Hill was manned by a detachment of the

U.S. Signal Corps. Mock air raids were held on the island in October as part of army maneuvers along the coast.

By November, rumors of evacuation plans for islanders had been in circulation for some time and were sufficiently upsetting to prompt an official denial. General William P. Ennis, chairman of the island's civil defense organization, pointed out that the island had no military importance, that many fishing craft and vessels were available to supply the population if steamboat service were to be suspended, and that the evacuation story was hampering civilian defense work because some were asking why they should prepare for defense if evacuation already had been decided upon.

Although it may have escaped attention beyond the perimeters of the island, Martha's Vineyard was, in fact, invaded in the late summer of 1941 — by the Japanese beetle. Alfred Norton, with whom I grew up in the Cromwell's Lane neighborhood, a gardener and landscaper, found several of them in an Edgartown garden, to the dismay of local horticulturists. It was believed the beetles had been shipped to the island as grubs in the soil of plants ordered from New Jersey, where they had been first found in this country twenty-five years before. They had been spreading through the East at the rate of five or ten miles a year.

That December, of course, produced the harsh realities, which the islanders, in characteristic fashion, took seriously, but in perspective. My father wrote:

A tremor of mixed excitement and dread swept the Vineyard on Sunday [December 7] when the first news of the Japanese attack on the Pacific islands became known through radio broadcasts. Not for eighty years has this island scene been duplicated, when the opening of the Civil War found Vineyard men at sea and in or near the war zone. The opening of this Far Eastern war likewise finds many Vineyard men in or near the scene, not merely in ships of commerce but in the armed forces of the country. The Vineyard is represented in the Army, the Navy, and the Marine Corps on duty in Hawaii and the Philippine islands.

The island joined the nation in an orderly but emphatic demonstration of indignation and determination to see the matter through to the finish. There was no note of worry or apprehension voiced, there was no hysteria shown. In many places on the Vineyard, the American flag was displayed at daylight on Monday morning. Civilian defense members responded to the first real call to duty about 1:30 Tuesday afternoon when air-raid signals were sounded the length of the East Coast, following a report of hostile planes off New York City, which proved to be unfounded. Some thought the incident was planned by the government as a test of air-raid facilities of the Northeast coast.

The Martha's Vineyard Rod and Gun Club, more than two hundred strong, declared in a resolution adopted December 10 that, in case of emergency, it would report as a shotgun brigade. A tally of the arms owned by the membership revealed at least one shotgun to a man and a number of rifles. It was announced that the club "discussed possibilities of an invasion with grim and practical earnestness before adopting the resolution. Given any sort of break, the club felt that its membership could add considerably to the unpleasant situation of an enemy should one appear."

On December 12, Cronig's Market in Vineyard Haven published a buy-at-home advertisement:

> *In mustering the land's resources*
> *Food, machinery, and horses*

The War Years

That place serves best which uses
Food that its own land produces.
So buy and live upon the bounty
Of food produced right in Dukes County.

By the close of the year, it was announced that island boats would be painted gray in compliance with wartime regulations of the United States Maritime Commission. Lights in their saloons and staterooms were dimmed, radios belonging to members of the crews were removed, the steamers' own radios were confined to listening, and passenger use of cameras and binoculars was restricted. Island householders were instructed to begin immediately preparing blackout rooms. Proprietors of stores were required to turn off all lights at closing time except for night-lights that were blue, ten watts or less, and shielded to prevent reflection.

"And ye shall hear of wars and rumours of wars," says the book of Matthew: "see that ye be not troubled: for all these things must come to pass, but the end is not yet." It was something like that in the first days of 1942. Among the rumors of the first week was one to the effect that a German submarine was off South Beach and was being fired on by the Coast Guard. An earlier report said that the public was being excluded from the beach in the vicinity of Tisbury Great Pond opening because the pond was being converted for use as a submarine base or hideout to be used either by the Germans or by the Americans.

The West Tisbury sheep farm, which had held first place in the rumor crop for some weeks, began to run behind, although it still was reported as actually (a) a site for a concentration camp; (b) an airfield for Germans, Russians, or any one of several other foreign nations; and (c) property into which the U.S. government, unbeknownst to the owners, had put a lot of money in order to have a suitable airport site.

It was rumored that a large number of German planes had flown over Oak Bluffs and photographed the town. Some-one, unnamed, saw the swastikas on the planes. Others noted that the planes were Japanese, with rising-sun insignia. An island resident was reported arrested for espionage; it was said that he had been spirited away in a plane. Gossip persisted that the nearly six thousand men, women, and children on the island were to be evacuated (under conditions varying according to the temperament and imagination of the story-teller), leaving the Vineyard uninhabited save for naval and military patrols until the end of the war.

Of course, all was not rumor; other things were going on.

A major part of the adult population of the Vineyard under-took some form of volunteer duty related to defense or the war effort, including everything from first-aid courses to man-ning civilian defense observation posts to joining the State Guard Reserve.

And John D. Bassett, the mayor of Wooton Bassett, sur-veyed the huge pile of fresh loam beside a gaping excavation at the rear of his house and took a fresh chew of tobacco. "Yes," he explained, in response to a question, "I am building a bomb shelter, the first one ever to be constructed in Dukes County, without a doubt, and it will be a masterpiece, too."

"Does the situation, then, appear so desperate to you?" he was asked.

"No, indeed," replied the mayor heartily, "it isn't that at all. I am merely combating this war of nerves that you hear so much about. You see," he went on, "the air is filled with rumors and predictions and people are being gallied by tales of startling nature. Only yesterday, a fellow went tearing through here, wild-eyed with a report that some kind of sub-marine was in port.

"I took a brief survey, just to satisfy myself, and located an otter swimming around down there, but it just goes to show the condition of people's nerves. So I am building a bomb shelter and a good one. Maybe I'll build a couple before I get through. People will learn about it and take comfort from the fact, which will ease their nerves, and that's all I want to accomplish. When spring comes, I'll probably use the shelters to smoke herring in or something like that, but as a morale-builder, they will serve their purpose."

In Chilmark, Article 22 of the town warrant concerned what action the town would take to afford protection for schoolchildren in the event of an air raid. A committee of five parents, together with the school committee members, presented to the meeting a report on the matter based on questionnaires sent to nineteen families in the town. It revealed that a large majority wanted their children sent home in case of an air raid in preference to having them removed to a bomb shelter, and those parents whose homes were distant from the school requested that their children be taken in by various residents living near the school.

Mrs. Jane Hope Whitney of the Falmouth USO visited the island to check on matters pertaining to the well-being of the detachment of soldiers stationed at Peaked Hill. She was pleased to learn that the uniform was the equivalent of a ticket of admission to many island affairs since this had not always proved to be the case on the mainland.

Manuel Swartz Roberts was scouting around looking for native Vineyard timber to go into a thirty-one-foot towing launch that he was building for the American West African Line. He was successful. The stern post, bow and stern knees, shaft log, and deadwood timbers were of such considerable dimensions as seven by nine, seven by thirteen, and nine by nine inches and they were cut from island-grown wood, all white oak except for the shaft log, which was of locust. When complete, the craft was scheduled to be taken to the coast of Africa and used in the discharge of cargo from freighters at locations where there were no port facilities.

"If I may, with due respect to officials," said Lucy Palmer Adams of Oak Bluffs in a letter to the *Gazette*,

I would like to ask why must we have a blackout [drill] at a time that interferes seriously with our church services? Last Sunday, in one town, it interfered with the time to start and in another, the services had to be cut short fifteen minutes out of one hour in order to give time for people to reach home in safety.

If we must have blackout on Sunday, our one day of worship, why must it interfere with the time of gathering or return? Part of our war cry is 'liberty and freedom to worship God' and it is the most important and surely, with our defense work, should be consistently adhered to and not interfered with when not necessary. Why not give us a chance and the encouragement we need?

Fifteen days later, General Ennis announced that Martha's Vineyard would participate in the first regional blackout drill of the area on Sunday, March 15. At 10:00 P.M.

Captain George Robinson of North Tisbury and Menemsha went to look at the wreck of an old building once owned by the late Onslow Stewart of Chilmark, with the idea of tearing it down and making some cords of fireplace wood. Inside, he found Mr. Stewart's No Mans Land boat, a good sixty-five years old, and decided to save her from the woodpile because her planking was still sound and her bronze fastenings were as good as ever. He pulled out and replaced some of her timbers, repaired the battered keel, installed a ten-horsepower engine, and said he expected to take her to the ledges for scup and tautog when the weather warmed up, thereby "helping out the defense program somewhat."

Sam Cronig, the first of Jewish faith ever to establish permanent residence in Vineyard Haven, observed his twenty-fifth anniversary as a market proprietor in that town. "When character among men is under discussion," my father wrote, "it is an everyday occurrence to hear Sam Cronig referred to in a manner that places his honesty and dependability upon a high plane. Tomorrow [March 7, 1942], he will greet his friends as an American among Americans at his market — a standing that he has well-earned and a far cry from the birthplace abroad that he knew, where today armies are battling."

Faced with the restrictions of tire rationing, Orin Norton, the Edgartown blacksmith, applied some characteristic ingenuity. He took old carriage wheel shoes, or iron rims, and welded them over the treads of the two rear tires of his light truck. The iron rim was about four inches wide and five-sixteenths of an inch thick. Before welding the rim around the rubber shoe, he deflated the tire somewhat, and then inflated it after welding to make a tight fit.

"I've reversed the usual process," he said. "The practice has been to put rubber on iron; I've put iron on rubber." Standing on his running board, he jumped up and down to show how flexible and resilient the device was. He explained that the shock of hitting such objects as rocks, instead of affecting the sidewalls of the tires, was distributed by the iron rim and that he had tried his appliance at speeds from ten to forty-five miles an hour and at the latter speed found the rumble of the iron-shod wheels virtually unnoticeable. He suggested the rim could be carried farther down the side of the tire to enclose most of the wall and thought the idea might be of value to army vehicles and that it would eliminate tread wear.

Orin did, in fact, help the army in another capacity, when it needed sheath knives. The specifications were explicit and somewhat difficult to meet; the blades were to be of a certain length and width and had to be capable of taking a keen edge yet could not be soft enough to bend without breaking. He took a contract to furnish some hundreds of the blades and they met every requirement. I do not know whether the army was aware of it but the knives were made of cross-arm braces junked by the telephone company. Orin had collected them a while back and he said, "I figured they'd come in handy sometime."

The Navy Department took Edgartown's newest dragger, the *Priscilla V*, whose captain was Jared L. Vincent, for conversion to war purposes. The federal government also took over the *Naushon*, pride of the island fleet of steamers since 1929. "So the Naushon has gone to war," observed the *Gazette*,

not to combat duty but to take her place among the auxiliary craft of service and supply which support the great effort of the war. What can one say, except good luck and farewell?

Good luck and farewell, then, to the Naushon, keeper of schedules, carrier of countless cars and tons of freight, main reliance of a legion of island people. She is more than a steamer; where she goes, something of the Vineyard must go, too. Between islands and their boats, there is a tie like that which binds families and life-long friends. It is never broken. Wherever the Naushon may steam on her new business of war, she is still our boat.

I had reason to remember that eventually: "she is still our boat." The next time I saw her, this is the way it was:

Sometime during the hours of fear and interminable explosion, of outrageous introduction to an outrageous world —

and do not ask me what time, for time was gone — something offshore in the gray, milling armada caught my eye. What a remarkable thing it is that a split-second glance at some familiar shape or line prods the subconscious. What was it I had seen that called me to look again?

Then I saw her, bright bone in her teeth, threading her way through the fleet and bound inshore, the 250-foot *Naushon*, once queen of the New Bedford, Martha's Vineyard and Nantucket Steamboat Line and requisitioned in 1942 by the War Shipping Administration for use as a hospital ship. She had come to Omaha Beach in Normandy to take back the first wounded to England.

Her lines were unmistakable as she stood in, and it just happened that she was starboard side to and turning, exactly as I used to see her day after day as she rounded the breakwater at Vineyard Haven with a long and two shorts of the whooping whistle to let everybody know she was coming.

Squatting among the broken poppies and the junk of war, I wept. It was sacrilege for this symbol of tanned women in summer hats, of laughing children making sand castles, to be in such a place and on such a bitter errand. It was unbearable to be reminded of a time when my principal concern was whether the mackerel were biting at the steamboat dock — and to try to relate that time, or myself, to the new corpse upon the gravel six feet away, a thing of open mouth and vacant eyes.

On the Vineyard, the navy also took over 683 acres of flat, scrubby terrain in the state reservation, an area where there had been only hawks, rabbits, and wild flowers for generations. What government acquisition of this land meant was that Martha's Vineyard acquired an airport that finally came to be county-owned. It has proved to be one of the major factors of change. Long after the war, a Vineyard businessman

RG 82

was asked what he thought of the island airport. "What do I
think about it?" he replied. "Try to imagine where we would
be without it. It's our link with the outside world. It makes us
a part of America."

Off and on, for the first six months of 1943, I was the
officer in charge of the Naval Intelligence office on Martha's
Vineyard, located in the Hinckley building on the Beach
Road in Vineyard Haven. My principal duty as I saw it was
to convince the navy to close the installation. I came to that
conclusion after no more than a few hours of searching for
"flashing lights" that proved to have logical explanations and
"guttural accents" that derived from Hoboken, not Hamburg.
It seemed to me possible that a spy, saboteur, or traitor might
show up on the island but I did not think that remote chance
justified maintaining a seven-day-a-week operation. I also had
a feeling that if one did show up, he (or she) probably would
not flash any lights or have a guttural accent.

About the most exciting thing to happen in that office,
which was up a flight of stairs over a lumberyard, was the
occasional arrival of Captain Vincent Astor, a tall, handsome
fellow who left a stream of Turkish cigarette smoke in his
wake. Captain Astor was concerned with organization of the
confidential fishing vessel observers, as part of the navy's anti-
submarine-warfare program.

What the navy did was to put radios on some fishing vessels.
If a fisherman spotted an enemy sub offshore, he could talk to
naval officials in Boston or New York and say "Hooligan 9"
or some such and that was the grid position of the sighting.
It did occur to some, however (including a knee-booted friend
of mine, neither coward nor fool, who spent half his life on
the Southwest Part of Georges Bank, haddock hunting), that
if a dragger opened up with its radio, the German sub nearby

might intercept the broadcast and sink the fishing vessel post-haste, with the idea of discouraging this kind of marine reporting.

From time to time, Captain Astor would put into Vineyard Haven and come to our headquarters to use the phone. Often, he would place several calls to Washington, be unable to reach whomever he wanted, and shortly thereafter, go to sea again. Over the next several days, high-ranking brass from the Navy Department would return his calls. As a brand-new ensign, I found this unnerving because I never could explain to them satisfactorily that Captain Astor was not present, that I did not know where he was, that I could not reach him, and had no idea when or whether he would return. It occurred to me that this seeming incompetence on my part might jeopardize my naval career but I also assumed that if I suggested to Captain Astor, however respectfully, that he hang around long enough to receive his calls from the admirals, et cetera, that might too.

A couple of items related to my brief tour of duty on the island are memorable. In assuming the command, I inherited the enthusiastic voluntary services of two or three Vineyarders who reported by phone every morning those events of the past twenty-four hours that seemed to them of possible government interest. I do not suppose I am violating security regulations if I reveal that one of them ceased calling me when his prime pro-German suspect received a U.S. Army commission, was ordered overseas and eventually decorated for gallantry in action.

But the call I enjoyed most each day was from a woman, probably in her sixties, an islander who had known my father and his father. These conversations — actually, I did not do much of the talking — tended to be lengthy, but more important, they were lively and colorful, reflecting the vitality of the informant. I sensed very quickly that the woman found it exciting to observe in behalf of the American government, that she took these matters of vessel and people movements very seriously, and spent at least twenty hours a day looking, listening, and taking notes. She conceded at one point that she did not "sleep very well or very much."

Unlike some volunteer informants who seem forever ill-tempered or unnecessarily neurotic, she was always very calm and methodical. I daresay she was probably the only government agent on the East Coast who could make a decent chowder. She was splendid about noting the precise times at which things happened, the compass bearing, if applicable, and she recited with what I thought considerable grace the manners and mannerisms of her subjects. Of one scholarly fellow whom she observed reading in a public place, she remarked, "Every time he wanted to turn a page, he licked his left forefinger and then darted it at the lower right-hand corner of the page and sort of hooked it up; it was just like a frog's tongue going after a bug in midair." Because of such observations, I tended to think of her as being less like Mata Hari than Samuel Pepys with an apron, teapot in one hand and pencil in the other.

I confess neither she nor I ever caught any spies or saboteurs but I did look forward to her accounts; they sparkled and brightened otherwise dull days.

Long afterward, her son said, "I do not know what my mother did for the government but I know what the government did for my mother. She had just lost my father; she was desolate. The opportunity to perform a service, to have something to do that occupied many hours of the day and that kept the senses alert — this was just what she needed at that time."

In due course, the navy did close the Vineyard office and assigned me elsewhere as a deck officer, which I had requested.

My last official act as commanding officer of the intelligence operation involved the destruction of classified documents. The cast of characters and sequence of events were something like this:

The only other occupant of the navy office was a handsome, invaluable first-class yeoman who wore tailored blues. He was invaluable because he was completely at home with such items in military correspondence as "Com One Ltr to DIO 1-ND" or "LANTFLTRECOFF" and he always knew where in the burgeoning files to find "Ref BuPers Dis 162133 Feb 42."

One day, the yeoman, whose name was George (I am aware that officers ordinarily do not address enlisted personnel by their first names but if there are two people in one small room several hours a day separated only by an empty wastebasket, too much formality becomes both burdensome and absurd), informed me that we were about to get a letter from headquarters ordering us to shut up shop. I do not know exactly how yeomen know these things before they happen but they do and we did. When the letter arrived, it also instructed that the secret files should be burned and that maximum-security precautions should be observed.

The magnitude of the task was obvious. The secret files referred to consisted of several hundred cards in drawers of a steel filing cabinet. Each card concerned an individual or group that some element of the national intelligence community thought ought to be there, the reason therefor being noted on the card. The only facility we had for burning was a rusty oil drum in the backyard.

"It will be a big job for us," I said.

"For you, sir," said George respectfully. "Those cards are for officers' eyes only."

"Perhaps I could get you commissioned," I said hopefully.

George put down his copy of the Boston *Daily Record* very carefully. "Don't you dare," he said. Then he added "sir" very quickly. "I like things just the way they are," George said.

I thought of blindfolding him while he helped me carry the cards out to the burn barrel, but he protested reasonably that the task required going down a flight of stairs and that if he could not see, he might fall and break a leg. Or his neck.

So I got a big carton with a cover on it, so that he could not read the contents. Over and over, I filled it with cards; we carried the stuff out to the barrel and I burned it. It was a boring, time-consuming job because many of the cards had to be pried apart, lest some survive the burning. I could visualize somebody coming by later, finding half-burned but legible cards bearing startling information about someone whom virtually everyone knew. "Whole governments might fall," I said to nobody in particular, fanning the smoke out of my eyes and watching weary George lope back to the office with the empty carton.

There was something else about those cards; when they burned, they not only smoked but smelled. Even in the filing cabinet, either the ink or the paper coating emitted a peculiar and not very pleasant odor. So I was not surprised when, after several days of the burning process, a civilian who apparently lived somewhere to leeward approached and asked politely, "What is making that awful smell?"

"I am burning official documents by order of the United States government," I said in an ensignly manner.

"Well," said he, "how long is this going on?"

"Until I finish," I said stoutly. "Unless you can get Washington to countermand the order to destroy this material."

"I have no intention of wasting my time with them damfools in Washington," he retorted. "Whatever you're burning stinks up my house and gives me a headache and if you don't finish pretty soon or get a shift of wind, I'm going to the selectmen and raise hell." And he stomped off.

As I remember, the wind shifted.

Almost every day, there were jolting reminders of war's grim aspects as they applied to Vineyarders. Eldon Willoughby was a paratrooper; he was hit by shrapnel in the successful drop on Sicily. Ernest Swartz, who was three years ahead of me in Tisbury High School and who once wrote in the school magazine, "We were all born for success . . . there is a certain maximum of attainment for each individual — in this sense, we can all succeed," was awarded the Silver Star for gallantry in action in Tunisia. Willard Durgin, who taught in the Oak Bluffs junior high and sang in the Vineyard Haven Baptist Church choir, received the Legion of Merit for remaining at his post as engineer of a landing boat for two and a half days, despite "gruelling hardships and exposure to hostile bombing and strafing," following the landings in French Morocco.

If you could remember those people — and many others gone to war — going about their ordinary business in island streets and shops, it was strange and sad to think of them far off, locked in murderous confrontation.

Still, there were everyday compensations, at least on the Vineyard.

On one of those many days when war gripped the world and the times were filled with generally gloomy overtones, Arthur B. Hillman, Edgartown banker, went to his camp at Wintucket and turned on the radio. A Romanian folk dance filled the air.

Mr. Hillman was outside the camp while the music played and soon he noticed a brown thrasher emerging from the woodland. Then came a robin, a song sparrow, and a chewink, and all four birds began to sing. "It was a pretty nice thing to hear," Mr. Hillman said. "It was as if each bird was trying in his own way to complement the music." While the music was playing and the birds were singing, a rabbit and a squirrel came out of the brush and sat around as if they thought pretty well of the occasion. Mr. Hillman said there had not been a squirrel around the place for weeks until that one came along. Things like that enable mankind to endure wars.

In Vineyard Haven harbor, where the bottom had not been disturbed within the memory of the living, the draggers were finding great quahaugging, some boats stocking as high as eight hundred to a thousand dollars a week. Some of them found things other than quahaugs. Captain Roland Authier, with whom I grew up, brought in a number of ancient bottles that he had dredged up. There were stone bottles of quart size, glazed earthenware containers with blue-tipped necks that once had been sealed with cork and wax to preserve the rum or gin they contained. There were jugs stamped with the long-forgotten names of Cantrell and Corcoran and a short, squat, hand-blown blue bottle with raised letters on the side: SODA WATER. It bore the date 1848.

Recovery of this fascinating junk pile from the past, recalling an era when deepwater windjammers anchored in the harbor at the beginning and ending of long voyages, was implicitly reassuring to those war-weary who were worried about the world's future. In 1848, at about the time when some unknown sailor had dropped the blue bottle over the side, revolutions had broken out in France, Germany, Austria, Hungary, Bohemia, and Italy, and he might well have been gloomy about the prospects for *his* tomorrow.

"Here's the way it is around these parts," said the *Gazette* in an early-1944 letter to service personnel all over.

January thaw on the Vineyard, with raw fog and melting snow and ice in the streets. There have been some nice sunrises recently, still after 8 o'clock. The island boat has been keeping the schedule better of late but the task is a hopeless one for a single boat. The Naushon might have made it pretty well but the Naushon is overseas.

The streets have brightened a lot as more dim-out cones have been removed from the street lights. You don't need a flashlight to get around town on a dark night now, which is lucky because flashlight batteries are hard to get. Candy bars are a fairly scarce item, too, and when one of the stores gets in a supply, word gets around fairly quickly.

Mrs. James B. Worden, Edgartown ornithologist, was thrilled by the sight of a pair of cardinals, the male a brilliant sight in his scarlet coat, in the yard off Pease's Point Way. She had never seen a cardinal on the island and had begun to think she never would because they were then only rare visitors to this section of the country.

Mrs. William T. Vincent was walking along South Summer Street in Edgartown when a jeep came by. "Monte," she cried out, "is that you, Monte Wells?" Lemont, employed at the navy air station, was, in fact, driving the vehicle. "Sure is," he said.

"I'd like to ride in that jeep," said Mrs. Vincent. "I am eighty-six years old and I'd like a ride in a jeep before I die."

She got her wish. Mr. Wells drove her to her home on High Street, courtesy of the U.S. Navy.

In the spring of '44, the Maritime Commission announced that two Liberty ships under construction would bear names of significance to the Vineyard. One was to be named for Captain George W. Eldridge, identified for the greater part of his life with Vineyard Haven, and the sponsor was to be a daughter of the captain, Mrs. Wilfrid O. White, also well known on the island.

Captain Eldridge was the son of the man who made the first charts of the Atlantic coast. Moving from the Cape to Vineyard Haven as agent for his father's charts in what was then a most important maritime center, he applied his own observations and ability to the problems of coastwise navigation. Sitting in the famous old ship chandlery of Charles Holmes one day, he made a rough sketch of a tide table. Shortly after, he worked out tables for the coast and publication of the famous Eldridge tide book began.

The second vessel was to be named for Lillian Nordica, the famed operatic soprano, who was born Lillian Norton, a member of the Vineyard's Norton family. She was a granddaughter of the well-known "Camp Meeting" John Allen of the Vineyard, who was some kind of forty-second cousin of my father, and she attended the academy at West Tisbury and often visited the island. She sang on the island several times, including a concert in the Union Chapel at Oak Bluffs and, for the last time, in the Methodist church at Vineyard Haven.

April came that year, as April always comes, even when its gay daffodils are in strange juxtaposition with human events: "Shot Down Over France. Tail Gunner on Fortress Missing in Action." Or, as Sergeant Elijah H. "Pete" Crowell, back from Guadalcanal, recalled, "We were bombed and shelled plenty and we couldn't do anything about it except run like hell and drop into our dugouts and wait for things to calm down."

By that time, of course, the pugs were biting. If you are by, of, and for the Vineyard, you know that the pug, or mud flounder, is the first fish to take a hook in the waters thereabouts and it tends to arrive about on time, war or no war.

For about a month in late April or early May, pugs lure the fisherman, in part, at least, because they signal that, after months of cold weather, the saltwater fishing season has begun.

Forehanded souls who plan far in advance will have a keg of scallop rims salted for bait, the cleanings from the harbor scallops saved from last fall. Others, perhaps from choice, will dig a pail of clams, and these appear to work well, too.

The pug is not a game fish; it is rather slow-moving and sluggish, particularly in spring when it is moving in cold water. And always the first expeditions for these fish are lean ones; perhaps two or three pugs will be taken by somebody — but then the word spreads and out come the boats. In the war years, few fishermen used rods and reels; mostly, they caught pugs with the old-style drop line and lead sinker. Some of the boats grouped off the Eastville shore were so close to the beach that conversation with people ashore was possible. Some days were chilly, some winds were bleak, but the fishermen were there — even though most of the pugs caught were given away — as if they welcomed the predictability of nature in a time when man was more unpredictable than usual.

Then there was D day in Europe.

In lines written about that event, the *Gazette* remarked:

Some must have known about it by 5 o'clock, or by 6, for Vineyarders are early risers, but it was probably 7 before the news spread generally. The church bells began to ring between 7 and 8, not in any special order, but spontaneously, as word went around and the intention was translated into action.

The morning was one of the characteristically beautiful mornings of early summer, when early summer is at its best. The sea was blue, the air was warm again after the recent chilly spell, for the temperature had risen in the night to around 55 or 60. The sun was bright and shadows were splattered on the grass by apple trees and on the streets by the elms. The sky was vast and clear blue. Such a bright island day, so much sunlight and warmth, so much of the blessing of Heaven. If there could be an omen, one believed this might be it. . . .

This was D-day on the Vineyard and weeks from now, we shall know what it was like for some of the island boys who crossed the English Channel by sea or by air to fight for freedom in the world.

Weeks from then, in a letter to my father — within security limits — I attempted to describe for him something of what the D-day landing at Omaha Beach, Normandy, was like. In passing, I must have responded to his earlier account of military maneuvers of the Vineyard's State Guard, in which he was a lieutenant. I had no intention of being other than complimentary, for I was aware of his dedication to the guard, and admired it, but I must have written in clumsy fashion. As only he could, my thoroughly Vineyard father placed in perspective what he and I were up to at the particular time, and Omaha Beach came off a poor second best:

You sound a bit sarcastic about the maneuvers! [he wrote]. Let me tell you that we were attacking the damned radar station at Peaked Hill and our own outfit, which is the 8th Company of the 30th Infantry now, was the only one that got anywhere near it. Boy, we blew up their damned power house, bushwacked their outposts, and we could have pitched grenades right into every strongpoint they had, if we had been real hostile.

This in spite of dirty work at the crossroads and disregard for the plans made at the war council by their commander. With one section of old A Company [his army outfit in Vancouver, Washington, circa 1913] and our regular equipment, I would guarantee to take the damned place, dogs and all.

Given time to reflect, I concluded that my father's reaction was native "Vineyardism" at its best. Over the centuries, there may have been some doubt as to the relationship of sun and earth but old Vineyarders knew that both sun and earth revolved about Martha's Vineyard, and that very likely if this were not so, neither sun nor earth would have endured. Nor am I suggesting that this is born of insularism — islanders have gone to the earth's far corners — but, rather, that it reflects a fierce spirit of self-reliance and independence. Traditionally, the Vineyarder has established his own models and manners and turned his attention to the world when it seemed reasonable or necessary to do so. When a young islander in the military wrote home in 1944 from an outpost thousands of miles away and said it reminded him of Quansoo, "only not so pretty," he was reaffirming the priorities of his heritage as well as expressing a touch of homesickness.

I am moved to complete these reflections upon the war and the Vineyard with some thoughts about Allan Gifford Keniston, for he symbolized the Vineyard youth removed from the Vineyard, and all that that means, and he was simultaneously an extraordinary individual. Assuredly, I have also chosen to write about "Giffy" because of an unforgettable moment that he and I shared when he was a little boy, living in West Tisbury.

From the beginning, he was exceptional. He broke island records by completing primary and grammar school work in four years. He was graduated from Tisbury High School, undoubtedly one of the most popular students ever to go there because he was as unassuming and good-natured as he was bright, and he entered Bowdoin College. When the war came at the beginning of his senior year, he enlisted in the Air Force.

As a staff sergeant, he was a member of the crew of a B-29,

and on their seventeenth mission, the plane was hit by heavy antiaircraft fire off the coast of Japan. "We had the choice of bailing out and maybe living or remaining in the plane and crashing with her," said Giffy.

They bailed out.

"We landed in a rice paddy near the town of Chiba," he related, "and all hands were prepared for a rough reception from the Japanese civilians. We got separated from the start and only the navigator and I were together. What was coming, we didn't know, but we were sure that it wouldn't be pleasant. However, the Jap soldiers got to us first and they protected us to a degree from the civilians."

As prisoners, with hands bound, the party started for Tokyo, traveling chiefly on foot, although they were put aboard a train eventually. The march took them through several villages and at some points, their guards encouraged the people to beat the Americans, who were bound and helpless. "They used clubs and their fists," he said.

In Tokyo, they were locked in a cellblock. Their cell was eight by ten feet and sixteen men were jammed into this space. Life in the cellblock was "frightful." They lived on rice and a small amount of dried fish. The men resembled walking skeletons — Giffy's weight dropped to a hundred pounds — and they were not allowed to join the prisoner working parties because the latter received larger food rations. Interrogation went on for hours, nearly every day. "They asked me the most idiotic questions," Giffy said, "concerning things that could not possibly matter to anyone."

Just in time to save two U.S. airmen who had diphtheria, they were removed to the prison camp at Omoi, located between Tokyo and Yokohama. Here, prisoners were treated better, although bomber crews were not favored and were restricted more than the others. They had rice, fish, and seaweed but never enough. By coincidence, on the day they were transferred, the war ended and the attitude of their captors underwent a distinct change.

"They treated us much better and acted friendly," Giffy said, "but it was not apparent that this change impressed anyone. They broke out a lot of supplies that they had evidently captured and never used and gave them to us — American uniforms, candy, cigarettes, and food.

"We were very lucky. We had only three months of being prisoners."

During those three months, Vineyarders knew only that Giffy had gotten clear of the falling plane and was listed as missing in action. The chaplain of his squadron wrote a comforting letter, observing that "all indications point to the probability that the crew of the plane reached the land." But no word came out of Japan and the island mourned with the Kenistons in the belief that he would not return.

When it was announced that the only Vineyarder captured by the Japanese was alive and free, island enthusiasm began to mount.

Giffy wrote to his parents from a San Francisco hospital; part of what he had to say he expressed in a poem:

> He shall recall this heart-destroying thing,
> The dying ship, her flaming, mangled wing;
> Majestic bird, plucked from the very sky
> By fire and screaming steel, to fall and die.
> He shall recall the fragile silken strands above him
> And the silent, hostile land that lay below.
> These things he shall recall for some brief time,
> The clearest thing of all he shall recall
> The bright rebirth of life, the swift, sharp joy

Keen as a gleaming knife that came on
  white-starred wings,
From crystal skies, where freedom's life had guided
Clear bright eyes
To victory. He shall forget the rest.
This crystal dawn he shall recall the best.

There was a deeply moved and cheering crowd, including the Tisbury school band, at the steamboat dock at Vineyard Haven when he came home. He was the first returning serviceman ever to be so welcomed by the town.

Giffy went back to Bowdoin, was on the dean's list throughout the remainder of his senior year, received his master's degree from Columbia in 1948, and taught English at South Deerfield (Mass.) High School. In 1955, he became ill on a Monday, was hospitalized with polio on Wednesday, and died on Friday, at the age of thirty-two.

Shortly before his death, he wrote some verse about the Vineyard, testimony to the deep feeling he always retained for it:

These we remember, open island spring
The song of robins in the country lane
Far-off sound of surf along the shore
The sound of brooks made deep with April rain.

I think that he was not even of school age when my father and I went to visit his father, Allan, and Giffy invited me out to the wooded area near the house, guiding me through the trees and past the brush, and making constant enthusiastic comment. It would have been unusual enough had his discourse been confined to an identification of leaves and grasses, a brief commentary on squirrels and acorns, and the location of a vacated robin's nest, all of which he did cover splendidly. But then he went beyond, and this is what I have never forgotten:

"Just through there," the little boy said, pointing beyond the scrub oak clump, "and around the bend, where you can't quite see it, is Rose MacIves's house. She comes to play with me every day. She's the same age as I am.

"And right here," he said, "is my lollipop garden. I have raspberry lollipops in that row, lime in that one, and all orange in this one. I think raspberry is my favorite."

There was no Rose MacIves. There was no house "around the bend," and, of course, no lollipop garden. There was nothing but the quietness of the wood, stretching away for miles. He had created in this place — which other children might have found lonely, even boring — a charming world of fantasy that revealed much about its intelligent young creator.

World War II ended, as journalists and historians hastened to assure us. Normalcy on the Vineyard, never more than just below the surface, reasserted itself.

In November, 1945, my father wrote:

Again, she walks the main drag, the first lady of the American stage, Katharine Cornell, one with the fresh and gusty autumn wind that swept through the village, tossing her hair and tugging at her characteristic dungaree suit in which she loves to hike.

Goddess of the autumn, indeed, and adding the crowning touch to such days as only the Vineyard knows at this time of year, bringing, too, a touch of that homely and intimate life beloved of all who know it, as she literally blows into Bangs' market before a heavy gust and says, "Paul, tell me, have you got any good potatoes this morning?"

I asked my sister, Marjorie Jo Wood, who is several years younger than I, how much of the "homely and intimate life" of that period she thought remained, what changes, in other words, she thought had taken place on the island since then.

She lived on the Vineyard from infancy, was graduated from Tisbury High School in the early forties, and she and her family have spent several weeks each summer on the island for more than thirty years, including much time at Potluck Point, Tashmoo. Her husband, my brother-in-law Bill, has been coming to the Vineyard for more than thirty-seven years.

"Much of island change began in the early forties," she says. "The war was on. Peaked Hill was established; the airport was built, soldiers from Camp Edwards came over here, and a USO opened on Main Street.

"Up to this time, or even slightly earlier, the churches played a large role in social activities. The Baptist parish house was opened to young people because they were beginning to have problems with them — nothing to do, no place to go, and some wanted to drink. The older people in town tried very hard to hold on to the young people and maintain this kind of influence, but it slipped away.

"Part of this goes back to the Depression. Island children never had gone to school with summer people until then. I went to school with many of their children who had been taken out of private schools for financial reasons. We visited their homes, where there were cooks and maids. We came to know these people who used to come in June and leave in September, because at that time, they stayed on the island all year. We realized there was something outside of the Vineyard that we did not have. I think that produced a certain amount of discontent, yet among those who thought they could emulate it, a good many did."

She thinks there might be less individuality among is-landers now, but adds, "I can't say that I would want to pre-serve some things that we had in order to preserve individual-ity. During the Depression, I can remember a great poorness about the whole island — buildings needing paint, stores not looking prosperous. I think the people are doing a better job of taking care of themselves."

Growing up, she "loved" summer people because they "generated a feeling of 'upness' that was never here in the winter. Winters now are not so dreary because islanders are more in touch with the outside world. The young people of my time were far less worldly than other young people of that time, even those as close as Cape Cod."

She thinks the islander probably is less happy now than then but adds, "That could be said of many people anyplace. There are pressures in our society that did not exist then.

"Tashmoo was really a place where you could see the move-ment and growth of population, which is one of those pres-sures. When we first went there, Fred Peakes was the only year-round resident on our end of the pond. Only twenty-eight years ago, early on a summer morning, the only sound would be the whispering of oars as Fred and George Dolby rowed up the pond to do some fishing.

"The last year we lived there [late seventies], every camp was rented during the summer and half of them had been turned into year-round homes. And a wharf was built two camps away from us and they were repairing engines and storing boats for the winter. It had become quite commercial and was not as quiet and tranquil as before. I found it un-comfortable but Bill did not, and that, of course, demonstrates what is probably simply a difference between individuals."

My brother-in-law acknowledges the changes, but he adds, "I have to say that I never found at Tashmoo something that

I didn't like. Although the changes came about, the noise was there, a lot more people, quite a bit of boat traffic, I guess that never bothered me. Everything in today's life, wherever you are, is marked by increase; there are more of a lot of things. I think I understand that this is the way it is, the way it's going to be, and to try to keep it the way it was is impossible.

"I'd rather be with people around me. I don't find any particular problem or difference from the time when I first came down here. I just don't see a tremendous overall change on the Vineyard in the way the people who live here conduct their lives."

One thing that has not changed at Tashmoo is the riprap that my father built (not "had" built) to keep the bank in front of his cottage at Potluck Point from eroding. The size of the stones, which he manhandled alone, is a testimonial to the strength and spirit of the builder. Nor does the bank wash away, in either calm or storm; it would not dare.

11. The Increasing Statistic

 THERE is the insistence of spring across the marsh and beyond in this Vineyard place, even if the pools are still cold and black and on the banks, the most stubborn of last year's husks rattle in the crisp westerly to remind one of what was and is no more.

In the decade of the '60s just past, [Phyllis Meras wrote], Gay Head has become a national landmark, the rolling moor, woods, and beach of Cedar Tree Neck have been preserved as a nature sanctuary. Felix Neck has become a preserve for wildlife; Wasque Point, the solitary, lonely end of Chappaquiddick, where the sea 'rolls like moving mountains on the shore,' has been saved for future generations by gifts that kept it from the hands of entrepreneurs.

Dodger Hole Swamp, where the pinkletinks 'sing like sleigh bells,' was a gift to the Sheriff's Meadow Foundation in memory of Mrs. Henry Beetle Hough, who liked so much to listen to the spring frogs there. The Seamen's Bethel, a home for weary, lonely mariners since the 1880s, not only gained reprieve from the wrecker's mallet, but along with the reprieve came remodeling.

Trustees of Reservations acquired as a gift 200 acres of Chilmark land and 6,000 feet of shore front.

The island's first cluster development, Waterview Farm, began to grow above Sengekontacket Pond, though many neighboring property holders nervously looked on.

The new season is still little more than an aura, sliding in sideways, almost as if one bird and one bud at a time tested the hospitality of the atmosphere, yet spring is like corn in a popper — first, nothing but kernel, hard and unpromising, then, in some moment to be remembered, an incredible puff and new prospect, and suddenly, an explosion of them, beyond counting. Branches here are still bare, yet they have lost the dark tones of winter, the attitude of suspension, and there is now some subtle anticipation in their waving.

Drastic change in the social scene of the 1960s has no precedence [The Vineyard Conservation Society concluded in late 1965]. Its pressures cannot be counted by traditional methods. The massive population explosion, increase in leisure time, with accompanying weekends and vacations, rise in income, with more money for travel and recreation and swift improvements in transportation on highways, waterways, and airways combine to transform the countryside. Towns and villages that had one character for many decades have been altered almost overnight.

If the Vineyard responds to these pressures as other communities have, unwittingly, unprepared, and unaware of the consequence, it will lose much of the cherished quality and unique assets. People who come to the island because of them will move away. Others will not consider it as a haven. Land now particularly valuable because of the island's character will eventually depreciate, after a quick profit for a few, to the level of the usual summer tourist place.

This winding path, just wide enough for one, will be muddy soon, as the sun comes northerly, but it is firm enough to walk on today. I tread quietly and slowly because spring is, after all, to savor and not to gulp. At a bend in the path, I come upon a Vineyard muskrat, sitting up and drying his shiny coat in such weak yellow light as the morning affords.

No matter, it is warm enough for him; he is well fed and well coated, and his haunches shine in the round. He would have been aware of my presence long before had he not been pleasantly preoccupied with the mating urge. Finally, he discovers me and jumps overboard with a fat plop, more annoyed than alarmed, I think.

In preparation for a cookout at Airport Beach [Mrs. Richard O. Bierregaard wrote in August, 1965], I spent one half-hour picking up the most appalling collection of garbage I have ever seen. In a small area, I picked up over fifty beer cans and soft drink cans, trash, and a large amount of broken bottles which had been deliberately broken and left lying half-submerged in the sand. In spite of all my efforts to rid the area of broken glass, a member of our party cut his foot. It is a crime and a disgrace to have a beautiful beach so desecrated. Over the years, the amount of trash has increased to the point that it is difficult to see the sand for the beer cans.

Along the shingle of winter-strewn beach, tumbled with windrows of dried weed, gray and black, layered with silvered driftwood worn smooth, and garnished with the litter of life from more seasons than I have known, there parade three enormous crows. I sit in a head-high stand of grasses, wind-stunted brush, and what all, and watch them come. There is a certain dignity about them as they eye the water's edge, looking for dinner — more dignity when they walk than when they hop, I think — and they look like clergymen or pall-bearers, not of this century but of the last.

[Following the West Tisbury town meeting in February, 1970, my father wrote:]

*It had to come. This quiet town for nearly eighty years
has been conducted by a group of thoughtful, gray-haired
seers,*

who met in unofficial style to decide on what was best,
then held town meeting that the whole might pass the legal
    test.
Yes, Rotch and Gifford, Mayhew, Luce, they are not there
    today,
but once in offices installed officially held sway.
At Gifford's store, and Sanderson's, they caucused every
    night,
to analyze each article, deciding what was right.
And through the generations, having mulled each matter
    o'er,
beside the stove in Sanderson's and down in Gifford's store,
they boasted of their record as a self-constructed boon
to finish all town business up and then get home by noon.

There were no contests for the seats of town officials then
when first the charter was obtained, they picked out leading
    men
and voted them to offices and kept them there forsooth
until grim death had cut them down and that's the gospel
    truth.
For no one questioned what they did, this group of trusted
    men
who held for public scrutiny the records now and then
to show department figures and resultant facts displayed
announcing "we have cash on hand and all the bills are
    paid."

But those men died, far gone in years, Luce, Gifford,
    Mayhew, Rotch
and presently new forms appeared, likewise a new approach.
The contests at election time and, as the town has grown
the town accounts are not the same as voters once had
    known.
For progress, ever on the move and never blocked or stayed

discounts the records of the past and whether bills are paid,
admonishing no soul to strive, economize and save
contrary to those ancient men long sleeping in the grave.

Within the realm of nature, it does not seem at all unreasonable to discover the generations, even the centuries,
overlapping, for surely the irresistible machinery of one spring
here is much like that of another. Such minor differences as
there may have been are obliterated in the pattern of the
whole, for natural sequences — having discovered what works
well, what is, in fact, practical truth — are willing to stick
with it, rather than forever experimenting each year.

Overhead, there is the lifting cry of geese and there they
are, three strung-out, wavering *V*'s, probably seventy-five birds,
high against the pale sky and pumping easily into the northeast, as their kind has done since before time recorded.

Most of the problems in life are not really between the
good and the wicked or between right and wrong [James
Reston, co-publisher of the *Vineyard Gazette*, observed in
January, 1970]; it is the conflict between one man's right
and another man's right that causes most of the trouble.

Take an ad in the Wall Street Journal the other day. It
read as follows: "Chilmark-West Tisbury, Martha's Vineyard. Unspoiled Colonial American countryside. Priceless
today, unattainable tomorrow. 100 prime acres, high knolls,
wide, distant, and uninterrupted views of rolling hills, open
and wooded land, stone walls, brooks, boulders, naturalistic
paradise. Owner will sacrifice for best offer over one million
dollars."

There are a number of ways to look at this. The obvious
way is to say that it's not a bad ad and not a bad price; it's
an arrangement between the buyer and seller, as private
as a love affair and nobody else's business, a question of

the rights and finances between men of property and nothing more.

Another way to look at this is as a symbol of inflation. Land is getting dearer, money cheaper, people and buyers are plentiful and at $10,000 an acre, who can afford not to sell? And yet there must be a community right here, somewhere.

The ad is not addressed merely to those readers of the Wall Street Journal who can afford to pay a million dollars for a private preserve, though that is a pleasant thought. The seller is clearly regarding the one hundred acres as an investment, so presumably potential buyers could do the same and try to recover or double their million by whatever means they can. They can use the land almost as they please in West Tisbury and Chilmark but can they exercise this right without imposing on the rights of others?

It is an old and controversial question on the Vineyard and as long as it was an abstract proposition, the island maintained its character without really facing up to unrestricted use of land and the rights of the community. But the Wall Street Journal ad brings the question down to the reality of the present and the future. The island cannot grow in size but it's bound to grow in numbers. The questions are how it grows and who decides.

Now, scientists suggest that the land may be much older than the oceans, rather than vice versa, and that by some massive processes that I do not understand fully, some leisurely, herculean turnings, foldings, uprisings, and sinkings, all of this oblate spheroid — and, as part of it, this island — on which we walk, eat, drink, love, hate, think, dream, struggle, and fear is constantly readjusting, making itself more comfortable, if you will.

I am glad that I do not have to watch movement of such proportions; it is unsettling to contemplate. Here, in this small spot, earth and sea seem stable enough, exchanging pebbles and curls of foam at intervals of about every thirty seconds; this has been going on, I suggest, since my predecessor stood in this place with a stone ax in hand and wondered whether an oyster was edible.

[In July, 1970, twenty-three young people involved in what the *Gazette* described as "the third great drug abuse roundup on the island," many of whom had been attending drug clinics on an unofficial probation arrangement by the district court, had their drivers' licenses suspended by the Registry of Motor Vehicles.

[Ten years later, Jack Burton, district court probation officer, concludes], With regard to young adults, the people who come in for drug crimes, we seem to have a very low statistic. We have had one heroin case since I came here eight years ago. The offending chemical is alcohol, without a doubt. Seventy to eighty percent of all the criminal cases are alcohol-related and on the juvenile side, this figure would be forty percent.

There is a lot of abuse of alcohol in the winter here. People experience a lot of boredom, depression, and loneliness. The resources of other activities are very limited. Social resources are much reduced. It seems that if a person has his or her own internal resources, he or she manages better, seeks his or her own pleasures, but otherwise, it is very difficult.

My feeling is that in the old days, the family network held a lot of that together better. There was not so much alcohol abuse because there were better family controls. Now, we have people here who do not have these limits placed on them by the family network. There has been a whole general breakdown of the family network.

There is more loneliness and depression here. This is not paradise. Here, these problems are a little more magnified by new people coming here without family ties.

The more serious crimes on the island appear to be com-

mitted by off-islanders, things such as rape and serious bur-
glary. There seem to be limits to the amount of violence
that an islander will participate in, and I think the crimes
here are more minor in degree.

I first came here in the summer of '58. The change I
noticed from then until 1972 was that people became a lot
more protective and sensitive about their property. Originally,
there was little feeling about walking across property; with
this influx of people, there is a lot more suspicion. The old-
timers might say, "My property is threatened. I feel
insecure."

The dunes, some hundreds of feet of sand above New
England's rock backbone, rise higher at this end of the beach.
Like French politics — any politics, I guess — they are change
that is no change. For, while they are never quite the same as
they were when I was here last, still, they are always here.
They are sufficiently fluid in their response to wind and sea
to survive, reshaped certainly, but still preserving their fundamental identity. In so doing, they are much aided by wind-
stunted growth, especially the tough-rooted, saber-edged grass
that is forever describing perfect sand arcs with its points and
will not let go, no matter what gale or pounding surf.

[In September, 1970, the *New York Times*'s Anthony
Lewis had recently ended a summer vacation at Deep Bottom Cove, on Tisbury Great Pond.] It's a private beach, isolated and somewhat hard to reach [he was moved to write].
Those who use it have always valued the feeling of seclusion.

This summer, dozens of young people came to the beach
uninvited. Their hair was long and they wore no clothes.
The head of the family stopped some of them eventually
and politely explained that it was private property and that
the family kept the place for themselves and their guests and

they wanted privacy. They asked if the uninvited people would go away. One answered, "You see, we don't have a beach," and they came on.

It was a summer of such confrontations. Some property owners called the police and on beaches that used to be summer frontiers for anyone to explore, young men and women were rounded up by the score and charged with trespass and so the beach became another battle ground of the generations. . . .

One woman, a gentle spirit, said, "I used to think of the population explosion as something that would happen long after I was gone. Now, suddenly, here it is."

Some of the young would say that population disposes of all the other questions. Pressures of numbers, they argue, inevitably must doom the concept of private property. Esthetic considerations are almost irrelevant in planning recreation for the future affluent millions. Privacy is dead.

The fact of population cannot be denied, but must we lose variety, need that mean that everyone has to live in an Aldous Huxley world, see alike, play alike? Will there be no isolated places, resistant, hard to reach? Are there no new forms of privacy to be developed? Must we lose variety, that beneficent result of private property?

It may be anti-democratic but I hope the answer is no.

Swinging in a cattail clump, a redwing blackbird gurgles *konk-la-ree* as insistently as the spring presses upon the consciousness. It is insistent, encouragingly so, yet obviously fragile by comparison with the insistence of human numbers here and the inevitable pressures that such numbers create.

Mrs. Elijah H. Crowell was a member of the class of 1923 of Tisbury High School. She lives in the house in which she was born and her father was born. It is located on Look Street, named for her father, the late Senator William J. Look.

She sang in the choir of the town's Christ United Methodist

Church for more than thirty years, was church secretary for twenty-six years, and communion steward for thirty-seven years. For forty-eight years, she worked for Smith, Bodfish and Swift Company on Main Street; she began as bookkeeper and ended as president of the firm, a post she held for seventeen years. She was secretary for the Tisbury Board of Selectmen for seventeen years and retired in 1975 as secretary for both selectmen and assessors. In part, she retired because "it became so I didn't know half the people. There are so many strangers in town now. I used to walk down the street and know everybody."

In April, 1976, Robert Lemire, addressing the members of the Martha's Vineyard Open Land Foundation and the Vineyard Conservation Society, concluded that the people of Martha's Vineyard "can have the kind of island they want it to be."

In a subsequent conversation, Mr. Lemire observed, "It's a New England tradition that what happens to the land is a private matter between the seller and the buyer. It isn't. It's a matter of deepest public interest. What must be developed is a methodology, a system of equity, so that the owner cannot be diminished and so that the developer can design with nature and be at peace with the island."

On the same date, Carolyn G. Goff of Chilmark wrote:

The recent gleeful article in the Gazette of April 23 "Smiles from Island Merchants Greet Glowing Prospect for Busy Season" sounds the death knell for all of us who remember and cherish glorious island summers of peace and tranquillity. When houses and cars could be left unlocked and unattended; when roads were uncrowded, when shopping could be accomplished with ease, when beaches were comfortably filled and respect was shown for private property.

Last summer was horrendous. Shopping was an aggravating chore because of crowded stores and unavailable parking spaces. Driving was an obstacle race — buses, hitchhikers, cars, cars, cars. It was often as abrasive an experience as driving in a metropolis during rush hour.

When will the promoters, those disturbers of the peace, realize that their shortsightedness needs correction?

Read and weep these quotations from your article of the 23d:

"The Chamber of Commerce office in Vineyard Haven looked a little like an overcrowded information booth in New York's Grand Central this week.

"On Beach Road, waves of cyclists pedaled off toward Oak Bluffs.

"An inn keeper said, 'I think this will be the biggest summer yet. Business is already running two to three times ahead of a year ago.'

"The Steamship Authority already has $100,000 in hand for prepaid reservations.

"Many businessmen report signs of an earlier beginning to the season and the peak summer activity will be sustained far longer into the autumn."

Statistics are something of an indicator of what has happened on the Vineyard.

In 1930, the total year-round island population was 4,953. In 1975, the same statistic, winter minimum, was 7,900. The Martha's Vineyard Commission predicts that by 1985, the year-round population will be in the range of 9,800 to 10,900. Some islanders, including realtor Carlyle Cronig, believe the latter figure already has been reached or even exceeded.

In 1975, the island summer population averaged 45,500. The commission estimates that by 1985, the Vineyard will have a summer population of 60,400.

Between 1950 and 1970, island population grew by 8 percent. During the period 1971–1976, the year-round population increased by 31.4 percent.

The 1980 federal census preliminary figures, challenged by some island officials as being low, report that the year-round population is 8,878, up 45.1 percent from 1970, with the greatest gains in West Tisbury, up from 453 to 1,006, a 122.1 percent increase; Edgartown, from 1,481 to 2,150, up 45.2 percent; Chilmark, from 340 to 489, up 43.8 percent; and Oak Bluffs, from 1,385 to 1,985, up 43.3 percent.

In 1930, Vindyarders in gainful occupations totaled 1,920, and of these, 474 were employed in agriculture, forestry, or fishing. By 1979, according to the commission, more than 95 percent of the total island economy was related directly or indirectly to the resort industry.

During the 1960s, an average of 65 dwellings per year were constructed on the island. The average during the 1970s was 251. According to the 1980 federal census preliminary figures, housing units on the Vineyard rose from 5,510 in 1970 to 8,811 in 1980, an increase of 39.9 percent. The greatest gain was in West Tisbury, from 461 to 911, up 97.6 percent.

The Steamship Authority carried 1,321,740 Vineyard passengers in 1976, and 1,422,692 in 1977, up 7.6 percent; 1,418,936 in 1978, off .3 percent, for which inflation was blamed; 1,470,232 in 1979, up 3.6 percent. From January through August, 1980, the number of passengers carried was up 10.4 percent over 1979.

Automobiles carried in 1976 totaled 218,201; in 1977, 227,227, up 4.2 percent; 230,767 in 1978, up 1.5 percent; and 237,170 in 1979, up 2.7 percent. From January through August, 1980, the number of automobiles carried was up 6.8 percent over 1979.

In presenting his 1979–1980 report on the Authority to the

Dukes County commissioners, Alfred F. Ferro, Authority member, urged the shaping of a growth policy that "reflects the thinking and wishes of the vast majority of our island families and businesses.

"If our island is to be united," Mr. Ferro declared, "it must be behind a realistic policy that recognizes that this is 1980 and that 1920 will never come again, that we are much closer to the 21st Century than we are to 1920 and that if we want to preserve much of what's best about 1980, we should be acting now."

It is, of course, impossible to know what everybody *does* on the Vineyard, but if you want a thumbnail sketch of summer goings-on, you could do worse than read the busy bulletin board outside Cronig's Market. This is what it had to say on a midsummer day selected at random in 1980:

> NAACP Kivie Kaplin scholarship dance in memory of Rufus B. Shorter, Tisbury Inn, bring your own favorite beverage; setups available. Tables $5. Music by Coy Shackley and his Roots. Raffle tickets three for $1. Prizes, 50 gallons of gasoline; 50 gallons of oil.
>
> Sailing lessons on a 19-foot sloop in Menemsha Pond.
>
> "I'm too busy." [Picture of a man hauling up a boat with a boy.] Most of us are but one of the nice things about being a Big Brother or Sister is that it takes so little time.
>
> Tisbury town picnic at the waterworks property. Bring your own picnic and enjoy. [Map shows Lake Tashmoo and picnic and play area.]
>
> Tom Thumb at the Tisbury gymnasium.
>
> Hear "The Connection" in concert at the First Baptist Church. Medieval and Renaissance music; American folk, sacred harp, spirituals; recorder, percussion and songs from Orff-Schulwerk.
>
> Glass recycling, West Tisbury landfill and Oak Bluffs bins. Clean glass only. Energy Resource Group, League of

Women Voters, Vineyard Conservation Society, and Martha's Vineyard Garden Club.

A special night at the Hot Tin Roof. Benefit of the Nathan Mayhew Seminars. Widespread Depression orchestra. Sounds of the '30s and '40s. Music for all ages. $8.50 per person. Dancing starts at 9.

Contra Dance with Roustabout. Traditional songs and tunes from the Ohio Valley to the Eastern Seaboard. Agricultural Hall, West Tisbury. Beginners welcome. All dances taught.

Lonely, depressed, suicidal? For someone to talk to in confidence, call the Samaritans.

Two male mongrel puppies free. Love children. Two and a half months old. Already know some training. Very smart. Already wormed also.

Nineteen-year-old female looking to share the rent with a group of young and hip collegians for the summer. Easygoing and promise not to be a pain in the neck. Duxbury.

Give me shelter! The storm is threating [sic] my very life today. Give me, give me shelter!? Or I'm going to fade away. I need a place to stay from now till Labor Day. Sharing a house is OK. Call Phil.

Reasonable housecleaning service $5 an hour. Veronica.

Flexible and responsible working male seeks summer home.

Girl, working in summertime, searching desperately for rooming situation (not expensive) with other informal type. Privacy not a big deal so long as the $ ain't.

Piano lessons. Jazz, classical, theory, composition, improvisation.

Car for sale. 1978 white with red trim Ford Mustang II. Excellent condition.

Chinese food catering. Diced chicken with pepper, shredded beef, steamed fish with sauce, sauteed bean curd, sweet and sour pork, egg rolls.

Complete electronic service. Stereo, radio, small appliances and general electronic repairs.

In November, 1970, the *Gazette* observed editorially, "We have room for only so many. Who is to be welcomed and who is to be excluded? Some said in 1964 — that was not the first year of consideration of the island's growth, but it was a year of omens — that the island should be for the right people. Who the right people are is difficult to define."

I thought about that on a summer Sunday morning in 1980 when I was on the Vineyard working on this book and discovered that, with bedding for seven to be laundered, my father's hot-water heater would not function. Accordingly, we went to an island launderette.

At some point, three shaggy motorcyclists — sawed-off jeans and boots — rumbled up with their girls and dismounted. They had been rained on during the night and they tossed everything they could reasonably get along without for the moment, including boots, shirts, sleeping bags, and socks, into the dryers. In various stages of dishabille, they stood about, chatting easily, and the leader of the clan, stripped to the waist, applied deodorant with total composure.

Unable to hear their conversation because of the general noise of laundry machinery and a roomful of people, I thought of the motorcyclists, "Their world and mine must be a thousand miles and perhaps even a thousand years apart. What do you suppose it would take to enable us to communicate, even a very little?"

I found out.

Once outside, our party decided to check the oil level in the automobile. The hood, once up, refused to come down. It resisted considerable effort; obviously, strength would only bend it and was not the answer. Worse still, it began to rain again.

At this point, the leader of the motorcyclists appeared: black mustache, long sideburns, hairy legs, and forty years younger than I. With no word spoken, he asked, "Got trouble?," did not wait for an answer, but leaned under the hood, fiddled expertly with springs and levers, and closed the hood carefully.

We thanked him (ever try to drive with your hood up?) and he said only, "Sokay," and disappeared into the steamy launderette in quest of shirt, boots, sleeping bag, and girl.

I make no more of the incident than it is worth, noting only that the *Gazette* went on to say, "The test [as to who are the right people] has nothing to do with ethnic origin, complexion, wealth, social position, politics, religion or genealogy. It concerns only the individual's attitude toward all that the Vineyard represents."

Of course that is so. However, the one aspect that attitude does not address is that of numbers. Any place on earth can have too many people even if they are all well-intentioned.

This is what worries Henry Beetle Hough.

Mr. Hough, editor, author, and conservationist, has been observing and recording island matters and his thoughts about them ever since he and his late wife, Elizabeth Bowie Hough, became publishers of the *Vineyard Gazette* in 1920. His writings concerning the island are much read and respected; they have won him deserved national recognition and he is properly regarded as an authority on Martha's Vineyard, a subject to which he has literally dedicated his life. For more than a half-century, Henry Hough and my father were friends and colleagues, jointly engaged in producing the *Gazette*.

It it noteworthy that Mr. Hough's book *Mostly on Martha's Vineyard*, a personal record of life on the island over the last sixty-odd years, is dedicated "To the Past." In it, he describes himself as "witness of a society and a world in decline," and he concludes — as I mentioned at the start of these reflections — "Considering everything, I should be sorry to have these memoirs end with the slightest note of optimism. Selfishly, I am sorrier about Martha's Vineyard than about the world."

Why does he feel this way?

"At Sengekontacket the other day," he says, "I saw a big cluster of mailboxes. I looked at them and there was not a familiar name on one of them. I read the town report recently and not one baby born last year bore any of the traditional Vineyard names — Allen, Pease, Norton, Vincent, for example — they had all disappeared. The names of the forefathers are still in the phone book but not in the birth lists.

"I say this, not snobbishly, but simply to emphasize that since World War II, there has been an explosive and complete change in the cast of characters. For the preceding three hundred years, there had been a homogeneity of culture; until the war, there was a long-lasting generation of leadership, all members of which had been born before 1900. Nor was this homogeneity of a provincial kind; blood from all quarters of the globe contributed to produce the fishing-farming Vineyard; consider that Dionis Riggs's grandfather met the woman who became her grandmother in Honolulu. We had a specific integrity; the island then was more the product of what it had been; now it is the product of what has been brought here from the mainland."

Mr. Hough alludes to remarks that he made twenty years before to the members of the Martha's Vineyard Garden Club concerning what he thought was ahead for the island:

"So we have this inevitable wasting of old values and ideas, this continual lopping off of memory, and we have the amazingly homogenous history of Martha's Vineyard broken and fragmented by changes in a single decade more radical than the changes of the preceding century.

"To those of us who can remember North Water Street in Edgartown, surely one of the most beautiful streets in America, when the line of trees and shipshape Vineyard houses was unbroken by a series of modern garages, the word *unspoiled* is bound to be a stricter term than it is for newcomers who discover the street as it is now, still beautiful, and can hardly miss or regret what they never knew.

"There is an erosion that goes with the passing of time and the inevitable acceptance of change. College courses used to teach, and I think they still do, that the human individual from the time of his conception must go through a complete recapitulation of the life of the race before he matures into a contemporary adult. Ontogenetic development recapitulates phylogenetic development. We may understand how the infant before and after birth can run easily through a rehearsal of the first few million years of human existence but how he can get through the past twenty years or even the past ten is beyond me.

"No wonder we have a problem of juvenile delinquency. What we have done to the lives of human beings in a short time is an entanglement that could not fail to snare the young, whose fate it is to endure and experience and somehow pass through it before they can come of age. And so this must be reckoned as something the future holds unsolved and if for no other reason than this, the need for locked gates and doors and no-trespassing signs and police protection will be on the increase. The old freedom is gone or going and what can we do about it?

"Here is one pressure, and another is the pressure of an in-

creasing population on the mainland, which, with the means
of easy communication now available, is bound to become
one of the most insistent factors in the future of the Vineyard.
We need here consider only the effect of a reasonable proportion of this rapidly increasing population looking for a place
to spend the summer, for a place to have a picnic, or a beach
to sit upon. No one has given much practical consideration to
the demand for space on the surface of the globe, including
the surface of Martha's Vineyard."

He notes that as long ago as 1960 total assessed valuation
figures in all the island towns had risen impressively within a
decade. Chilmark's, for example, had more than doubled, and
of this growth, Mr. Hough adds, "In a society such as that in
which we live, no one would want to see anything but growth
of this kind. Yet when valuations double, the result is, in effect, that a man who owns a piece of land can sell half of it
for as much as the whole piece of it originally cost him. Who,
among our community, enlightened as it is, can count on holding intact many large tracts of land when economic law says
there is a one hundred percent profit in selling off half?

"The two terms of the equation operate together — a rapidly
multiplying population with a demand for space, and a profit
to be made by supplying this demand through dividing available land into continually smaller parcels. Who is optimistic
enough to think that this equation will not make a marked
difference on Martha's Vineyard within a fairly short span
of years?"

He cites the tourist industry as a major factor of change.
"This was always a summer resort but now, visitors are in and
out of here all the time. The Steamship Authority finds it
more profitable to carry excursion passengers. It is more profitable for hotels to cater to weekenders than to those who spend
all summer here. They raised their rates and excluded the

easy, old-fashioned people. I went through an island hotel and the rooms were furnished austerely. The manager said, 'Our patrons want to be outdoors all the time.' The hotel attitude had to be turned around; if it hadn't been, the hotel would have been dead, but keeping up with the times has deprived us of our islandness.

"Once, we had the steamer *Martha's Vineyard*. She was conservative and dignified. You got on, you traveled, you took a journey. There was always a stewardess; this emphasized the voyage. There was a ladies' cabin. You couldn't smoke above the main deck; the drummers were always below, playing cards on their suitcases and smoking. You would never think of not dressing properly for the trip.

"Now, we have a ferry. What do you call it? You get on and suffer a little while. It is better than a bridge." Of the Steamship Authority's second slip at Vineyard Haven, the subject of long controversy before its construction began, he says, "They wanted it while they reconstructed the present slip, to use for a backup. But there is provision for growth here; if you have it, you must use it, especially if a couple of million dollars is involved in its construction.

"It is a whole new route, an effort by some to sacrifice us to more growth. Where is the space to come from? We had space and people marveled at it. The Supreme Judicial Court of Massachusetts ruled that fair market value must be the basis standard of assessment. So we must develop space so that it can pay its way. The developers used up Cape Cod and now they have come here. The canny natives sell out for what they can get and are willing to let the speculators make what they can. And the devotees of modern architecture are having their say — and perhaps they should — and are endeavoring to make this place resemble their own suburbs.

"There have been clamor and petitions because Vineyard

Haven was trying to change the boat schedule so the town can get the crowds [of newly landed visitors], and so they are asking for more traffic. Where my uncle Ben [Benjamin Coffin Cromwell I, father of Big Ben] lived, next to where you lived in Cromwell's Lane, what a pretty place that was; I remember the long green lawn running down toward the water. Now there is a supermarket, department store, and parking lot there.

"There is so much of that, visual pollution. It sounds like an elitist term but there is so much of it. The old things were not necessarily beautiful in themselves but they had character. Even a boat hauled out on the beach to decay — you might wish that somebody had taken care of it, but probably there was a reason for its decaying and even so, you didn't mind looking at it."

Mr. Hough refers to the "unfortunate disfigurement" of the Beach Road in Vineyard Haven, adding, "Once there were the blacksmith shops of Prentiss Bodfish and Elmer Chadwick, and my uncle Ben's junk pile. [Part of Uncle Ben's "junk" was a shedful of shooks — brand-new staves, hoops, and headings for barrels.] One concedes that the oil tanks of today are functional but the bizarre shops and the service stations are poor successors to the ship chandleries and marine railways that were there.

"Most islanders who have leadership qualities now leave; there are a few notable exceptions but it has been said in recent years that the principal export is young men. It was not so in whaling times when it was possible for a young man to become master at twenty. Now, they have to scratch for opportunities.

"In 1925, it was fine, coming along. The Depression enforced a period of restraint and the only people who came here were those who loved the island. They were lovely summers. The war, too, was a factor because it was a deterrent to travel; gasoline was in short supply. Immediately after the war, even the first of inflation was a boon.

"Then," says Mr. Hough, "people started coming."

12. The Leave-Takings

I HAVE taken leave of this place, this Vineyard, on four occasions of consequence and if one is to understand what the island means to those who are of it, it is essential to know what the going away is like — not simply going away for a trip or until next summer, but really going away.

The first time was to go to school, and even though it was fall, I was still full of the June before, simply because I had never had another such June.

"The Senior Class of Tisbury High School requests your presence at its commencement exercises on Thursday, June 15, 1933, at eight o'clock, Town Hall. Class motto: Finimus Coepturi (We finish to begin); class colors, blue and gold; class flower, carnation."

Even now, it is easy to remember the smell of flowers, the soft sounds of night through the open windows, and how warm it was. The hall was full; the wooden folding seats creaked as the men in their dark suits shifted uneasily and the women in their flowered dresses fanned themselves with their programs.

My good friend Wesley Martin, whose sister Letha had taught us in the fourth grade and whose father was superintendent of schools, played the saxophone as did I, and sat near me in the orchestra. Mrs. Marguerite Allen Johnson, the island's music supervisor, was directing; her daughter Phyllis was the pianist — we had been dating since the fall before, and eventually married. The program began with a Mendelssohn march, and after that had ended, those of us who were graduating went to a room where the selectmen ordinarily met, to join the rest of our class.

There were eighteen of us; it was a large class for an island high school. Henry Ritter, the principal, had told my father that he was more moved than usual by the fact of our graduation because he had had so much to do with us, on Sunday as well as school days. He stood before us, hand on hip, feet apart, mouth working a little with emotion, and he said, "Well, take a good look at each other because you'll never be all together again." Then he swallowed a couple of times and added, "Good luck to every one of you." He was torn between wanting to prolong the moment and not wanting to, and we sensed it. "Let's get going," he said quickly, and we followed him, lining up to march into the auditorium.

It seemed incredible that we would never all be together again; there were really so few of us, we all came from the same small place, and we had been together so long. It was sad to think about and I would have felt even worse had I known that he was absolutely right or had I been able to envision that, at this date, more than a third of the class would be dead, and no war casualties among them.

The theme of our graduation essays was "Century of Progress" and I won the DAR prize, which was presented to me by Emma Cromwell, for a piece that began, "Oddly enough the field of journalism, which is one of the most important phases of our modern life, is seldom brought to the public notice." As I think about the statement, I am not sure that it was true or that I know what it means.

A number of other essays were recited. Evelyn Alley spoke on "Century of Progress in Music" and Lawrence Athearn, who lived next door in Mary Abby Norton's house, talked about "Progress in Construction." Wesley played a saxophone solo because he did not want to write and memorize an essay.

Dr. Alfred Fairbrother, a member of the school committee, gave the commencement address; he was widely traveled, erudite, and the only person in town whom I knew whose house contained a room full of books. The town was fortunate to have his scholarly counsel; I wish I knew what message he gave us that night but I do not. Perhaps I may be forgiven for not knowing because there is no graduation, at whatever level, that signals such irrevocable change in the lives involved as that from high school — and from a Vineyard high school at that time, it was far more critical than it is now.

For the first time, a disquieting sense of differences among us surfaced at that commencement; it was still vague, but it would not go away. It seemed to involve things that either had not mattered much before or that had not even been thought about. It was an abrupt introduction to the truth that differences are an iron-bound element of adult life and we had not had to consider that before. This is how it was:

Now, in this moment, we know, as the principal congratulates the class ("Yours is a journey, not ending, but commencing . . ."), who is going to college and who is staying home, who was accepted and who wasn't, who has money and who hasn't. There is a sudden sense of cruel distinction between popularity in Tisbury High School, casually accepted, and the demands of post–high school society, whatever they may be. The era of a reasonably tolerant microcosm, sustainable because of its size and simplicity, in which most values have turned on the fact that we have known each other since we were little and our fathers and mothers know each other, is fragmenting in this very hour. Whatever is replacing it is still vague, but definite enough to be strange and frightening.

The speaker is saying something about tomorrow but his words are drowned in a surging tide of desires to have it become yesterday again. Images from a past that now seems comfortably uncomplicated tumble into the mind in almost unbearable dimensions. The first prom in the new school building, with twisted crepe-paper streamers and Japanese lanterns, and Evangeline Ritter, always daring to be distinctive, in the lace collar and cuffs that were her trademark. A party at Eleanor Luce's, the first ever at which there were cigarettes on the coffee table for the taking; some parents were concerned when they found out about it. A winter evening when South Main Street was closed from the Edgartown Road to Dukes County Garage and everybody, adults and all, went sliding; Carey Luce had a toboggan. The smell of smoke from a beach-party fire and voices, very warm and personal voices, in the shadows. Some games, some cheering, some cold-sweat examinations, the pink of girls' cheeks in the operetta chorus — straws, every one, blown by the wind, blown forever.

That summer, I worked for Phil Mosher, developing film in his photography studio; my father was borrowing money to send me to school and even that was not nearly enough to pay for a single year. One day, Dorothy Lair, with whom I worked, sat at a table straightening newly dried prints and she said quietly, "You will go away to school and you will forget all about us." I protested; I had not thought about such a possibility, but once expressed, it sounded to me like unwelcome truth. I did not want to forget anything or anybody; I wished I were not going away, yet that was the only course there was for me and I was coming to realize that once it was taken, nothing would ever be the same again.

On the first day away at school on the mainland, with my still-packed footlocker in the middle of the room, the smell of fresh varnish everywhere, and rain slashing at the window, I could think only that forty-eight hours before, I had been sitting in Laura Johnson's hammock with Phyllis, dreading the next morning and boarding the steamer. I wanted to run home.

Instead, I went to the school library and took out a copy of Hardy's *Jude the Obscure;* it matched my mood and I thought, "If I am going to be gloomy, I will be damned gloomy and be done with it."

Still, although going away to school set a course for departure from the island, it was not immediately a complete break because one came back for vacations. Five years later, however, it was different. I had a degree and several hundred dollars of indebtedness; I had spent the summer as harbor patrol in Vineyard Haven, getting browner by the day and accumulating letters that began, "We regret that we have no openings at present . . ." But as fall came, and with it, the hour for hauling up the boat and putting the oars in the cellar, the New Bedford *Standard-Times* did, in fact, hire me.

In those days, the steamboat left at six in the morning. If one's feelings were mixed, that was probably a bad time of day, although if an island means something to you, there is no good hour for leaving it if you know that you are not coming back. I knew that, because I could come back only in failure.

My father got up with me and we stood there in the kitchen, drinking coffee. Even for two people who talked a lot, and we did normally, there wasn't much to say. He had been newly married, to Anna, for about a year; they were very compatible, afloat or ashore, and, as they should have been under such circumstances, self-contained. I was twenty-one and very conscious of the fact that I had attained my majority. It was time, in terms of both mathematics and circumstances, for me to leave home for good. Even if I had had no job, I would have done so, and left the island as well, for I sensed no opportunity there for me. I was not full of self-confidence. I had talked recently with an islander with whom I had gone to school and he had left a mainland job to come back to the Vineyard "to work for groceries," as he put it, but I thought that at least my failures would be less obvious off-island. I had twenty dollars in cash.

We finished our coffee. "Do you want me to walk down to the wharf with you?" my father asked.

"No," I said. "You stay here." I picked up my bag; he put his hand on my shoulder and said, "Give 'em hell, boy." I walked out into the morning.

Once aboard the steamer, I went to the upper deck so that there would be nothing between me and the Vineyard sky. I went all the way aft so that I was as close as possible to the Vineyard shore.

There the town lay, my town, its spires, shingles, and clapboards tucked into the trees. Mostly, I knew who was up and who was not, and the names of all the boats in the basin, and what the people looked like who owned them. I knew how the streets looked at this hour, quiet and easy, with nothing much moving but somebody's mongrel, running the sidewalk scent of a last-night's rabbit. I knew what October would be like, washed blue-clean overhead and leaf-buried below, with a great quietness settling upon the land. I would not be here then.

Beneath my feet, the throb of the engine; astern, green and white water swirling; the dripping lines were hauled aboard and the distance to the beach widened. Past the dock end, the breakwater, past the power plant and the Lagoon bridge, and the details of the village melded into its green and white wholeness. "The *Uncatena* is long gone," I thought. "A lot of time is gone." And after we had left West Chop behind and thus were less departing from the Vineyard than approaching

Woods Hole, I thought, "When I was a child, I spake as a child, I understood as a child, I thought as a child: but when I became a man, I put away childish things." I had first heard that from our pastor, Willard Johnson; when I was fifteen, he had asked me whether I had ever given any thought to entering the ministry. I was not sure that what I felt for the Vineyard was a "childish thing" but whatever it was, there was no turning back. There isn't for anybody, but especially for islanders, there isn't — either you stay or you go, and that makes the difference.

It was a third kind of leave-taking when I left the island in early '43 in uniform, knowing that I was going somewhere out of the country. Having had recent opportunity to observe the Vineyard and Vineyarders at close hand in a wartime atmosphere, I had come to regard them as admirable examples of what the nation had to represent during its ordeal: durability, determination, and common sense. I thought, as we sailed, "It is of little consequence, except to me, whether I ever return here but it is of great consequence in terms of what this war is about that what the Vineyard represents at its best should be preserved for those who *do* come here in the future."

My father had not wanted me to volunteer for military service. I think this was because my birth had prevented him from serving in World War I, and now, he was too old. I do not think he was fearful that something untoward might happen to me. He always assumed that Americans would win every military engagement with a minimum of casualties and that the war would end before most people thought it would. He buttressed this positive outlook with an unshakable reaffirmation of his ties to the enduring past, in which Allens did not really die, either in war or in peace, not ever.

Late in 1943, in England, I received a letter from him, dated December 16:

I have been out with Anna picking greens with which to decorate the church for Christmas. While picking greens, I walked over to the cellar hole where the Allens lived for close to two hundred years and took a look at the place. I stood on the doorsteps, front and back, over which they walked and I paused at the well which my father filled in and covered with a rock. And I looked down into the crumbling cellars; there are two, as you may recall, one for vegetables, the other for the grog. And I said things, somewhat under my breath, although there was no one around to hear except the ghosts of old Allens, whom I felt I would like to attract for I suspect that any place which has been lived in or on for centuries possesses its characteristics absorbed from the people who lived there.

I know that I never visited such a place that I couldn't feel something so human about it that I unconsciously looked around to see if anyone was near. Well, I couldn't see them but I suspect they were there just the same and maybe heard and saw me. So I stood there in the snow — it's a couple of inches deep — for a minute or two and just wished that I could get that land back into the family again so that it could be passed on and on.

Realistically, that possibility had died long since. My grandfather sold the place for something in five figures and the last time around, it went for something in six.

The fourth leave-taking from the Vineyard was in two parts, essentially indivisible. First, Anna died, after more than forty years of marriage to my father, and this is how one recalls it:

Sometimes, distance is the best thing, even though you might not think so at the moment. Which is a way of addressing the fact that the grandmother — a good and gentle woman sufficiently courageous to knit afghans for all her children's children, even though blind — finally surrendered to a totally unfair number of ailments.

The Leave-Takings

Each of us is remembered by those who know us best, not as suspended in a vacuum, but in characteristic pose — the musician, with his instrument; the mother dressing her child; the aficionado of football, beer in hand, before the television set. The familiar gesture, set of the head, manner of speaking — all of these are part of what the mind retrieves as it tries to determine, for the sake of its own well-being, what is left after death.

So this was indeed her kitchen and it is easier than not to place her here in imagination, for so many hours over the years were spent in seeing her here, just so, very likely with spoon in hand, stirring and tasting, talking and laughing. And in the living room, this is the chair in which she sat, first being able to see and then not being able to. For some time after the loss of sight — no one really knows how much time because she was not given to complaining or self-pity — she was depressed. But the woman had uncommon faith, not perhaps so much in the notion that she would be able to see again, but, rather, in herself. She was much at home with the Bible; more important than being simply aware of the tribulations of Job, she understood how he found the strength to endure, to salvage something of value from adversity. "There are those far worse off," she would say, even when she was not very well off at all.

Then there were the remembrances of things said and done. "She always said —" someone began, and there followed the relating of one of those curious coincidences or uncannily accurate predictions that seem to occur in life, leaving them all to wonder to what degree humankind may, on occasion, pierce the veil of cosmic truth. And because most lives are blessed with the lubricant of humor, sooner or later the memories stumbled upon the laughable. "It really was the funniest thing and especially her comment . . ." So they laughed, not too long, being reprimanded by grief and propriety, yet with relief, believing that if she had been there, she would have had them laugh, at least a little, and perhaps a lot.

They were all gathered there, feeling comfort from the togetherness, from the crowded room and the buzz of voices, from the meetings with those not seen recently ("How you have grown! You *do* look so like your father!"), and from the warm reaching-in of society — the dining room table was covered with steaming dishes, good home cooking prepared with love by the women of her church.

Still, there was one with Vineyard ties who was not there. She is the dark-haired, green-eyed one in jeans, the one with the long-nosed cat and the garden apartment in San Francisco, the first of the clan to round Cape Horn since great-great-great-grandfather Captain Elijah Howland of Tisbury. As he also knew, San Francisco is a continent away from the island; so, because she could not be with them, she did the next best thing, which may, in fact, have been the best thing — she wrote what she felt when word came that the woman was dead.

Sitting cross-legged on a folding Japanese creation that serves as bed and chair, gray cat watching the pen move, she wrote to her grandfather:

> *It is this void that brings pain*
> *That alwaysness vanished*
> *Leaving us empty.*
> *But she didn't tell*
> *Us, before she left*
> *That in her giving us this empty space*
> *She has opened doors inside ourselves*
> *To fill this empty place*
> *Not with more grief, old beliefs or sorrow*

But an opportunity to do
Her good and our good
Today, not tomorrow
Filling our hollowness
It will hold
What hasn't yet been built
To manifest in life
Our sights of newness and old.

My father, then more than sixty years her senior, said to me, "I thought you would like to read this poem. It is filled with good words. But I just cannot write thank-you notes at all. Any mention of Anna breaks me up and makes me maudlin and worse. The poem reminds me of something, somewhere, sometime. Was it — well, I cannot remember. It does not do to think too hard."

So, to the green-eyed girl, my daughter, Stephanie, I sent his thanks. And mine. And then I left the island once more.

Two months later, there was the second part:

It was March. The house in Cromwell's Lane was years behind us.

Standing in my father's Main Street living room, a high-posted affair dominated by a massive fireplace with a touch of Tudor, it seemed to me that the house had come to a halt.

I looked at my watch. He had been out of the place no more than three hours, yet with his departure, its vitality was gone as well. It was now no more than rooms of echoes, of clock hands sweeping without meaning.

The photographs on the mantel were where they had been, just so, except for dusting, for thirty years. Weddings, houses, children, grandchildren, boats — all of the landmarks of life of which people customarily take pictures. The pictures prop up an illusion of permanence. We really know that nothing is going on forever but most of us are willing to be lulled into believing that what is, given certain minor changes such as wrinkles and glasses, may endure for a very long time.

The old man's vigor had encouraged such thinking. One blue eye had fallen to cataracts, yet the other burned as fiercely as ever under the bushy white brow. In recent years, he had walked with a cane and strode the windswept beaches no more; he deplored movement of the post office from downtown to the Five Corners to ease traffic congestion, because his legs bothered him. Yet his complexion, born of island weather, remained ruddy and he continued to articulate his views with the same splendid inflexibility that had always been his trademark.

There once was a New York drinking place on East Fifty-seventh Street, somehow Vineyard-inspired and therefore called the Menemsha Bar. Touched with nostalgia by the name, I walked in there one afternoon, probably in the early sixties. On each table, there was a little folder, with a cover drawing titled, "Menemsha Harbor, Martha's Vineyard" — vessel at the dock, boathouse with a sign LOBSTERS — and I discovered that my father had written the brief text inside.

Joe Allen says [it read] the atmosphere of Menemsha is such that in mid-summer, no one can tell who is the fisherman or who is the summer guest. Both wear with pride their patched and salt-stained dungarees and rubber boots. Both are sunburned to the color of a tan-barked sail and both, having absorbed to the full the spirit that predominates the place, live up to the old proverb which says:

"Live every day so that you can look every damned man in the eye and tell him to go to hell."

I do not know how "old" that proverb is. I wouldn't be surprised if my father invented it. It fitted him, or part of him.

Eventually, the young woman who had been housekeeping for my father came into the living room. There was in her face that look of sadness reserved for those who have not yet had much sadness.

"He had been downstairs working," she said. "He was in his office, writing his column for the *Gazette*. He took off his red smoking jacket — you know, the one with the black piping — and hung it over the back of a chair, the way he always did, and then he went upstairs for something.

"All I heard was a thump and I ran and there he was, lying on the floor. I tried to talk to him but I couldn't understand what he said. I wanted to pick him up but he was too heavy. I put a pillow under his head and called the police for an ambulance. They came in just a few minutes." She paused, pale hands in her lap like white flowers. "That's all," she said, as if there ought to be a lot more, considering the importance of what had happened.

Conscious of the finality in what had to be said, I weighed very carefully how to tell her about my father.

"You could begin," I thought, "by telling her what a stroke is, what the dictionary says it is, sudden diminution or loss of consciousness, sensation, and voluntary motion caused by rupture or obstruction of an artery to the brain.

"Then I suppose you could convey to her gently what the first findings indicate: massive, irreversible damage to the centers of intelligence. It is highly unlikely that he will ever again remember, comprehend, recognize, or communicate, or that any kind of rehabilitation of consequence will be possible. How do you convey that gently?

"Then you could point out what pertains to her directly. No matter how long the old man may live, he will never be coming home again."

Apparently she had assumed all of this, instinctively. "Last night, we were sitting here in this room," she said. "We were both tired of winter and cold weather and I said I wished spring would come. So he said, 'We'll start spring on the way. You just go get a pad of paper and a pencil and we'll figure out what we're going to plant in the garden this year and where we're going to put all of it.'

"He used to joke with me about the garden," she said, "because maybe he'd have a row of cucumbers that he'd tend and I'd have a row and sometimes mine would come out better. That was because it was hard for him to bend down and tend the plants and he'd get tired — things like that — and I used to like to go out there and spend a couple of hours a day. You know, working with the dirt and green things. I like nature. A lot."

She went to the mantel, found a piece of folded paper behind one of the pictures, and brought it to me. "Here's what I drew for him last night. Lettuce here. A row of Kentucky Wonder beans —" She stopped abruptly, reality washing over her like a cruel sea. "I guess we don't need this piece of paper anymore," she said. She tore it this way and that very slowly and dropped the pieces into the fireplace.

She did not say anything more about the old man before she left, closing the front door behind her quite carefully, but what she did was better than words. Somewhere in the back-yard's late-winter bleakness — where the garden would have been, given time — she found a sheaf of dried grasses, tucked them into a green ceramic umbrella stand on the front-hall stair landing, and left them behind her as a mute note of caring and farewell.

That time when I took the ferry to the mainland, I spent much of the trip thinking about the old man, not only because he was my father but because somebody once described the Vineyard as "Joe Allen surrounded by water." In a fundamental sense, the man was inseparable from those ways and words that most people consider to be especially of the island.

In essence, that was my last island leave-taking, because something that began on Martha's Vineyard in the seventeenth century and had survived wars, political crises, depressions, and the gales of winter was ended.

When I left, West Chop light was silver in the fog and the pines were dark banks, sharply etched. Mist like smoke hung over the rips, the rolling water was hard against the leaning marker, and our horn *whoo-oo*-ing. When the land faded to a blur, there remained only the brightness of two dimensions, light gray sky and dark gray sea. Occasionally, the sun made itself felt from somewhere, hot and bright, but never breaking through. It was not a day for the sun to be breaking through.

Close aboard, a buoy emerged, lifting, sloshing, clanging in its lonely way, but it was gone from sight in an instant and we moved within curtains and without time or dimension.

For the last time, good-bye.

Still, if one *must* look back, there is the urge to look ahead as well, and Dr. Milton Mazer is very helpful in this — and he knows what was.

Dr. Mazer, who lives in West Tisbury, is founder and director of the Martha's Vineyard Mental Health Center, a staff psychiatrist at the Martha's Vineyard Hospital and Massachusetts General Hospital, former assistant clinical professor of psychiatry at the Harvard Medical School, and was for ten years moderator of the West Tisbury town meeting. In short, he came from off-island but through an extraordinary combination of compassion, insight, and patience, he has won not only acceptance but respect from islanders.

Dr. Mazer moves easily within both winter and summer populations, something that most do not. Those who know him, and many do, recognize him as both personable and professional; he sails his own boat, has a sense of humor, and there is nothing formidable or pretentious about him. Although many would have predicted otherwise in the beginning (1961), islanders in respectable and increasing numbers come to his clinic.

He came to the Vineyard to live in '61 and had summered on the island earlier than that. I ask him what thoughts he has about change over the years.

"When I first came here," he says, "there were congregating places, for example, the café in Edgartown, on North Water Street. Elderly people had their dinner there; when men were not working or were out of work, they would sit around and talk.

"The drugstore had a soda fountain. I said to Pete Vincent, 'Does this soda fountain pay for itself?' and he said, 'It doesn't pay at all.' I said, 'Why do you have it, then?' and he said, 'The store wouldn't be any fun if I couldn't stand behind the counter and talk to people.'

"Now we have lost all this and I understand the Barnacle Club in Vineyard Haven may go under. [Author's note: It did.] We have libraries but they have a different aura. So we have some loss of the sense of community.

"Another change is this. When I first came here, invariably when we were driving along the highway, we would wave to another car, even before we could see who was driving it. There were two traditional ways of waving: one was that you would lift your left hand from the wheel; the other was that you would keep your thumbs on the wheel and open your left hand. We no longer feel that we know who the other person is.

"Also, there has been a change in speech pattern. In 1962, a Columbia University linguist did some research on the island on this. It was concluded that Chilmark speech was the most distinctive and traditional. In considering high school youngsters, he found those with more traditional speech patterns were more likely to remain on the island, those with less traditional speech were more likely to leave. Probably this represents a collection of values.

"During my first years here, the island conversation was full of distinctive speech patterns. They used to say, 'That is some good' and 'finest kind.' Now, the colloquialisms have tended to disappear. My impression is that the talk is closer to radio English than it was."

Why?

"First, we hear more standard English on radio and television, and second, a smaller proportion of the island population is native. Consider the recent election for selectman in Chilmark. Betty Ann Bryant was running against Jonathan Mayhew and there were some, perhaps many, who thought she didn't stand a chance because of the historic importance of the Mayhew name in Chilmark. [Author's note: There have been Mayhews on Martha's Vineyard since 1642.] But I wasn't sure because so many people had moved into Chilmark; there is a smaller proportion of natives. She won."

Who sets island directions these days?

"Probably not the Chamber of Commerce. Probably citizen action groups, as well as official groups. There is more contesting for public office. The Martha's Vineyard Commission also is concerned."

With regard to citizen action, I cite the controversy in the late seventies over the proposal to establish a McDonald's restaurant on the island. The anti-McDonald's forces were led by Henry Hough, who characterized the company's gold arches as "a symbol of the asphalt and chrome culture that we do not have here, a symbol of peril to the island, and of all the forces that endanger the island." Among the supporters of the No Mac Committee's petition were Mia Farrow and Ruth Gordon, authors Vance Packard, William Styron, and John Updike, singers James Taylor and Carly Simon, then husband and wife, and cartoonist Jules Feiffer. The anti-Mac forces won and McDonald's gave up.

How did he feel about that situation?

"The surprising thing about the McDonald's conflict was that it was so one-sided, publicly at least. There was virtually no support expressed for having a McDonald's restaurant on the island. That interested me because it would have been a place where a workingman could take his family out to dinner — one of the very few such places on the island — and get away with a reasonable check. And certainly the success of the McDonald's enterprise indicates that its product has great public acceptance. But the people who might have patronized a McDonald's were virtually silent. Perhaps they did not have readily at hand pen, notepaper, and postage stamps or the time or assurance to engage in the conflict. And most of them were too busy just earning a living. I am told they had the same fuss when A and P scheduled their first store here.

"We pay higher prices here than they do on the mainland. For example, the *New York Times* is forty cents and in Falmouth, it is thirty; it doesn't cost ten cents to ship it here. The gas pumps on the island all register the same price. An old commission survey showed that two importers of fuel charged the same price to a hundredth of a cent.

"New Bedford, for example, has different prices for the same commodity. Comparable mainland communities have a bigger scope, a choice of more movies, the opportunity to shop advantageously in more stores, and their people can look for more jobs in more areas. Some of our people shop as a form of recreation in the big supermarkets in New Bedford; they take along a portable refrigerator and save enough to pay for a little holiday.

"Vineyarders are harder hit by an economic decline. An auto mechanic who is fired has only a limited number of places to go and he probably knows all the mechanics. There is a limitation in the use of skills; the same thing is true in recreation and in restaurants; they are limited areas.

"The visible affluence of non-natives has deleterious effects. Yachts cost more to maintain than families earn in a full year. Few local people are invited to join the yacht club. Native children soon discover the matter of loyalty; they will not be disloyal to year-round friends by forsaking them for seasonal friends."

I say some have suggested to me that island natives lack initiative or courage and that those who hold this view point out how many new commercial enterprises have been established and operated successfully by non-natives.

"I think that is probably more related to Vineyard traits, and the native is heavily laden with them," he says. "Non-natives, the average middle-class Americans, believe they can conquer nature, can make it rain, can go to the moon. The native works harmoniously with nature, the storm at sea, and so on. The non-native believes that progress must always go on, that it is infinite. The native is not even sure that progress is always good, let alone infinite. It's what you're taught when you're growing up that influences your idea of free enterprise."

Acknowledging change, Dr. Mazer is positive about the island and its people.

"I think often that what is, is better than what was. Then, many teenagers had never been off-island, not even to Boston. At present, a high school class is visiting Spain; that would have been unheard-of then. The school system is improved. It used to be that teachers were islanders who had lived here a long time. Then, students were advised to go to schools in Maine, Vermont, New Hampshire, or normal schools. The island was often afraid to compare itself to other places. Schools used college catalogues from colleges you never heard of. Later, we got a superintendent who advertised for teachers in the *New York Times* and we got better teachers. Kids here are as bright as any others and they are now going away to better schools."

Dr. Mazer adds a footnote about people on the island, suggesting it reveals something characteristic: There was a baby party in West Tisbury and a man who was divorced brought his infant boy, who was a nursing baby. A woman who was present was nursing a baby and she also nursed the infant boy. She did the same thing for a woman friend, saying, "It's time that you went to the movies, to get a little change." The friend said of her baby, "She's going to get hungry while we're gone."

"My baby will share it with her," said the other woman.

For profound reasons, I find that reassuring because it re-affirms the spirit of caring that has been, unevenly perhaps but persistently, a bright thread of Vineyard tradition. It reminds me of my father and the flower.

A woman of approximately his generation had loved sun-flowers since childhood because to her they epitomized cheer and gladness. In his small backyard, my father raised one for her, nurturing it with tender care through the season. When it was higher than his head, he cut it, this fellow with one good eye and so lame that he could no longer walk to the post office daily. And he put on his white Stetson, grasped his cane firmly in one hand and the great yellow bloom in the other, and made his laborious way through Main Street to her home triumphantly — old man, new flower, bent on a bright mission of neighborliness.

13. The Longer Look

 THE Vineyard that my father knew for much of his life, the island atmosphere in which I grew up, these are gone and one must say good-bye to them. Hattie Tilton and Henry Beetle Hough were right, of course, in mentioning the world and the Vineyard in the same breath because something of what has happened to the island is what has happened elsewhere, especially in America. Those new matters that pose problems anywhere are more difficult on Martha's Vineyard principally because it is smaller and can grow no larger.

Within the space of only a few midsummer weeks last year, those who care about the island were reminded of the pressures upon it, the results of drastic and continuing change.

In leaving his post as director of the Vineyard Conservation Society after twelve years of service, Bob Woodruff noted that during his tenure, thousands of building lots had been carved from open land in the six island towns. Though it is increasingly expensive, people still want a piece of the Vineyard. Mr. Woodruff referred to the increase in growth from year to year as geometric; he sees the next five to ten years as being critical in the survival of the island as a high-quality place in which to live, or as a summer resort.

"Interest in Martha's Vineyard is growing," he commented, "and with it grow the numbers of people who want to see and touch the island for a day or for a lifetime. Even in the un-

likely event that a growth rate is approved islandwide, there
is still the question of what to do with the thousands who
simply want to come to the Vineyard. They're either going to
be sitting around playing cards in a hotel room or leaking
onto private property. It comes down to access. I think a limit
on the number of cars on the island should be explored.

"I think one thing that needs to be done is for everyone
from the Chamber of Commerce to the *Vineyard Gazette* to
be conscious of the publicity. Every article draws people's
attention."

At about the same time, it was reported that the popularity
of the island was at an all-time high, that further records for
tourism were expected to be shattered in the future, and that
the four ferry lines alone spend well over $160,000 a year on
their advertising, mostly during the summer.

Alarmed by the frequency and seriousness of accidents
involving mopeds, members of the All-Island Selectmen's
Association resolved that the towns must act soon to upgrade
moped safety laws. And the Martha's Vineyard Commission
placed growth-rate limits on two large Oak Bluffs subdivisions.

In Edgartown, selectmen's phones rang, and the *Gazette*'s
letters page was filled with complaints that the town was
taking on a honky-tonk air, that its streets were clogged with
day-trippers, and that unpleasant sounds disturbed the night.
Police Chief Bruce Pratt said the Edgartown Yacht Club's
annual regatta, July 20–25, made that the worst single week
of the summer, with twenty-eight arrests "and every one of
them associated with the regatta. Thank God we didn't get
Marblehead and the New York Yacht Club this summer."

Edgartown's 4,300-foot South Beach and an adjacent strip
of county-owned beach in front of Katama Bay were the only
Atlantic shore beaches on the island open to the general public
and easily accessible from a paved road. The surf there drew

as many as 7,000 people on a good weekend, taxing the town's ability to police, protect, and clean up the beach.

Island selectmen, worried about increased pressure on town services and public facilities, criticized the Steamship Authority, the summer ferry lines, the Chamber of Commerce, and the State Department of Commerce for advertising the Vineyard's charms abroad and exacerbating problems at home.

Island businessmen criticized the selectmen for not projecting a more hospitable attitude.

John Broderick, Chamber of Commerce executive director, attributed a significant part of the island's exposure to the names of celebrities who go there, to the Chappaquiddick incident, to the fight against McDonald's, to the making of the film *Jaws* on the island, and to the Vineyard's threat to secede from Massachusetts when redistricting cost it a resident legislator in the state house of representatives. And finally, he asked, "How does the island survive economically without tourism? I have yet to hear anyone answer that question."

Moreover, by fall, the *Gazette* was warning somberly: "Wastes we deposit in Vineyard soil pose an environmental threat that promises only to increase. Experts can describe the threat but can point to no simple or inexpensive solution, for there is none. This is part of a larger question: How shall we live responsibly in this place?"

A friend, whose ties to the Vineyard span several generations, wrote to me in September, 1981:

I am sure that if you visited the island this summer, you found it an absolute madhouse. It has gotten so bad, even though we live in a highly protected area of the island, that my family and I are seriously considering, because of the overcrowding, not coming to the Vineyard at all during July and August and taking our vacations in June and September. I mention this because, in talking to other long-time summer residents, they spoke of the same dilemma and were considering the same decision. Many up-islanders that I talked to have refused to go down-island at all during July and August.

Inevitably, in attempting to measure some of the things that have occurred since 1925, I returned to personal beginnings; I went back to Cromwell's Lane. Its onetime ruts and meanderings, cinders, grasses, and overhanging boughs are no more; what was half hidden, irregular, softened by clumps, tufts, piles of this and that, now lies bald and stark. The area is dominated by vehicles, a supermarket, a restaurant, and a department store.

Where Emma Cromwell's roses spilled over the wire fence, there is a dirt parking lot. Next to the rose garden, there was an arbor of Concord grapes, powdery-skinned and sweet. A half hour within its cool shadows, plucking and eating, would remove the wrinkles of anxiety, only most people did not have any then. The vines are gone; the arbor is gone. Somewhere under this new tarred surface of civilization lies what was Emma's magnificent lawn, stretching toward the harbor. The lawn is gone. The Cromwell house, a venerable, Victorian mansion, has been bulldozed in deference to more practical matters.

It is interesting to conjecture whether the pieces of Emma's ivory Mah-Jongg set are still in their box, reminiscently intact and orderly, or whether they were scattered wherever. I have to wonder about this because the last time I saw the oil painting of the gallant, sunlighted square-rigger that hung in the Cromwell dining room, it was like this:

On a May Day afternoon a few years ago, they excluded motor vehicles from five blocks of Boston's Newbury Street and turned over its clutch of art galleries, faded brick, side-

walk pansy beds, and verdigris on eighteenth-century copper
sheathing to the mind and eye. Hundreds, complete with dogs
and children, swarmed through the galleries, devouring popcorn and pictures, sculpture and beer, and listening to the
street music.

In the street, always the restless drum and guitar beating.
Red and yellow balloons, a yard across; some young, dungareed
unwashed on the sidewalk; a Robin Hood girl in olive-green
hat and smashing black stockings with runs; a warm-eyed
donkey with a cerise ribbon proclaiming MATISSE across his
furry chest. The bicyclist in shorts blew a police whistle and
sold penny candy for art's sake; on the iron fire escapes, students in T-shirts photographed the street flow, and a little boy
with a sweater labeled WINNIPESAUKEE asked, "Where are the
animals?"

The man, class of '35, who made one think of dry sherry
and British biscuits, said, "He wasn't very good at math so they
made him an accountant." Trickle of small laughter: colored
jumping jacks bouncing on the pavement, and the guitarist
biting his nails between numbers. The guest book at 175
Newbury read, "Ho Chi Minh, Hanoi." On the sidewalk, two
boys fenced with bamboo canes bearing Matisse pennants; a
father retied a little girl's hair ribbon and looked at the photograph in deep darks of a woman, limp cigarette streaming,
with black hair across her eyes.

PLEASE KNOCK, it said on the gallery door. I entered, seeing,
on the wall beyond, a gold-plated column of rods entitled
Homage to the Vertical, and then seeing, with a catch of
breath, the picture of the Cromwell ship, still aristocratic
under her cloud of sail, but now a homeless aristocrat, dis-
placed by time and circumstance, gone from the island to the
city, probably forever.

I left Newbury Street with the taste of life's hard iron in

my mouth, having stumbled upon the one among those scores of pictures that signaled the pride of intimate yesterday brought to its knees. And more, I suppose, for as I left, the undeniable guitar was beating in my ears and I thought, "How the things of the world and the things of the Vineyard now are juxtaposed, even to unlikely degree."

In the lane, the stump on the Cromwell lawn is gone, too. I suppose it had been an elm and its prime also was of an earlier society. It must have been six or seven feet high, barkless and silvered by weather, and more than four feet in diameter. In childhood, we drove spikes into it so that we could climb it and sit on top. Once there, facing outward like a covey of quail, we surveyed the world and remarked upon its goods and bads, having learned even by then that height is helpful if you want to see how things really look.

The house of Dolph Manning, who knew all about horses, is gone, too. So is the cellar hole that contained the wreck of an ancient dray and a bush of white lilacs; the place is now a parking lot. Tom Tilton's old house is gone, where my father stayed when my sister had scarlet fever. The yellow archway over our gate, on which the clematis rambled, is gone, and in its place, there is a high board fence that shuts out the passerby. I do not know what Lucy Cooper's cat would have thought of a high board fence.

The fact that Luther Athearn's little workshop is gone (replaced by a parking lot) is not so strange. One understands that old men die and if no one remains to work in their shops, the shops come down, or even fall down. But the atmosphere of the lane today is not conducive to what he did in his shop; he spent many of his days whittling wooden puzzles to give to children. They were simple puzzles, made of sticks, strings, and washers that he had at hand. Whether there still are children somewhere who would play with such homemade things, or even find them puzzling, is not certain.

The lane thus far has escaped hot-topping, but these days, it is no more than a way of getting from one place to another.

Having said all this, and confessing that I have no idea how the pressures upon the Vineyard of numbers and attitudes during the critical eighties may evolve, I find that I cannot end these reflections upon an inflexible negative note. The first reason I cannot is that I owe my father something better.

Granted that thirty years ago is not now, yet he faced the reality of considerable island change then, liked some of it and disliked some, accepted the fact that islanders left and off-islanders came, and that summer was an exhausting experience, and he retained a perspective.

In the spring of 1955, he wrote,

Life moves faster today than it did thirty years ago. There is less time in which to look at sunsets, tie up the honeysuckle, or lean on the fence to talk to neighbors; there are no more old whiskery characters, picturesque in dirty overalls, and no more children standing spellbound to watch a horse trot down the village street. At night, both towns and long stretches of highway are illuminated, and the whippoorwills retreat to the shadows when they sing their evening song.

But there is not the distress or the need that was apparent thirty years ago or the lackadaisical attitude with which such things were viewed.

Today, life moves even faster and there is less time than ever; there are more people, automobiles, buildings, and things in general that get in the way of sunset-looking. Yet I also owe my children, Stephanie and Christopher, and my grandchildren, Kimberly, Jennifer, and Joshua, all possessing a Vineyard heritage, something like a balanced judgment in trying to look ahead. In '55, my father saw a Vineyard passing through social and economic convulsions but he concluded that it was "more vigorous, more modern in all respects, yet never entirely relinquishing the hold on the old practices and character that constitute its charm." As a sentimental realist, I can believe no less — at least for now. It is a fact that people who care about the island still go there — and many remain there — because they find on the Vineyard that same charm.

As a means of crystallizing some of the diverse thoughts that have emerged in this book, I sought the views of two island women, whose backgrounds and life-styles are different, but who know the Vineyard and its people well, to find out how they feel about what has happened and is happening.

Elizabeth Ann Bryant was born and raised on the Vineyard and has lived in Chilmark, where she is a member of the board of selectmen, for more than twenty-one years. For several years, she was a member of the Chilmark and Union school committees and of the regional school committee. She has been the selectmen's representative to the Dukes County Advisory Board and is a corporator of the Martha's Vineyard Hospital. She was a member of the Youth Center Operating Committee and the Committee on Drugs and Alcohol of Martha's Vineyard Community Services. She was the director and counselor of the first family-planning clinic on the island, a former VISTA worker, and a paralegal working for low-income families on the Vineyard. She was involved in the anti–Vietnam war movement.

I interview Ms. Bryant at Menemsha's Dutcher Dock while she eats her noonday sandwich; hers is a busy life involving much public service, and she enjoys it.

"In the sixties," she says, "the Establishment was the enemy.

I am part of the new Establishment. In the antiwar movement, I met a lot of new young people summering here and
got to know them.

"One-third of the island population is not native anymore.
The results of the influx of new people here are mostly positive. I don't care as long as they don't spoil the environment
and I think it is good for our kids to see different life-styles.
When I grew up, there was a lot of discrimination here and I
rebelled against it. I don't want to see houses built on wetlands
but new people are healthy for me. Alternative life-styles were
not accepted even in the sixties. I feel good about helping
these people to live here in peace.

"We have problems like any other place. Growing up, I
knew who the vandals were; then we had one kid and ten
homes and now we have ten kids and a hundred houses; they
are both native and in-migrant kids. Both natives and non-
natives are among those who have alcohol problems; these are
more magnified here because of the smallness of the place.

"I finally discovered that I am comfortable with change. I
am liberal about people. I'm for windmills and young police
departments; I care about how kids feel in their school system.

"But a way of life is being taken away here; there is no
question about that. The price of real estate is prohibitive.
The young are devastated. They can't stay here. They see this
society as not giving young people a piece of the action and
they are angry as hell. They're worried about whether they
can live here; we have to provide for that. I understand that
the rich can't afford to be Santa Claus but whoever dreamed
of double-digit inflation and twenty percent interest?

"Frustration because of visible affluence is absolutely deva-
stating for some; it lowers their motivation, so they go to a
barroom and blow their paycheck. The impact is greater here
than off-island because, although the trade-off from the influx

of new people may be positive, there is only so much land and there is fierce competition for it. Many are not even in the running for land."

Of her election to the board of selectmen, she comments, "I learned organizing during the anti-Vietnam effort, built a political nucleus, and my people organized in Chilmark, and elected." But she adds, "The twenty-four-to-thirty age group on the island can't even find rentals and is too frustrated, for example, to bother with politicizing. Islandwide, people are too busy just trying to survive. The Vineyard is big business now; there's no time to get caught up.

"I bought my husband a pair of binoculars for Christmas. That day, we went to Chilmark Pond, Quansoo, Crab Creek, West Tisbury Pond, and Black Point Pond. We were so high because we were alone on Martha's Vineyard; we never saw a living soul and then we came home and caught a Joan Baez concert. It was a perfect day. There's no place anymore where you can walk alone.

"My husband and I can probably survive the eighties here. My daughter probably will have to stay home and that's not good but that's because of real estate prices. We have a little boat. We have always lived off the land. My husband has felt a crunch; young people and retirees here are antihunting. Some people came down to the beach where he was gunning, waved their arms to scare the ducks away, and said to him, 'What the hell are you doing?' He may not be so happy in ten years.

"There is distrust and alienation in groupings. Some people, instead of trying to communicate, stay in their niches. If I'm going to survive on Martha's Vineyard, I feel that we must work together. What happens depends on how people relate to each other. What has happened is that those things the native Vineyarder looked upon as fundamentals of the Vineyard way of life are now gone and it seems unlikely that the coming generations can have them.

"The big need now is for communication, understanding, and working together, since these are necessary to survive."

Barbara Cottle Child's ancestors came to the Vineyard about 1680 and there have been Cottles on the island ever since. She was graduated from Tisbury High School, attended art school in Boston, and lived with her husband, Edward, in Troy, New York, and Westfield, Massachusetts, before they moved to the Vineyard in 1954 as permanent residents. She and her husband live on the Lambert's Cove Road, maintain a continuing interest in land use, animals, and nature, have raised purebred Herefords and chickens, and now have a small flock of sheep. They are parents and grandparents. Mrs. Child is employed at the Bunch of Grapes bookstore in Vineyard Haven.

"My feelings about island population growth are mixed," she says, "but perhaps more negative than positive. My immediate feeling is one of resentment, to find strangers speaking of 'discovering' the Vineyard after a few days here; to think of the island as just another resort saddens me. The island is a part of me that is fundamental and probably this has also made me overly possessive and protective of it as one would be about a dearly loved child.

"The growth affects me in countless ways, in not being able to open a gate and walk through to a stretch of beach, in walking down a street and recognizing no one or, at best, very few. There is a feeling of suburbia, that my husband and I tried to escape, following us here.

"In a positive way, we have found new people who treasure this delicate spot as much as we do and, perhaps more from realization of what has happened to their favorite places off-island, are working hard to preserve the Vineyard. There is also an influx of talented young people, teachers, artists, and musicians, who enrich our lives.

"The regional concept here makes sense in a lot of ways. The island fire departments work together, the regional high school was probably the only way to procure top-notch teachers, and even the churches had to move toward this by sharing pastors. I don't necessarily think that all island functions should be regionalized, because each town has its own individuality and problems, but we should share concerns such as problems of waste disposal and clean air, which seems to be happening.

"We have drawn together as an islandwide community in the last ten to fifteen years and are interested in the whole Vineyard far more than in my growing-up years when West Tisbury was the whole world until the time came when we went to the "city" of Vineyard Haven. Our provincialism has not disappeared, but has lessened.

"The increase in alcohol abuse, crime, and marital difficulties here is consistent, I believe, with mainland trends. I believe there are several factors involved. Many come here for a happier island life — retirees, divorcées, or young people — and they find their problems are still with them. Expectation of respite and discouragement about coping may contribute to renewed heartbreak.

"Another group of the population are islanders who, financially, are barely eking out an existence and who come in contact continuously with affluence, which seems to be a constant affront to them. This contrast is a daily experience that in another area would not be so obvious. This leads to a hopeless, helpless attitude and often results in alcohol or drug abuse and also marital difficulties. Other factors enter the picture: television influence, movies, parents working so hard they have little time or energy for listening to their children, and church attendance is down, too.

"Island changes are not in degree as great, for instance, as those of a suburb of Boston that has been engulfed by the city, but they are comparable in some ways. Our little strip of ocean has been our biggest defense and ally; it prevents easy access and discourages those who don't really want to be here. (Perhaps the exception would be the tour buses.) I think we have become aware of the needs and priorities in the last few years and the changes are not all bad. For example, the 'No Macs' stand and now a realization that we need a home for our elderly; this is a true picture of our thinking now.

"The island has lost its insular quality, its provincialism to some extent, and become more cosmopolitan. The whaling days were also like that here. Perhaps we have also lost a narrowness and a tendency toward malicious gossip since the Depression era. Outside influences have changed us. Our children go to Europe with a French class, we have fine restaurants, see famous people; there is a lively, intelligent interest in what is happening.

"For the most part, there still is a fine, friendly feeling that draws one to live here and to come back again and again, a feeling that is not felt in many places. Many visitors and acquaintances remark about this.

"On any morning, as people pass the door of the bookstore, smiles, laughter, and helpfulness occur far more than frowns and indifference. It's that island magic and it's still here.

"At the moment, the scales of change are very delicately balanced; so many events can tip them one way or the other.

World chaos, inflation, gas and oil dependency, all will affect this fragile outpost as they do the rest of the nation. Maybe being vigilant will be the key to *real* progress."

I submit that both women are realists, both recognize the problems and pitfalls, and both are essentially positive in their outlook.

I hope for the Vineyard, as do they. Over the course of this book, I have asked myself repeatedly what is gone from the island that used to be there. I have concluded that, as with much of the world, it has lost innocence, which, however comfortably gentle in retrospect, was essentially crippling and carried a terrible price tag, and a certain nobility that derived from elbow room and general willingness to accept the status quo. When we are crowded and challenged, we tend to become less than noble, principally because we become more than indifferent or resigned.

It is too easy and too simple for one of my age to look upon the creators of island change as barbarians at the gates. That is a historic reaction that history itself has refuted more often than not. Obviously, what is happening at the gates is tomorrow, which clearly will be different and — given thoughtful human involvement — offers some promise of being better, despite bigger problems. I do not know how well tomorrow's islanders will solve them — nor do they.

On the morning when I completed the research for this book, I stood on the steps of the Vineyard Haven library to consider this place in which I grew up. It was a good moment to stand there. There had been rain the night before and all the trees and flowers that I could see were lush and dripping. A male cardinal, dramatic red note against the green, was calling persistently: *Wheet, wheet, chu, chu, chu.*

A bearded young man in the ubiquitous jeans approached. "Hello, sir," he said, and I responded agreeably.

"I am a teacher," he said, "and I am taking a year off to live on the Vineyard. I wondered if you knew anyone who had a room to rent."

I gave him a couple of places to try. Then I said, "Why are you coming to the Vineyard for your year off?"

"I want to think," he said. "This is a good place to think."

I thought that was a sensible answer. The Vineyard has always been a good place in which to think and it has produced some good thoughts. Some of those thoughts over the last half-century translate today into greater island social awareness, added concern for the environment, increased interest in growth planning, new opportunities for youth, and more cultural activity. In thinking, obviously, there lies the salvation of the Vineyard. And of the world, for that matter.

Still, the Vineyard's tomorrow, whatever it is, will differ much from its yesterday, and that is why this is an elegy. What is gone, is gone, and some of what is gone was good. I am sorry that those who come after cannot know the Vineyard that I have known, but I look back without anger because much of what one remembers fondly was at best mixed and some of it never even existed. When I was growing up, the whole island never really did belong to us from Labor Day to June, but, as islanders, we were allowed the illusion for an incredible number of years.

So my elegy is without anger. Yet I think it no more than reasonable to request respectfully that I be allowed to shed one tear for the dear imperfect past.

The author is grateful to the following publishers and individuals for permission to quote material as follows:

Country Journal for an excerpt from "A Square Yard of the World." Reprinted with permission from Blair & Ketchum's COUNTRY JOURNAL, September 1978. Copyright by Country Journal Publishing Company, Inc.

The New Bedford Standard Times for the interview with the Reverend Guy Willis Holmes, from the September 27, 1925, issue.

Northeast Folklore Society, Inc., for the song "Rolling Home" by Alton Tilton, which appeared in FOLKSONGS FROM MARTHA'S VINEYARD, Vol. VIII, by Gale Huntington (1966).

Dorothy Cottle Poole for the use of an excerpt entitled "Free Fare" from VINEYARD SAMPLER, Copyright 1964 by Dorothy Cottle Poole.

Mr. James Reston for an excerpt from *The New York Times* September 1970 issue by Anthony Lewis, and for an excerpt from *The New York Times* January 1970 issue by James Reston.

Dionis Coffin Riggs for the poem "Blueberrying," first published in *The Vineyard Gazette*.

The Tudor Press for the poem "Josiah Torrey Hancock" by Joseph Chase Allen from VINEYARD POEMS AND PRINTS.

The Vineyard Gazette for permission to reprint various articles, letters, editorials and advertising texts including material by Joseph Chase Allen, Henry Beetle Hough, Phyllis Meras, and Clifford A. Kaye for his poem, "Passing of the Red Spur."

The author is also grateful to Mrs. Elizabeth M. Keniston and to the Vineyard Conservation Society for permission to use material owned by them.